Holt Spanish 3

Assessment Program with Differentiated Assessment for Slower-Paced and Advanced Learners

HOLT, RINEHART AND WINSTON
A Harcourt Education Company
Orlando • **Austin** • New York • San Diego • Toronto • London

Photo Credits
Page 253 (5) PhotoDisc/gettyimages; (6) © Royalty-Free/CORBIS; (7) Don Couch/HRW; (8) Peter Van Steen/HRW.

Printed in the United States of America

ISBN 0-03-074429-6

6 7 8 170 10 09

Table of Contents

CHAPTER QUIZZES

Each Chapter has a set of nine different quizzes.

- Prueba: **Vocabulario 1**
- Prueba: **Gramática 1**
- Prueba: **Aplicación 1**
- Prueba: **Vocabulario 2**
- Prueba: **Gramática 2**
- Prueba: **Aplicación 2**
- Prueba: **Lectura**
- Prueba: **Escritura**
- Prueba: **Geocultura**

CHAPTER TESTS

Table of Contents *continued*

To the Teacher

In the ***¡Exprésate!*** *Assessment Program,* content is tested in the same manner that it is presented and practiced in the *Student Edition.* All test activities are related to the chapter theme, direction lines provide a context for each test activity, and all items within a test activity are within the context of the activity, that is, all items are thematically related and not random.

The *Assessment Program* consists of a set of quizzes for each chapter, chapter tests that are skills-based and assess the material presented and practiced in the entire chapter, speaking tests for each chapter, midterm and final exams, and alternative assessment: portfolio suggestions, performance assessment, and picture sequences to assess the students' ability to describe and to narrate. There are score sheets, scripts, and answers for all of the tests.

For each chapter there are nine quizzes:

Pruebas: Vocabulario 1 and **Vocabulario 2** contain primarily discrete items that focus on the vocabulary and functional expressions presented and practiced in each section of the chapter.

Pruebas: Gramática 1 and **Gramática 2** test the grammar concepts presented and practiced in each section of the chapter. All three grammar concepts are included in the quiz. The vocabulary in these activities is vocabulary that has already been presented, either in the corresponding chapter or in previous chapters.

Pruebas: Aplicación 1 and **Aplicación 2** are skills-based quizzes. They test the material from each chapter section by integrating the vocabulary items, functional expressions, and grammar in communicative contexts. The skills quizzes do not test discrete vocabulary items, functional expressions, or grammar points. They test the skills of listening, reading, and writing. Each quiz contains one listening, one reading, and one writing activity.

The points for the three quizzes for a chapter section add up to 100. Each vocabulary quiz has a value of 30 points, and the grammar and skills-based quizzes have a value of 35 points each.

In addition to the chapter section quizzes described above, there is also a reading quiz, a writing quiz, and a **Geocultura** quiz for each chapter.

Prueba: Lectura tests reading skills and the reading strategy presented in the *Student Edition* chapter. This is a one-page quiz consisting of three activities. Readings for this quiz will include various types of texts (realia, letters, short stories, and/or fables, for example) that provide an opportunity to apply the strategy learned in the chapter. Students are asked to produce something that shows that they understand the strategy and can apply it to new reading material. This quiz contains, along with the reading text, a pre-reading activity, a comprehension activity, and a post-reading activity.

Prueba: Escritura tests writing skills to fulfill a specific purpose. In the earlier chapters, students are asked to demonstrate their ability to use the chapter functions in writing, then gradually move toward writing text that persuades, narrates, informs, and so on. This one-page quiz consists of one or two open-ended writing prompts that are linked to the *Student Edition* chapter. The writing prompts for Levels 1, 2, and 3 are in English and ask students to write the following types of text: dialogues, advertisements, notes, letters, postcards, paragraphs, and so on, progressing to stories and essays.

The **Geocultura** quiz tests the information presented in the **Geocultura** section that precedes each chapter. The first activity in this quiz is a map activity, in which students are asked to identify cities, countries, or regions based on the information presented in the **Geocultura** pages. Other activities in the quiz will assess the student's knowledge of certain basic facts presented either in the almanac or the captions on those pages. This quiz is a combination of closed-ended and open-ended activities.

The **Lectura** and **Escritura** quizzes have a point value of 35 points each, and the **Geocultura** quiz is worth 30 points, so that these three quizzes added together are worth 100 points.

For each chapter, there is one chapter test (**Examen**). The chapter tests assess discrete vocabulary items, functional phrases, and grammar concepts, as well as listening, reading, writing, and speaking skills, by integrating the language learned in the chapter.

Each test has six sections that appear in the following order: Listening, Reading, Culture, Vocabulary, Grammar, and Writing. The total number of points on a test is 100. Direction lines for Levels 1, 2, and 3 are in English. The two activities in the **listening** section of the chapter test integrate vocabulary, functional expressions, and grammar from the entire chapter. Assessment in this section is for global comprehension; it does not test discrete vocabulary items or grammar concepts. The **vocabulary** and **grammar** sections of the test focus on the vocabulary items and grammar concepts covered in the chapter. The **reading** section assesses the student's reading skills and integrates the vocabulary, functional expressions, and grammar from the chapter.

The **culture** section of the chapter test assesses the information in the culture notes. The **writing** section integrates the vocabulary, functional expressions, and grammar from the chapter.

Each chapter test is followed by a speaking test (**Examen oral**) which globally assesses oral production. Students are asked to integrate the vocabulary, functional expressions, and grammar concepts in the chapter. This is a one-page test that consists of an interview, a role-playing activity, and a rubric for easy grading. The situations in the *Activities for Communication* ancillary are designed to prepare students for this test.

The midterm and final exams test the material presented and practiced in Chapters 1–5 and Chapters 6–10, respectively. In these exams (**Examen parcial** and **Examen final**), both discrete items and skills are tested. In the skills sections (listening, reading, and writing), language from the five chapters covered is integrated. Each of these exams is an eight-page test. Included in the *Assessment Program* are the score sheets, scripts, and answers needed for each exam.

Alternative Assessment

The purpose of the alternative assessment in this program is to provide the teacher with assessment tools that accommodate students' individual needs, ways of learning, and rates of learning when testing students' mastery of each chapter's vocabulary, functions, and grammar. The three types of alternative assessment provided (portfolio suggestions, performance assessment, and picture sequences) assess students' ability to describe and/or narrate. Each of these will be discussed in more detail in the "To the Teacher" section that precedes the Alternative Assessment section of this *Assessment Program.*

Quizzes

Table of Contents

CHAPTER QUIZZES

Each Chapter has a set of nine different quizzes.

- Prueba: **Vocabulario 1**
- Prueba: **Gramática 1**
- Prueba: **Aplicación 1**
- Prueba: **Vocabulario 2**
- Prueba: **Gramática 2**
- Prueba: **Aplicación 2**
- Prueba: **Lectura**
- Prueba: **Escritura**
- Prueba: **Geocultura**

To the Teacher

Evaluating the Quizzes

The nine quizzes for each chapter thoroughly cover the material in the chapter (**Geocultura,** vocabulary, functional expressions, grammar, and culture), so that a student who does well on the quizzes is amply prepared for the chapter test, midterm, and final. The discrete items on the vocabulary and grammar quizzes prepare the student for those same sections on the chapter test, while the skills-based quizzes and the reading and writing quizzes prepare students for the skills-based sections of the chapter tests and midterm and final exams.

The 30 points of the **Vocabulario** quizzes are distributed among four activities as appropriate to reflect the difficulty of the task. A simple multiple-choice activity with five items might be worth five points, whereas a more difficult vocabulary activity with five items that requires the student to write sentences using the new vocabulary might be worth a total of 10 points.

The same system of assigning points is true for the **Gramática** quizzes. Each **Gramática** quiz is worth 35 points, and those points are distributed among four activities to reflect the difficulty of the task and whether the task is at the recognition or the production level.

The **Aplicación** quizzes for each chapter section are also worth a total of 35 points. As a rule of thumb, a listening activity with five items is worth 10 points (2 points per item), a reading activity that requires understanding a short passage and writing short answers to five comprehension questions is worth 10 points (2 points each), while a writing activity that requires the student to write a paragraph on a specific topic is worth 15 points.

The **Lectura** and **Escritura** quizzes are worth 35 points each and the **Geocultura** quiz is worth 30 points. Possible points on the three quizzes add up to 100, just as the three quizzes for the chapter sections add up to 100.

The quizzes are written so that students can complete them in no more than 20 minutes.

Nombre ______________________ Clase ______________ Fecha ____________

CAPÍTULO 1

Vocabulario 1

PRUEBA

A Write the letter of the word that best completes each sentence.

a. naipes
b. windsurfing
c. disfrutamos
d. caracoles
e. truenos

____ **1.** En mi viaje a España, hice ___ en la playa.

____ **2.** A mi mamá no le gusta nadar, así que coleccionó ___.

____ **3.** Una noche llovió mucho y escuchamos ___.

____ **4.** Nos quedamos en casa jugando ___.

____ **5.** Nosotros ___ mucho de las vacaciones.

SCORE /5

B Read each definition and choose the correct word.

____ **6.** En este edificio, las personas celebran ritos religiosos.
a. la catedral **b.** la estación de trenes **c.** el bosque

____ **7.** Este juego es un juego de palabras.
a. el crucigrama **b.** la natación **c.** el esquí acuático

____ **8.** En este lugar puedes hacer actividades acuáticas.
a. el bosque **b.** las montañas **c.** la costa

____ **9.** Esta frase significa pasear por un lugar.
a. divertirse mucho **b.** coleccionar caracoles **c.** dar una caminata

____ **10.** Cuando esto ocurre, hay lluvia, viento y relámpagos.
a. el río **b.** la tormenta **c.** la costa

SCORE /5

PRUEBA: VOCABULARIO 1

C Answer the following questions about your summer.

11. ¿Qué hiciste en julio?

____

12. ¿Qué tal lo pasaste?

____

13. ¿Adónde fuiste en agosto?

____

14. ¿Qué te pareció la última película que viste durante el verano?

____

15. ¿Qué hiciste cuando hubo una tormenta?

____

SCORE /10

D You are telling a Spanish exchange student about your childhood. Write how you would say the following things.

16. I used to like to roller blade as a child.

____

17. I thought camping in the woods was great.

____

18. When I was young, I usually went to the beach with my family.

____

19. When I was six, I used to play cards with my dad.

____

20. I usually went horseback riding with my cousin on the weekends.

____

SCORE /10 TOTAL SCORE /30

Nombre ______________________ Clase ______________ Fecha ______________

Gramática 1

A Marta is taking a poll in her school about what teachers and students did last summer. Complete the answers with the **preterite and imperfect** of the verbs in parentheses.

Marta Luis, ¿fuiste al final con tus padres a Costa Rica este verano?

Luis Sí, nosotros (**1**) ______________ (viajar) a Costa Rica en agosto.

Marta Aída, tú solías acampar en el bosque con tu familia, ¿verdad?

Aída Sí, pero este año (yo) (**2**) ______________ (acampar) con unos amigos junto a la playa.

Marta Luis y Pepe, ¿ustedes no montaban a caballo por las praderas del Norte?

Luis y Pepe Sí, (nosotros) (**3**) ______________ (montar) a caballo de niños, pero ahora nos da miedo.

Marta Señor Díaz, ¿qué solía hacer usted durante los meses de verano?

Señor Díaz Yo (**4**) ______________ (hacer) viajes al extranjero, pero este año me quedé en mi país.

Marta Diana, tú caminas con frecuencia con tus amigos, ¿pudiste caminar en tus vacaciones?

Diana Sí, nosotros (**5**) ______________ (dar) muchas caminatas juntos por la orilla de la playa.

SCORE ____ /5

B Complete Sonia's short essay with the **preterite** of the verbs from the box.

recorrer	**organizar**	**hacer**	**montar**	**estar**

¡El pasado fin de semana yo (**6**) ______________ con mis padres en la costa de Puerto Rico! Nuestro monitor nos (**7**) ______________ actividades al aire libre muy divertidas: Mi hermana y yo (**8**) ______________ a caballo por la playa y mi hermano (**9**) ______________ esquí acuático. Para mis padres (**10**) ______________ un tour al Morro, una fortaleza muy antigua en San Juan, la capital de Puerto Rico. Nunca olvidaremos este fin de semana.

SCORE ____ /10

PRUEBA: GRAMÁTICA 1

C During Pablo's family reunion, he is asked all kinds of questions. For each item, decide whether he should use **ser** or **estar** in his response. Write the correct verb in the blank.

__________ **11.** su tía le pide que describa a su novia

__________ **12.** su abuela quiere saber su profesión

__________ **13.** su tío quiere saber cómo se siente

__________ **14.** su mamá quiere saber cómo quedó la comida

__________ **15.** su primo quiere saber la hora

SCORE ____ /5

D Read each sentence. Then give advice to each person using the verb in parentheses, the **present subjunctive,** and **Vocabulario.**

16. Pedro quiere aprender a patinar en línea, pero no tiene patines. (es importante)

____

17. Ana quiere viajar a Chile, pero no tiene dinero. (aconsejar)

____

18. Esteban quiere divertirse este fin de semana, pero no sabe qué hacer. (recomendar)

____

19. Laura no sabe nadar, pero quiere aprender. (ser buena idea)

____

20. Cristóbal quiere ir al cine con su novia, pero no tiene carro. (sugerir)

____

SCORE ____ /15 TOTAL SCORE ____ /35

Nombre ______________________ Clase ______________ Fecha ______________

Aplicación 1

Escuchemos

A Listen to Irene's statements about her weekend plans with her friends, and choose **a**) for **cierto** or **b**) for **falso.**

_____ **1.** Gloria montó a caballo el sábado pasado.

_____ **2.** Laura nunca montó a caballo.

_____ **3.** A Jorge le parece genial el esquí acuático.

_____ **4.** A Tina le interesan mucho los deportes.

_____ **5.** Raúl no quiere ir a la playa.

SCORE /5

Leamos

B Read Lucía's letter to her friend and answer the questions that follow.

Querida Verónica:

El verano pasado viajé a España con mi familia y lo pasé de maravilla. Fuimos a la ciudad de Toledo y la encontré muy interesante. La ciudad está en la región de Castilla-La Mancha. Llegamos a la estación de trenes y me quedé impresionada porque es tan bella. Estaba lloviendo cuando llegamos, pero luego salió el sol y hacía mucho calor. Di una caminata por la ciudad y conocí a un chico español. Se llama Ramón y es alto y guapo. Todavía no se lo dije a nadie. ¡Quiero que vengas a mi casa para enseñarte las fotos!

Con mucho cariño,

Lucía

PRUEBA: APLICACIÓN 1

6. ¿Adónde fue Lucía con su familia el verano pasado?

____

7. ¿Qué le pareció la estación de trenes de Toledo?

____

8. ¿Qué tiempo hacía cuando llegaron a la estación de trenes?

____

9. ¿Dijo algo Lucía a sus otros amigos sobre Ramón?

____

10. ¿Cómo es Ramón?

____

SCORE /15

Escribamos

C Write an essay about yourself for the class yearbook. Be sure to include a description of yourself, what you used to do as a child, and the activities you enjoy now. Tell about some of the things you did last year and express some of your hopes and wishes for this year.

____

____

____

____

____

____

____

____

____

SCORE /15 TOTAL SCORE /35

Nombre ______________________ Clase ______________ Fecha ______________

Vocabulario 2

A Choose the phrase that does not logically fit with the others.

____ **1.** ¿Cuál no es parte de estar saludable?
a. mantenerse en forma **b.** la dieta balanceada **c.** el club de debate

____ **2.** ¿Cuál no es una actividad tecnológica?
a. diseñar páginas Web **b.** saltar a la cuerda **c.** hacer diseño por computadora

____ **3.** ¿Cuál no es una actividad atlética?
a. hacer gimnasia **b.** practicar atletismo **c.** observar la naturaleza

____ **4.** ¿En cuál de estos lugares no es importante hablar bien?
a. la estación de trenes **b.** el club de debate **c.** la clase de oratoria

____ **5.** ¿Qué cosas no puedes coleccionar?
a. las estampillas **b.** las monedas **c.** los truenos

SCORE ____ /5

B Match each problem below with the most appropriate advice from the box that follows.

____ **6.** Quiero mantenerme en forma, pero no sé cómo hacerlo.

____ **7.** Me encanta el centro recreativo, pero no tengo con quién ir.

____ **8.** Siempre me pongo muy nervioso cuando tengo que hacer una presentación en clase.

____ **9.** Tengo ganas de participar en alguna actividad en el colegio, pero no me gustan los deportes.

____ **10.** Me gusta el arte, pero no dibujo muy bien. Trabajo mejor en la computadora.

a. Te recomiendo que diseñes páginas Web.
b. Puedes participar en la banda escolar o en un club como el club de español.
c. Te aconsejo que te hagas amigo(a) de alguien a quien le gusten los deportes y que vayas con él (ella).
d. Te recomiendo que hagas ejercicios aeróbicos y sigas una dieta balanceada.
e. Debes tomar una clase de oratoria.

SCORE ____ /5

PRUEBA: VOCABULARIO 2

C You are advising new students about the activities available at your school. Based on their interests, give them advice on what activities to participate in.

11. Manuela / tocar música

____

12. Ignacio / correr

____

13. Mónica / hablar en público

____

14. Lorenzo / usar la computadora

____

15. Anita / participar en un club

____

SCORE /10

D Answer the following questions about your plans for this year.

16. ¿Qué vas a hacer los fines de semana?

____

17. ¿Adónde piensas ir durante las vacaciones?

____

18. ¿Cómo vas a mantenerte en forma?

____

19. ¿Qué cambios vas a hacer de hoy en adelante?

____

20. ¿Qué piensas hacer en tu tiempo libre?

____

SCORE /10 TOTAL SCORE /30

Nombre ______________________ Clase ______________ Fecha ______________

Gramática 2

A Luz and Ana are shopping. Complete the conversation using the correct word in parentheses.

Luz ¡Ay, qué blusa más linda! Voy a comprarla.

Ana ¿Cuál, (**1**) ____________ (aquel / aquélla) que está allá?

Luz No, (**2**) ____________ (éste / ésta) que tengo en mis manos. Aquélla no me gusta para nada. Creo que es (**3**) ____________ (menos / más) atractiva que ésta. ¿Y tú, no vas a comprar nada?

Ana Estaba pensando en comprar (**4**) ____________ (este / éste) suéter o estos pantalones, pero los pantalones son más caros (**5**) ____________ (que / menos) el suéter.

Luz Pues, te recomiendo que compres el suéter.

SCORE ____ /5

B Using **hacer** and time constructions, how would you tell someone… ?

6. what you did three days ago

____

7. how long your family has been living here

____

8. something you haven't done for a week or more

____

9. how long ago you and your family went out to eat together

____

10. how long ago you met your best friend

____

SCORE ____ /10

PRUEBA: GRAMÁTICA 2

C Read the sentences and then rewrite them, replacing the **subject** and **object** with the correct **pronouns.**

11. Esmeralda tiene que hacer la tarea para mañana.

____

12. ¿Paulina y Alicia vieron a Manuel en la tienda?

____

13. Los músicos practicaron la presentación musical.

____

14. Emilio diseña las páginas Web para el club de computación.

____

15. Mis amigos y yo hacemos ejercicios aeróbicos.

____

SCORE /15

D Complete the letter to the advice columnist by filling in the blanks with the appropriate word from the box.

ninguna	**jamás**	**ningún**	**nadie**	**tampoco**

Querida Paquita:

Te escribo para saber qué consejos me puedes dar. El problema es que soy muy solitario y no tengo (**16**) ____________ amigo. También quiero ser más divertido, pero (**17**) ____________ actividad me gusta. Hace dos meses, me hice miembro del club de debate de mi colegio, pero la oratoria no me gustó para nada. Después, me hice miembro de la banda escolar, pero a (**18**) ____________ le gustó cómo tocaba la trompeta. No pinté (**19**) ____________ en mi vida, pero hace poco me hice miembro del club de arte. (**20**) ____________ tuve éxito en la pintura. No tengo remedio alguno. ¿Qué debo hacer?

El chico más solitario del mundo,

Jorge

SCORE /5 TOTAL SCORE /35

Nombre ______________________________ Clase ______________ Fecha ____________

CAPÍTULO 1

Aplicación 2

PRUEBA

Escuchemos

A Listen to some friends talk about their travel experience. Then, choose the correct answer to each question.

____ **1.** ¿Fue Tito a Europa?
a. sí **b.** no

____ **2.** ¿Hace cuánto tiempo fue Elena a América del Sur?
a. hace un mes **b.** hace un año

____ **3.** ¿Quién viajó más?
a. Fernando **b.** Catalina

____ **4.** ¿Dónde está Patricia ahora?
a. Nueva York **b.** México

____ **5.** ¿Cuál de las oraciones sobre Ricardo es cierta?
a. Fue al Caribe. **b.** No salió del país jamás.

SCORE ____ /10

Leamos

B Read the conversation and answer the questions.

Felipe Oye, este centro recreativo es fabuloso. Pablo me lo recomendó.

Silvia Sí, hace un año que hago gimnasia aquí. Es la mejor manera de mantenerse en forma.

Felipe Yo nunca hice gimnasia. Juego al golf con mis amigos durante el verano, pero ninguno de ellos hace ejercicio durante el invierno.

Silvia Te aconsejo que vayas a la presentación sobre el centro. Rita te explicará todas las actividades que hay.

Felipe No sé quién es. ¿Es esa chica rubia que está haciendo ejercicios aeróbicos?

Silvia No, es aquella chica morena que está saltando a la cuerda al otro lado del centro. Ella es la directora del centro.

PRUEBA: APLICACIÓN 2

6. ¿Dónde están Felipe y Silvia?

7. ¿Felipe hizo gimnasia alguna vez?

8. ¿Cuánto tiempo hace que Silvia hace gimnasia en el centro?

9. ¿Qué le recomienda Silvia a Felipe?

10. ¿Quién es Rita? ¿Cómo es?

SCORE /10

Escribamos

C You've been doing the same activities forever and you want to try something you've never done before. Write a letter to a friend telling him or her about your problem. Describe your interests and ask for advice.

SCORE /15

TOTAL SCORE /35

Lectura

A Read this essay using the verbs to determine if the article is written in the first or third person. Explain why you think the author wrote from that point of view.

Las artesanías de Toledo por José López

Creo que la tradición artesana de Toledo es una de las más antiguas; sus espadas y su cerámica son famosas por su calidad, al igual que el arte del damasquinado, traído por los árabes. La técnica de este arte consiste en incrustar oro, plata o cobre sobre otros metales más duros, como el acero. Esta industria fue muy importante durante los siglos XV, XVI y XVII cuando vinieron a Toledo artesanos de toda Europa y del Oriente para aprender los secretos de aquellos artistas. Otra cosa espectacular que encontramos en Toledo son las armaduras, o vestidos de hierro de tamaño natural al estilo medieval y renacentista, hechas a mano por sus artesanos.

____

____

SCORE /10

B Based on the reading, match the terms from the left column with the descriptions in the right column.

____ **1.** espadas de Toledo

____ **2.** damasquinado

____ **3.** tradición artesana

____ **4.** oro y plata

____ **5.** un secreto

a. arte de hacer cosas a mano

b. técnica de incrustar metales como el oro sobre otros metales más duros

c. son las mejores del mundo

d. algo que pocos saben

e. metales que tienen mucho valor

SCORE /10

C Answer the following questions in complete sentences.

6. ¿Cuándo y por qué fue importante la industria artesanal en Toledo?

____

7. ¿Qué indica que los árabes vivieron en Toledo alguna vez en la historia?

____

8. ¿Qué otra cosa de hierro está hecha a mano por los artesanos de Toledo?

____

SCORE /15 TOTAL SCORE /35

Escritura

A Felipe felt bored and lonely last year. Now he is starting high school and he wants to be more active than he was in junior high. He has started thinking about what activities he might participate in. Write a letter from Felipe to his friend Marcos, who is a junior in high school, telling him about past experiences at school and asking for advice about how to make his freshman year a good one.

____

____

____

____

____

____

____

____

____

____

SCORE /20

B Write a response to Felipe from Marcos giving him advice for his first year in high school. Include information about what activities he has participated in and for how long.

____

____

____

____

____

____

____

____

____

SCORE /15 TOTAL SCORE /35

Nombre ______________________ Clase ______________ Fecha ______________

CAPÍTULO 1

Geocultura

PRUEBA

A Match each letter on the map of **Castilla-La Mancha** with the name of the place or area it represents.

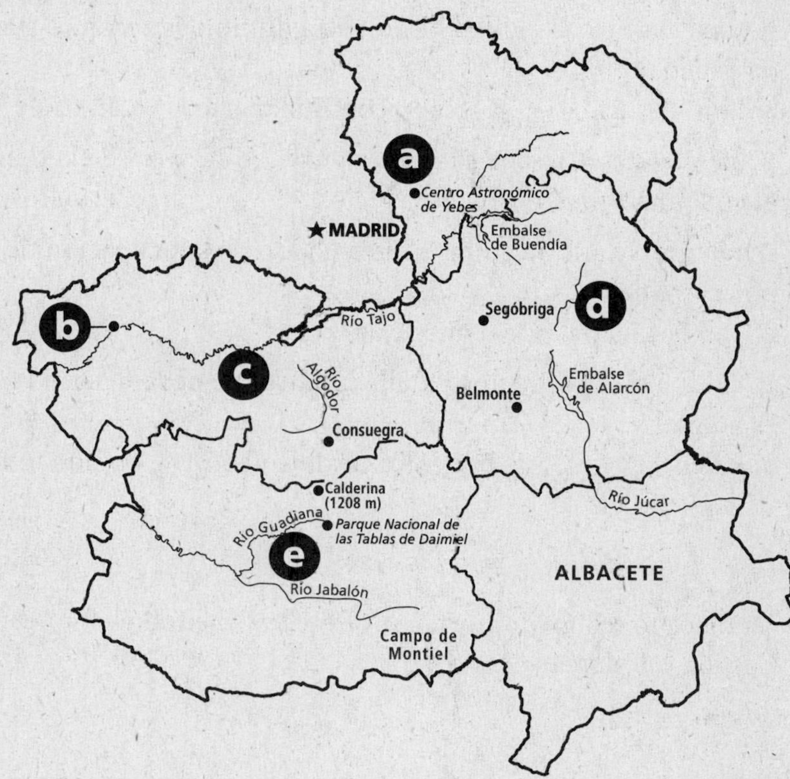

_____ **1.** Toledo

_____ **2.** Ciudad Real

_____ **3.** Talavera de la Reina

_____ **4.** Guadalajara

_____ **5.** Cuenca

SCORE /5

B Read each statement and write **cierto** or **falso.**

__________ **6.** El azafrán viene de las uvas.

__________ **7.** Albacete es la capital de la provincia de Albacete.

__________ **8.** Alfonso VI también es conocido como El Cid.

__________ **9.** El Greco vivió en Toledo por casi 40 años.

__________ **10.** Felipe II cambió la capital de España de Toledo a Madrid.

SCORE /5

PRUEBA: GEOCULTURA

C Choose the correct answer to each of the following questions.

____ **11.** ¿Cuál de estos lugares NO es una provincia de Castilla-La Mancha?
a. Segóbriga **b.** Ciudad Real **c.** Guadalajara

____ **12.** ¿Quién capturó la ciudad de Valencia durante la reconquista cristiana de España?
a. Luis Tristán **b.** Napoleón Bonaparte **c.** El Cid

____ **13.** ¿Cuál de estas artesanías famosas viene de Talavera de la Reina?
a. el damasquinado **b.** los azulejos **c.** el claroscuro

____ **14.** ¿Qué tipo de arquitectura es el resultado de la ocupación de España por parte de los musulmanes?
a. barroca **b.** mudéjar **c.** gótica

____ **15.** ¿Cuál fue el lugar de una batalla importante de la Guerra Civil española?
a. Valencia **b.** el Alcázar de Toledo **c.** Ciudad Real

SCORE ____ /5

D Write one sentence to tell the importance of each of the following people in the history of Castilla-La Mancha.

16. los visigodos

____

17. El Greco

____

18. Napoleón Bonaparte

____

19. Francisco Franco

____

20. Alfonso VI

____

SCORE ____ /15 TOTAL SCORE ____ /30

Vocabulario 1

A. (5 points)

1. b **2.** d **3.** e **4.** a **5.** c

B. (5 points)

6. a **7.** a **8.** c **9.** c **10.** b

C. (10 points) Answers will vary. Possible answers:

11. Viajé a Francia.

12. Lo pasé de película.

13. En agosto fui al parque de diversiones.

14. Me pareció un poco aburrida. No me interesó mucho.

15. Me quedé en casa y jugué naipes con mi familia.

D. (10 points)

16. De niño(a), me gustaba el patinaje en línea.

17. De pequeño(a), encontraba fascinante acampar en el bosque.

18. Cuando yo era niño(a), solía ir a la playa con mi familia.

19. Cuando tenía seis años, jugaba naipes con mi papá.

20. Los fines de semana, solía montar a caballo con mi primo(a).

Gramática 1

A. (5 points)

1. viajamos **2.** acampé

3. montábamos **4.** hacía **5.** dimos

B. (10 points)

6. estuve **7.** organizó **8.** montamos

9. hizo **10.** Recorrieron

C. (5 points)

11. ser **12.** ser **13.** estar

14. estar **15.** ser

D. (15 points) Answers will vary. Possible answers:

16. Es importante que compres patines.

17. Te aconsejo que ahorres dinero.

18. Te recomiendo que hagas windsurfing.

19. Es una buena idea que tomes clases de natación.

20. Te sugiero que tomes el autobús.

Aplicación 1

A. (5 points)

1. b

2. b

3. a

4. b

5. b

B. (15 points)

6. Fue a España, a la ciudad de Toledo.

7. Le pareció muy bella.

8. Estaba lloviendo.

9. No, no le dijo nada a nadie.

10. Es alto y guapo.

C. (15 points)

Answers will vary.

Vocabulario 2

A. (5 points)

1. c **2.** b **3.** c **4.** a **5.** c

B. (5 points)

6. d **7.** c **8.** e **9.** b **10.** a

C. (10 points) Answers will vary.
Possible answers:

11. Manuela, te aconsejo que toques música con la banda.

12. Ignacio, debes correr en el equipo de atletismo.

13. Mónica, debes tomar clases de oratoria.

14. Lorenzo, te aconsejo que diseñes páginas Web.

15. Anita, te recomiendo que participes en el club de debate.

D. (10 points) Answers will vary.
Possible answers:

16. Tengo ganas de ir al monte para observar la naturaleza.

17. Pienso ir a la costa para tomar el sol.

18. Voy a hacer ejercicios aeróbicos y practicar atletismo.

19. De hoy en adelante seguiré una dieta balanceada.

20. Pienso diseñar una página Web para todas mis fotos.

Gramática 2

A. (5 points)

1. aquélla **2.** ésta **3.** menos

4. este **5.** que

B. (10 points) Answers will vary.
Possible answers:

6. Hace tres días, fui al centro comercial con mis amigos.

7. Hace diez años que mi familia vive en Kirkwood.

8. Hace una semana que no practico atletismo.

9. Hace dos días, mi familia y yo fuimos a un restaurante para el desayuno.

10. Hace cinco años, conocí a mi mejor amigo.

C. (15 points)

11. Ella la tiene que hacer para mañana. / Ella tiene que hacerla para mañana.

12. ¿Ellas lo vieron en la tienda?

13. Ellos la practicaron.

14. Él las diseña para el club de computación.

15. Nosotros los hacemos.

D. (5 points)

16. ningún

17. ninguna

18. nadie

19. jamás

20. Tampoco

Aplicación 2

A. (10 points)

1. a **2.** b **3.** a **4.** b **5.** b

B. (10 points)

6. Están en el centro recreativo.

7. No, nunca hizo gimnasia.

8. Hace un año que Silvia hace gimnasia.

9. Le recomienda que vaya a la presentación sobre el centro.

10. Rita es la directora del centro. Es morena.

C. (15 points)
Answers will vary.

Lectura

A. (10 points) Answers may vary. Possible answer:

El autor usa los verbos en primera persona en el ensayo. Usa la primera persona para contar su opinión personal del tema.

B. (10 points)

1. c **2.** b **3.** a **4.** e **5.** d

C. (15 points)

6. La industria artesanal fue importante durante los siglos XV, XVI y XVII porque vinieron a Toledo artesanos de toda Europa y del Oriente, para aprender los secretos de los artistas de Toledo.

7. El arte del damasquinado indica que los árabes vivieron en Toledo alguna vez.

8. La armadura, o los vestidos de hierro, están hechos a mano por los artesanos de Toledo.

Escritura

A. (20 points) Answers will vary.

B. (15 points) Answers will vary.

Geocultura

A. (5 points)

1. c **2.** e **3.** b **4.** a **5.** d

B. (5 points)

6. falso

7. cierto

8. falso

9. falso

10. cierto

C. (5 points)

11. a **12.** c **13.** b **14.** b **15.** b

D. (15 points) Answers may vary.

16. Los visigodos invadieron la península ibérica y nombraron Toledo su capital.

17. El Greco es considerado como el primer genio de la escuela española de pintura al principio del movimiento barroco.

18. Napoleón Bonaparte controló la mayor parte de Europa durante la primera parte de los años 1800, pero fue derrotado en la batalla de Talavera.

19. Francisco Franco ganó la batalla del Alcázar de Toledo durante la Guerra Civil española y tomó control del país.

20. Alfonso VI encabezó la reconquista de España y capturó la ciudad de Toledo en 1085.

Aplicación 1

Escuchemos

A Listen to Irene's statements about her weekend plans with her friends, and choose **a)** for **cierto** or **b)** for **falso.**

1. Gloria quiere que montemos a caballo el sábado porque nunca lo hizo.
2. Laura siempre montaba a caballo de niña y le encantaba. Dice que es genial.
3. Jorge prefiere que practiquemos el esquí acuático. Dice que es muy divertido.
4. Tina está nerviosa porque no le gustan los deportes. No sabe hacer el esquí acuático.
5. Raúl sugiere que todos vayamos a la playa y que Tina coleccione caracoles.

Aplicación 2

Escuchemos

A Listen to some friends talk about their travel experience. Then, choose the correct answer to each question.

1. Hace tres años Tito fue a Europa con su familia. Disfrutaron mucho del viaje.
2. Elena fue a América del Sur el año pasado. Ella quiere regresar pronto.
3. Fernando viajó más que Catalina el verano pasado. Él fue a Europa, África y Latinoamérica.
4. Hace una semana, Patricia salió para México. Ella regresa a Nueva York en dos meses.
5. Ricardo nunca salió del país. Tiene muchas ganas de viajar al Caribe.

Nombre ______________________ Clase ____________ Fecha ____________

Vocabulario 1

A Complete each sentence with the correct vocabulary word.

a. el kárate
b. me aburro
c. esquí acuático
d. me la paso
e. ciclismo

_____ **1.** ¿Quieres ir a la playa a practicar ___ ?

_____ **2.** No aguanto el senderismo. ___ mucho.

_____ **3.** Estoy loco por la escalada deportiva. ___ escalando.

_____ **4.** Me encantan las artes marciales como ___ .

_____ **5.** Me la paso montando en bicicleta. Soy un fanático del ___ .

SCORE | /5

B Choose the correct expression for each of the following situations.

a. El boliche me deja frío(a).
b. Estoy loco(a) por el salto de altura.
c. Eres muy bueno(a) para escalar, ¿verdad?
d. No, gracias, iba a jugar al boliche con los amigos.
e. ¿Te gustaría ir al cine? Yo te invito.

_____ **6.** to invite someone to go to the movies with you, your treat

_____ **7.** to respond that you have other plans

_____ **8.** to ask someone if he or she is good at climbing

_____ **9.** to say you are crazy about the high jump

_____ **10.** to say that bowling doesn't do anything for you

SCORE | /5

PRUEBA: VOCABULARIO 1

C Write a conversation between Javier and Olga based on the following prompts.

11. Javier invites Olga to go hiking on Saturday.

____

12. Olga tells Javier she already has plans but asks him to go biking with her on Sunday.

____

13. Javier agrees, and asks when she wants to meet.

____

14. Olga says she'll meet whenever he wants, it's all the same to her.

____

15. Javier remembers that Olga is a good biker and asks her if it's true. He says he'd better rest up.

____

SCORE /10

D Complete the following conversation with the appropriate questions.

Edgar Soy un fanático de los deportes.

(16) ____

Maya Pues, la verdad es que los deportes me dejan fría.

(17) ____

Edgar Sí, me la paso escalando. Pero también me gustan otras actividades como ir al cine.

(18) ____

Maya Sí, gracias. ¡Pero no tienes que invitarme!

(19) ____

Edgar Como quieras. Me da lo mismo. Escoge la película tú.

(20) ____

Maya No, no aguanto las películas de acción.

SCORE /10 TOTAL SCORE /30

Gramática 1

A In the blank, write **presente** if an activity is currently done by the person, or **pasado** if the activity was done in the past.

______________ **1.** Jaime y Alejandro juegan al boliche casi todos los días.

______________ **2.** De niña, Lucy jugaba al dominó.

______________ **3.** Cuando tenía diez años, me la pasaba haciendo rompecabezas.

______________ **4.** Eduardo hace senderismo todos los veranos.

______________ **5.** Antes, los estudiantes estudiaban para los exámenes.

SCORE ______ /5

B Complete the answers to the questions by filling in the blank with the **nosotros** command of the verbs in parentheses.

6. Soy un gran aficionado al jai-alai. ¿Qué podemos hacer para ver un partido?

(comprar) ______________ boletos para el partido o

(ir) ______________ al frontón en la plaza.

7. Estoy aburrida con el atletismo. ¿Qué podemos hacer para mantenernos en forma sin aburrirnos?

(hacer) ______________ senderismo o

(practicar) ______________ el ciclismo.

8. No hay nada interesante que hacer este fin de semana ¿Qué hacemos?

(comer) ______________ con un grupo de amigos o

(ver) ______________ una película.

9. Nuestro televisor se rompió ayer. ¿Qué podemos hacer para divertirnos?

(jugar) ______________ al dominó o

(escuchar) ______________ la radio.

10. Soy un gran fanático de los deportes acuáticos. ¿Qué podemos hacer este verano?

(remar) ______________ en el lago u

(organizar) ______________ una excursión a la playa.

SCORE ______ /10

PRUEBA: GRAMÁTICA 1

C Make sentences using the phrases to tell what the Martínez family planned to do and why they couldn't do it. Use **ir a** + the infinitive in the past tense.

11. Sara / ver una película / tener que hacer su tarea

____

12. Jaime y Eduardo / escalar / tener que limpiar sus cuartos

____

13. Mamá y yo / hacer unas compras / sentirse muy cansadas

____

14. Papá / lavar el carro / tener que cocinar

____

15. Abuela / llamar a su amiga / no tener su número de teléfono

____

SCORE /10

D Complete the conversation by filling in the blank with the imperfect or a **nosotros** command of the verbs in the box.

pasar	**remar**	**jugar**	**fascinar**	**ir**

Alejandra Hola José, ¿cómo estás?

José Me siento aburrido. Tengo ganas de hacer algo pero no sé qué.

Alejandra (**16**) ____________ al parque. Soy una fanática del béisbol y hay un partido que me gustaría ver.

José No, gracias. Cuando era niño, me (**17**) ____________ el béisbol, pero ahora me deja frío. En vez de ver el partido, mejor (**18**) ____________ al boliche.

Alejandra La verdad es que antes me la (**19**) ____________ jugando al boliche, pero ahora no. ¿No te gustaría ir al lago a remar?

José ¡Qué idea genial! ¿Pero cómo sabías que soy aficionado al remo?

Alejandra Pues, el año pasado me contaste que cuando vivías cerca del lago (**20**) ____________ todos los días.

SCORE /10 TOTAL SCORE /35

Nombre ______________________ Clase ______________ Fecha ______________

CAPÍTULO 2

Aplicación 1

PRUEBA

Escuchemos

A Listen to the conversation between Gabriela and Carlos and answer the following questions.

____ **1.** ¿Qué quiere hacer Gabriela el sábado?
a. jugar al boliche
b. practicar el tiro con arco
c. hacer senderismo

____ **2.** ¿Qué iba a hacer Carlos el sábado?
a. iba a hacer senderismo
b. iba a jugar al boliche
c. iba a practicar atletismo

____ **3.** ¿Por qué no quiere jugar al boliche Gabriela?
a. nunca ha jugado al boliche
b. jugó mucho durante el verano
c. ya tiene planes

____ **4.** ¿Qué sugiere Carlos al final?
a. que vayan el próximo fin de semana
b. que no inviten a Pablo
c. que no hagan senderismo

____ **5.** ¿Qué quiere hacer Gabriela?
a. ir al bosque
b. escalar
c. ir a las montañas

SCORE /10

PRUEBA: APLICACIÓN 1

Leamos

B Read Zoila's essay about herself. Then, read the statements that follow and choose **a)** for **cierto** or **b)** for **falso.**

Soy una gran aficionada a las artes marciales. De niña, iba todos los días a clases de kárate. Cuando empecé en el colegio, iba a seguir tomando clases, pero el equipo de atletismo necesitaba más chicas. Soy muy buena para el salto de altura y también corro muy rápido. Estoy loca por el atletismo. Ahora estoy en la universidad y me la paso haciendo atletismo. Todavía me gustan las artes marciales y de vez en cuando, voy a clases de kárate también.

____ **6.** A Zoila le dejan fría las artes marciales.

____ **7.** Zoila nunca hacía kárate de niña.

____ **8.** Zoila iba a clases de kárate en el colegio.

____ **9.** Zoila es muy buena para el salto de altura.

____ **10.** Zoila está loca por el atletismo.

SCORE ____ /10

Escribamos

C Last weekend you had many plans but things kept coming up, and your plans kept changing. Write a paragraph telling about five activities you had planned on doing and explain why you didn't do them.

____

____

____

____

____

____

____

____

SCORE ____ /15

TOTAL SCORE ____ /35

Vocabulario 2

A Read María's descriptions of several people and decide which adjective best describes each person.

_____ **1.** Juan Miguel es muy buen amigo. Siempre dice la verdad y sé que puedo confiar en él.
a. creído **b.** honesto **c.** grosero

_____ **2.** Antonio quiere que yo salga solamente con él. Siempre peleamos si me ve hablando con otros amigos.
a. celoso **b.** desleal **c.** confiable

_____ **3.** Maribel no sabe guardar los secretos. Si le digo algo privado, siempre se lo dice a todo el mundo. Siempre está hablando mal de los amigos.
a. generosa **b.** seca **c.** chismosa

_____ **4.** Lola siempre comparte lo que tiene. Si necesito algo, me ayuda.
a. terca **b.** honesta **c.** generosa

_____ **5.** Luis cree que es el chico más guapo del colegio. Se considera superior a todos.
a. desleal **b.** creído **c.** atento

SCORE ____ /5

B Read each statement or question and choose the most logical response.

_____ **6.** Te veo de buen humor.
a. Sí, estoy decepcionada porque Luisa nunca me apoya.
b. Sí, estoy entusiasmada porque Luisa y yo hemos hecho las paces.

_____ **7.** ¿Qué te pasa? ¿Estás dolida?
a. Sí, me siento mal porque Eduardo no respeta mis sentimientos.
b. Sí, estoy feliz porque Eduardo es muy atento.

_____ **8.** ¿Cómo debe ser un buen amigo?
a. Un buen amigo debe ser muy criticón.
b. Un buen amigo no debe ser creído.

_____ **9.** ¿Qué buscas en un novio?
a. Busco uno que sea confiable y leal.
b. Busco uno que no sea grosero.

_____ **10.** ¿Por qué crees que Laura no es confiable?
a. Porque siempre es muy solidaria.
b. Porque miente muy a menudo.

SCORE ____ /5

Nombre ______________________ Clase ______________ Fecha ______________

CAPÍTULO 2

PRUEBA: VOCABULARIO 2

C Write what you would say in Spanish in the following situations.

11. Tell a friend that you are disappointed because Sara is very cold toward you.

____

12. Say that you and Rosa have a lot in common.

____

13. Explain that you think Alejo is very rude.

____

14. Tell someone that your friend Sonia broke up with her boyfriend Víctor.

____

15. Say that you have not made up with David.

____

SCORE /10

D Write a sentence describing each person with the adjective provided, and explain why it applies to him or her.

16. Diego / maleducado

____

17. Rita / insegura

____

18. Eva / abierta

____

19. Fernando / terco

____

20. Miguel / leal

____

SCORE /10 TOTAL SCORE /30

Gramática 2

A Read each statement. In the blank, write **a)** if the person expresses a belief, or **b)** if the person expresses an emotion.

____ **1.** Me encanta que seas una amiga leal.

____ **2.** Creo que llegamos tarde a la escuela.

____ **3.** Ella se alegra de que sus amigas vengan a la fiesta.

____ **4.** Mis padres temen que yo sea maleducado.

____ **5.** A mi parecer, tu novio es un chico muy celoso.

SCORE ____ /5

B Complete the conversation by filling in the blank with the subjunctive or the indicative of the verbs in parentheses.

Roberto Bárbara, ¿qué buscas en un novio?

Bárbara Pues, quiero un novio que (**6**) ____________ (es / sea) leal. Mi último novio fue desleal y rompí con él. ¿Cómo debe ser tu novia?

Roberto Para mí, lo más importante es el sentido del humor. Quiero que mi novia me (**7**) ____________ (haga / hace) reír. También quiero que no (**8**) ____________ (tiene / tenga) celos. Mi novia (**9**) ____________ (sea / es) muy celosa y no me deja salir con mis amigos. Tampoco tiene un buen sentido del humor.

Bárbara ¡Qué lástima! Pero, ¿por qué no rompes con ella?

Roberto No sé. A lo mejor es porque ella (**10**) ____________ (sabe / sepa) algo de deportes y a mí me gustan los deportes.

Bárbara ¡Ay, Roberto, para ti no hay remedio!

SCORE ____ /10

PRUEBA: GRAMÁTICA 2

C Rewrite the sentences by replacing the direct and indirect objects with direct and indirect object pronouns.

11. Carmen le dio los libros a su hermana.

____

12. Mi amiga me prestó la cámara a mí.

____

13. Mis hermanos les enviaron cartas a mis padres.

____

14. Mis tías nos dieron regalos a mí y a mi hermano.

____

15. José le dijo el secreto a su primo.

____

SCORE /10

D Complete Jessica's letter to Ana by filling in the blank with the correct form of the indicative or the subjunctive of the verbs in the box.

devolver	**ser**	**hacer**	**poder**	**tener**

Querida Ana:

Te escribo para darte las gracias por el buen consejo que me diste. Ayer, rompí con Alejandro. La verdad es que él es muy celoso y además, no (**16**) ____________ nada en común. Yo necesito alguien con quien (**17**) ____________ practicar deportes y pasarlo bien. Ahora busco un novio que no (**18**) ____________ inseguro y que me apoye en todo. Hoy le voy a pedir a Alejandro que me (**19**) ____________ las fotos que le he dado. Él me dijo que mañana va a hacerlo. Espero que (**20**) ____________ lo que me prometió. Pues te mantendré al tanto de los acontecimientos. Hasta luego.

Tu amiga,

Jessica

SCORE /10 TOTAL SCORE /35

Nombre ______________________ Clase ______________ Fecha ____________

CAPÍTULO **2**

Aplicación 2

PRUEBA

Escuchemos

A Listen to each person talk about their friends or someone they know. Then, read the questions and choose the appropriate answer.

_____ **1.** ¿Cuál es el problema con Felipe?
a. Es creído. **b.** Es chismoso. **c.** Es confiable.

_____ **2.** ¿Cómo es Alicia?
a. Es seca. **b.** Es sociable. **c.** Es amigable.

_____ **3.** ¿Por qué no se puede confiar en Isabel?
a. Es chismosa. **b.** Es grosera. **c.** Es maleducada.

_____ **4.** ¿Por qué Yolanda no quiere hacer las paces con Pepe?
a. Es infiel. **b.** Es atenta. **c.** Es terca.

_____ **5.** ¿Por qué Lorenzo no cree en sí mismo?
a. Es maleducado. **b.** Es abierto. **c.** Es inseguro.

SCORE /10

Leamos

B Read the following conversation and answer the questions.

Julia Oye, Silvia, ¿qué te pasa? ¿Estás dolida?

Silvia Sí, estoy triste porque mi novio Roberto le regaló flores a Carmen. Estoy muy decepcionada de él.

Julia ¿Por qué hizo algo así? Él no es muy confiable. Además, me parece muy maleducado. Cuéntame, ¿qué pasó?

Silvia Salí de clases a las dos y me fui a verlo. Lo vi de lejos. Estaba regalándole flores a Carmen. Me molesta que él le diga una cosa a Carmen y me diga otra cosa a mí. Nos miente a las dos. No hablemos de eso porque me dan ganas de llorar.

Julia No puedes confiar en él. Debes buscar un novio que sea leal y solidario.

PRUEBA: APLICACIÓN 2

6. ¿Por qué está triste Silvia?

____

7. ¿Cómo se siente Silvia?

____

8. ¿Qué dice Julia acerca de Roberto?

____

9. ¿Por qué está decepcionada Silvia de Roberto?

____

10. ¿Cómo es el novio que Julia sugiere que busque Silvia?

____

SCORE /10

Escribamos

C Rosana is going to try a dating service at her school. Write an ad for her describing the kind of boyfriend she is looking for, and describe her personality.

____

____

____

____

____

____

____

____

____

SCORE /15 TOTAL SCORE /35

Nombre ______________________ Clase ______________ Fecha ______________

CAPÍTULO **2**

Lectura

PRUEBA

A Read this advertisement about a cycling club. As you read, look for the main idea of the ad. Once you finish, write the main idea on the line below.

> **¡Únete a nuestro club de ciclismo!**
>
> Si tienes entre 15 y 17 años, y si eres muy bueno para el ciclismo, tú eres la persona que buscamos. Disfruta con nosotros de paseos de 40 a 45 kilómetros diarios por los caminos de Castilla-La Mancha. Somos unos fanáticos de este deporte y queremos tener más miembros en el club. Todos los fines de semana, el club hace un paseo. Este sábado saldremos temprano para Consuegra. Vamos a almorzar junto a los molinos y regresaremos al colegio por la tarde. ¿Qué estás esperando? Tendrás la oportunidad de hacer amigos y mantenerte en forma al mismo tiempo. Recuerda que necesitas permiso de tus padres, así que debes tener una carta firmada por ellos que te dé autorización para integrarte al club. ¡Esperamos verte pronto!

Main idea: ____

SCORE ____ /10

B Read each statement, and choose **a**) for **cierto** or **b**) for **falso.**

____ **1.** Para pertenecer al club de ciclismo debes tener menos de 15 años.

____ **2.** El club de ciclismo hace paseos diarios de 40 a 45 kilómetros.

____ **3.** Todos los fines de semana el club de ciclismo va a Consuegra.

____ **4.** El club es una buena oportunidad para mantenerse en forma.

____ **5.** Para ser miembro del club necesitas una autorización de tus padres.

SCORE ____ /10

C Answer the following questions in complete sentences.

6. ¿Por qué crees que uno tiene que ser muy bueno(a) para el ciclismo para ser miembro del club?

____

7. Describe la persona ideal para el club de ciclismo.

____

8. ¿Qué tienen en común los miembros del club de ciclismo?

____

SCORE ____ /15 TOTAL SCORE ____ /35

Escritura

A Write a conversation between Sofía and Ángel. Sofía is upset and she is telling Ángel why she broke up with her boyfriend, Jorge. Ángel starts asking her what kind of boyfriend she is looking for and they realize they have a lot in common. Finally, Ángel invites Sofía to do something on Saturday and she accepts the invitation.

Sofía ____

____

Ángel ____

____

Sofía ____

____

Ángel ____

____

Sofía ____

SCORE /20

B David is remembering his college days. Write a letter from David to his friend Mark in which he talks about some of the sports they used to do together. Include some sports they both really liked and were good at and some that either David or Mark disliked or found boring.

____

____

____

____

____

____

____

____

____

____

SCORE /15

TOTAL SCORE /35

Nombre ______________________ Clase ______________ Fecha ______________

Geocultura

A Match each letter on the map of Castilla-La Mancha with the name of the place or area it represents.

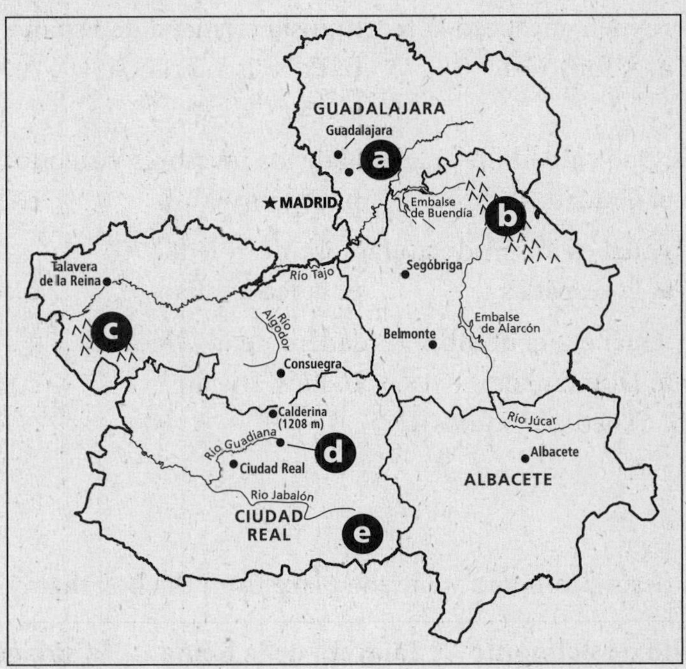

_____ **1.** Parque Nacional de las Tablas de Daimiel

_____ **2.** Serranía de Cuenca

_____ **3.** Campo de Montiel

_____ **4.** Centro Astronómico de Yebes

_____ **5.** Montes de Toledo

SCORE /5

B Read each sentence, and choose **a**) for **cierto** and **b**) for **falso.**

_____ **6.** La ciudad de Toledo está ubicada en un precipicio a orillas del río Tajo.

_____ **7.** Los molinos de viento se encuentran en las montañas de Castilla-La Mancha.

_____ **8.** Para obtener un kilo de azafrán hay que recoger casi 45.000 flores.

_____ **9.** Las casas colgadas están en la ciudad de Cuenca.

_____ **10.** La Corona de Recesvinto es uno de los tesoros visigodos que queda de la ocupación germánica en España.

SCORE /10

PRUEBA: GEOCULTURA

C Read the following questions and choose the correct answer.

____ **11.** ¿A qué grupo expulsaron los musulmanes de Castilla-La Mancha?
a. los romanos **b.** los visigodos **c.** los franceses

____ **12.** ¿Quién encabezó la reconquista cristiana de España?
a. Alfonso VI **b.** Francisco Franco **c.** Rodrigo Díaz de Vivar

____ **13.** ¿Qué ciudad fue la capital de los invasores visigodos?
a. Ciudad Real **b.** Segóbriga **c.** Toledo

____ **14.** ¿Cuál es un producto famoso de Toledo?
a. las espadas **b.** la fotografía **c.** los azulejos

____ **15.** ¿Cuál era el nombre verdadero de El Greco?
a. Domenikos Theotocopoulos **b.** Luis Tristán **c.** El Greco de la Mancha

SCORE ____ /5

D Read each description and write the place from the box that best fits each one.

el Castillo de Belmonte	**Talavera de la Reina**	**la sinagoga del Tránsito**
el Alcázar de Toledo	**Ciudad Real**	**Segóbriga** **Toledo**

________________ **16.** Esta ciudad es muy conocida por sus cerámicas y azulejos. Aquí, las tropas inglesas y españolas pelearon en la guerra contra Napoleón.

________________ **17.** La catedral de esta ciudad fue construida entre 1226 y 1493.

________________ **18.** Este edificio es un ejemplo de arquitectura mudéjar. Tiene muchos arcos y diseños geométricos típicos de la época.

________________ **19.** Este edificio fue construido en el siglo XV. Tiene una mezcla de estilos gótico, mudéjar y renacentista, y está muy bien conservado.

________________ **20.** En este pueblo se encuentran las ruinas de una poderosa civilización. El anfiteatro y los baños públicos, construidos hace más de 1.500 años, atraen a muchos turistas a este pueblo.

SCORE ____ /10 TOTAL SCORE ____ /30

Vocabulario 1

A. (5 points)

1. c **2.** b **3.** d **4.** a **5.** e

B. (5 points)

6. e **7.** d **8.** c **9.** b **10.** a

C. (10 points)

11. ¿Te gustaría hacer senderismo el sábado?

12. No, gracias. Ya tengo planes. ¿Quieres practicar ciclismo conmigo el domingo?

13. ¡Sí! ¿A qué hora?

14. Como quieras. Me da lo mismo.

15. Eres muy buena para el ciclismo, ¿verdad? Debo descansar mucho.

D. (10 points) Answers will vary. Possible answers:

16. ¿Qué deporte te gusta a ti?

17. Eres muy bueno para la escalada deportiva, ¿verdad?

18. ¿Te gustaría ir al cine? Yo te invito.

19. ¿Qué película quieres ver?

20. ¿Te gustan las películas de acción?

Gramática 1

A. (5 points)

1. presente **2.** pasado **3.** pasado
4. presente **5.** pasado

B. (10 points)

6. Compremos, vamos

7. Hagamos, practiquemos

8. Comamos, veamos

9. Juguemos, escuchemos

10. Rememos, organicemos

C. (10 points)

11. Sara iba a ver una película, pero tuvo que hacer su tarea.

12. Jaime y Eduardo iban a escalar, pero tuvieron que limpiar sus cuartos.

13. Mamá y yo íbamos a hacer unas compras, pero nos sentimos muy cansadas.

14. Papá iba a lavar el carro, pero tuvo que cocinar.

15. Abuela iba a llamar a su amiga, pero no tenía su número de teléfono.

D. (10 points)

16. Vamos

17. fascinaba

18. juguemos

19. pasaba

20. remabas

Aplicación 1

A. (10 points)

1. c

2. b

3. b

4. a

5. a

B. (10 points)

6. b

7. b

8. b

9. a

10. a

C. (15 points)

Answers will vary.

Vocabulario 2

A. (5 points)

1. b **2.** a **3.** c **4.** c **5.** b

B. (5 points)

6. b **7.** a **8.** b **9.** a **10.** b

C. (10 points)

11. Estoy decepcionada porque Sara es muy fría y seca conmigo.

12. Rosa y yo tenemos mucho en común.

13. Creo que Alejo es muy maleducado/grosero.

14. Sonia rompió con Víctor.

15. David y yo no hemos hecho las paces.

D. (10 points)

Answers will vary. Possible answers:

16. Diego es muy maleducado porque no respeta los sentimientos de los demás.

17. Rita es insegura porque cree que todo el mundo es superior a ella.

18. Eva es muy abierta, habla con todo el mundo y no tiene miedo de expresar sus sentimientos.

19. Fernando es muy terco porque nunca cambia sus ideas.

20. Miguel es leal y confiable. Siempre guarda los secretos.

Gramática 2

A. (5 points)

1. b **2.** a **3.** b **4.** b **5.** a

B. (10 points)

6. sea

7. haga

8. tenga

9. es

10. sabe

C. (10 points)

11. Carmen se los dio.

12. Mi amiga me la prestó.

13. Mis hermanos se las enviaron.

14. Mis tías nos los dieron.

15. José se lo dijo.

D. (10 points)

16. tenemos

17. pueda

18. sea

19. devuelva

20. haga

Aplicación 2

A. (10 points)

1. a

2. b

3. a

4. c

5. c

B. (10 points)

6. Está triste porque Roberto le regaló flores a Carmen.

7. Silvia se siente muy decepcionada de Roberto.

8. Dice que no es confiable y que es un maleducado.

9. Está decepcionada porque Roberto les miente a las dos.

10. Es una persona leal y solidaria.

C. (15 points)

Answers will vary.

Lectura

A. (10 points) Answers will vary. Possible answer: La idea principal son las ventajas de practicar ciclismo y de hacerse miembro de un club de ciclismo.

B. (10 points)

1. b **2.** a **3.** b **4.** a **5.** a

C. (15 points) Answers will vary.

6. Uno(a) tiene que ser muy bueno(a) para el ciclismo porque los paseos son largos.

7. La persona ideal para el club de ciclismo debe ser muy buena para montar en bicicleta y un(a) fanático(a) de ese deporte.

8. Los miembros tienen en común su dedicación al ciclismo y el deseo de mantenerse en forma.

Escritura

A. (20 points)
Answers will vary. Possible answers may include: decepcionada, romper con, ¿Qué buscas en un novio?, tener mucho en común, invitar

B. (15 points)
Answers will vary. Possible answers may include: practicábamos las artes marciales, íbamos a remar, sí, estaba entusiasmado porque..., éramos muy buenos para... ¿verdad? estábamos locos por..., lo pasábamos bien..., éramos unos fanáticos / aficionados a..., no aguantabas.. me/te aburría… el atletismo, el ciclismo, la escalada deportiva, la esgrima, el salto de altura, el senderismo.

Geocultura

A. (5 points)

1. d **2.** b **3.** e **4.** a **5.** c

B. (10 points)

6. a

7. b

8. b

9. a

10. a

C. (5 points)

11. b **12.** a **13.** c **14.** a **15.** a

D. (10 points)

16. Talavera de la Reina

17. Toledo

18. la Sinagoga del Tránsito

19. el Castillo de Belmonte

20. Segóbriga

Aplicación 1

Escuchemos

A. Listen to the conversation between Gabriela and Carlos and answer the following questions.

Gabriela ¿Quieres hacer senderismo este sábado, Carlos?

Carlos Pues, iba a jugar al boliche con Pablo, pero estoy loco por el senderismo. ¿Quieres ir el domingo?

Gabriela No puedo. Samuel me va a enseñar el tiro con arco el domingo.

Carlos ¿Quieres jugar al boliche con Pablo y conmigo?

Gabriela No, gracias. Jugué al boliche todos los fines de semana del verano y no aguanto más.

Carlos Dejémoslo para el próximo fin de semana entonces e invitemos a Pablo también. Podemos ir a las montañas porque conozco un lugar perfecto para hacer senderismo.

Gabriela ¿Ah, sí? Pues, yo creo que debemos ir al bosque.

Carlos Como quieras. Me da lo mismo.

Gabriela Bueno, te llamo. ¡Hasta luego!

Aplicación 2

Escuchemos

A. Listen to each person talk about their friends or someone they know. Then, read the questions and choose the appropriate answer.

1. Ya no soy amigo de Felipe. Él siempre pensaba que él era mejor que nadie y yo no aguantaba más. No conozco a ningún chico que sea tan creído como él.
2. Mi amiga Alicia es muy sociable. Me alegra que venga a la fiesta. De hecho, ella no iba a ir a la fiesta pero la convencí.
3. Estoy decepcionada porque no puedo contar con Isabel para nada. Le conté que salí con Daniel y se lo dijo a todas las chicas del salón. Es una chismosa de primera.
4. Me irrita que Yolanda no quiera hacer las paces con Pepe. Ella es tan terca. En realidad, Pepe no hizo nada malo.
5. No me gusta la actitud de Lorenzo. Él no cree en sí mismo. Se lo he dicho muchas veces. Me frustra que él sea tan inseguro.

Nombre ______________________ Clase ______________ Fecha ______________

CAPÍTULO

Vocabulario 1

PRUEBA

A Read the sentences below. Choose the word that best summarizes each sentence.

_____ **1.** El señor Gutiérrez me da consejos sobre los cursos que debo tomar.
a. el profesor **b.** el consejero **c.** el director

_____ **2.** Saqué una mala nota en este curso, y ahora tengo que tomarlo de nuevo.
a. suspender **b.** combatir **c.** tomar apuntes

_____ **3.** El año escolar está dividido en dos partes de seis meses cada una.
a. la universidad **b.** el horario **c.** el semestre

_____ **4.** El gobierno de un país no respeta la igualdad de cierto grupo social o étnico.
a. el director **b.** la fama **c.** la discriminación

_____ **5.** La gente forma una idea particular de un grupo con base en la televisión o los periódicos.
a. la física **b.** la imagen **c.** el colmo

SCORE ____ /5

B María is writing to her pen pal about what her semester is like. Read her message, and choose the words from the box to complete it.

horario	**ciencias sociales**	**aprobar**	**prueba**	**la universidad**

Hola Karla:

¿Qué tal? ¿Cómo van tus clases? Pues, a mí me gusta mi (**6**) ______________ este semestre. Tengo cálculo, (**7**) ______________ y literatura por las mañanas. Tengo español y geografía por las tardes. El consejero insiste en que tome geografía porque es necesario para entrar a (**8**) ______________. De hecho, mañana vamos a tener otra (**9**) ______________ en esa clase. Es muy importante para mí (**10**) ______________ esta materia. ¡Tengo que estudiar!

Nos vemos,

María

SCORE ____ /5

PRUEBA: VOCABULARIO 1

C Below is part of a conversation between Alberto and Javier. Read the conversation, then choose a word from the box that best completes each sentence.

falta de respeto	**estereotipos**	**juzgarme**
actitud negativa	**impresión equivocada**	

Alberto Yo creo que Paula tiene una (**11**) ______________ de mí, ¿no piensas?

Javier ¿Por qué? ¿Qué pasó?

Alberto Ella me dijo que tengo una (**12**) ______________ hacia las mujeres. ¡Qué (**13**) ______________! No me conoce tan bien como para (**14**) ______________ así.

Javier ¿Qué le dijiste?

Alberto Pues, le dije que las mujeres no deben jugar al fútbol con nosotros. Y me dijo que debo olvidar los (**15**) ______________ tontos de las mujeres y dejarla jugar.

SCORE /10

D Write what you would say in Spanish in the following situations.

16. You do not think it is fair that you have another test in geometry.

____

17. Someone tells you something that is obviously completely untrue.

____

18. You've had it up to here and you can't take it anymore!

____

19. You really dislike Hugo's attitude toward sports.

____

20. In your opinion, there's no equality between soccer and football.

____

SCORE /10 TOTAL SCORE /30

Gramática 1

A Read each statement. In the blank, write **a**) if it is an **affirmation**, or **b**) if it is a **denial.**

_____ **1.** Estoy seguro de que la discriminación ha terminado.

_____ **2.** No es cierto que todos los hombres sean ignorantes.

_____ **3.** Él no cree que haya desigualdad entre los sexos.

_____ **4.** Estamos de acuerdo en que debemos luchar por la libertad.

_____ **5.** Ellos afirman que estaban equivocados.

SCORE /5

B State whether you agree or disagree with the statement by using a phrase of affirmation or negation in your sentence. Be sure to use a different phrase for each answer and pay attention to the use of the indicative and the subjunctive.

Es verdad que	**Estoy de acuerdo que**	**Creo que**
No estoy de acuerdo que	**No es verdad que**	**No creo que**

6. Los estudiantes de hoy no aprenden nada en el colegio.

____

7. La discriminación no existe en Estados Unidos.

____

8. Hay estereotipos de la gente hispana en la televisión.

____

9. Las clases de arte y música no son necesarias para los estudiantes.

____

10. Los horarios de clase deben ser extendidos.

____

SCORE /10

PRUEBA: GRAMÁTICA 1

C In September, everyone has different wishes for the coming school year. Fill in the blank with the correct conjugation of the verb to find out what the wishes are.

11. Los estudiantes esperan que sus horarios no (ser) ______________ difíciles.

12. Los profesores insisten en que los estudiantes (tomar) ______________ apuntes.

13. Los padres quieren que sus hijos (aprobar) ______________ todos sus exámenes.

14. Los estudiantes esperan que las vacaciones (llegar) ______________ pronto.

15. Los padres sueñan con tener un hijo(a) que (ir) ______________ a una buena universidad.

SCORE ____ /10

D Complete Tito's advice by using phrases from the first column and the **subjunctive** or the **infinitive** of the verbs in the phrases of the second column.

debes pedirle que	tomar apuntes en el cuaderno
tienes que	haber igualdad para mujeres y hombres en el trabajo
deben insistir en que	ayudar a tus padres en casa
debes aprender a	permitir tomar otra clase
debes tratar de	estudiar más para el próximo examen

Luz María No aprobé el último examen de álgebra. ¿Qué debo hacer?

Tito (16) ____

Rogelio No recuerdo nada de la clase. ¿Cómo puedo recordar las lecciones?

Tito (17) ____

Silvia y Ana Nuestro jefe trata a los hombres mejor que a las mujeres. ¿Qué debemos hacer para combatir su ignorancia?

Tito (18) ____

Virginia Mi consejero insiste en que tome la clase de álgebra aunque ya la tomé el año pasado. ¿Qué debo hacer?

Tito (19) ____

Daniel Mamá y papá siempre llegan muy cansados del trabajo. ¿Cómo puedo mejorar la situación?

Tito (20) ____

SCORE ____ /10 TOTAL SCORE ____ /35

Aplicación 1

Escuchemos

A Listen to Rocío's conversation with her guidance counselor. Then, read the statements that follow and choose **a)** for **cierto** or **b)** for **falso.**

_____ **1.** Rocío piensa ir a la universidad.

_____ **2.** Rocío no aprobó una clase de matemáticas el semestre pasado.

_____ **3.** Rocío piensa tomar geometría y cálculo este semestre.

_____ **4.** El consejero insiste en que tome geografía y física también.

_____ **5.** El consejero quiere que Rocío tome buenos apuntes.

SCORE ____ /10

Leamos

B Read the conversation. Then, read the statements below and choose **a)** for **cierto** or **b)** for **falso.**

Jaime Hola, Cristián. Oye, voy a jugar al fútbol al rato y quiero que me acompañes. Hace falta otro jugador. ¿Qué dices?

Cristián Hoy no puedo. Tengo que estudiar para el examen de física. Mis papás insisten en que yo apruebe ese examen.

Karla Yo te acompaño. A mí me encanta el fútbol y no tengo planes.

Jaime ¿Tú? No creo que puedas jugar con nosotros. Eres una mujer. Estoy seguro que no sabes jugar bien.

Karla No puedo creer que me hayas dicho eso. ¡Qué falta de respeto, Jaime! Me choca tu actitud hacia las mujeres. Tú tienes una impresión muy equivocada.

Jaime Lo siento Karla. No te ofendas. Bueno, vamos al campo de fútbol.

_____ **6.** Para empezar, Jaime le pide a Cristián y a Karla que lo acompañen a jugar al fútbol.

_____ **7.** Cristián no puede jugar porque va a estudiar para un examen.

_____ **8.** Karla no tiene planes y quiere jugar al fútbol.

_____ **9.** Jaime piensa que una mujer puede jugar bien al fútbol.

_____ **10.** Karla se siente muy ofendida con el comentario de Jaime.

SCORE ____ /10

PRUEBA: APLICACIÓN 1

Escribamos

C Imagine that you are a reporter for the school newspaper. You are doing a report on stereotypes in school. Write your view of stereotypes and what you and the people in your school do to eliminate them.

SCORE /15 TOTAL SCORE /35

Vocabulario 2

A Read each conversation and choose an expression from the box that best completes each one.

lo volveré a hacer	**dejó de hablarme**	**un detalle**
la comunicación	**le dio un beso**	**no creo que**

1. Érica y yo discutimos hace una semana y ella ________________.
2. Sí, ya sé, sería buena idea hablar con ella y decirle cómo me siento. ________________ es muy importante.
3. Tengo que decirle a Roberto que siento mucho lo que hice y que no ________________.
4. Tal vez ________________ como una rosa sea una buena manera de decirle que cometiste un error.
5. No puedo creer que Lorena me haya hecho esto. La vi con otro chico y ________________.

SCORE ____ /5

B Olivia's friends are asking her for advice. Read what her friends say, and write a response using an expression from **¡Exprésate!**

6. Le compré un regalo a Paulina para su cumpleaños. ¿Qué más falta?

____

7. Alicia me ha dejado de hablar. Le canté una canción y todavía está resentida. ¿Qué hago?

____

8. Mario me hirió mucho con lo que me dijo. Pienso romper con él. ¿Qué dices?

____

9. Escuché el rumor de que Alonso anda con otra chica. ¡Me dan ganas de llorar!

____

10. Estoy enojado con Sara. Discutimos y me ofendió. Voy a dejar de hablarle.

____

SCORE ____ /10

Nombre ______________________ Clase ____________ Fecha __________

CAPÍTULO **3**

PRUEBA: VOCABULARIO 2

C Complete the conversation with the correct form of the words in the box below.

cometer un error	**estar pensando**	**herir**
darse tiempo para pensarlo	**no volverlo a hacer**	

Guillermo Raquel, siento mucho haberte ofendido. Perdóname. Te juro que (**11**) ______________ .

Raquel Fuiste muy grosero comigo, Guillermo. Me (**12**) ______________ con tus comentarios. Hiciste caso a los rumores en vez de hablar conmigo primero. ¡Qué falta de respeto!

Guillermo Perdóname, Raquel. No sé en qué (**13**) ______________ . Ya sé que (**14**) ______________ . No quise hacerte daño. ¿Me perdonas?

Raquel No sé. Tengo que (**15**) ______________ . Estoy resentida contigo todavía.

Guillermo Espero que podamos reconciliarnos pronto.

SCORE ____ /5

D Write what you would say in Spanish in the following situations.

16. Ofendiste a tu amiga y quieres decirle que no pasará otra vez.

____

17. Dejaste a tu novio(a) plantado(a) y quieres decirle que no fue intencional.

____

18. Dijiste algo a un(a) amigo(a) que lo (la) ofendió, pero no fue a propósito.

____

19. Quieres decirle a alguien que cometiste un error y le pides perdón.

____

20. Se te olvidó el cumpleaños de tu mejor amigo(a). Él (ella) no puede creer que lo olvidaste.

____

SCORE ____ /10 TOTAL SCORE ____ /30

Nombre ______________________ Clase ______________ Fecha ______________

CAPÍTULO 3

Gramática 2

PRUEBA

A Read each statement. In the blank, write **futuro** if the action will happen, or **pasado** if the action has already occurred.

_________ **1.** Eliezer y María se reconciliaron ayer.

_________ **2.** Ellos irán al concierto este sábado.

_________ **3.** Ella estuvo muy dolida después de que discutieron.

_________ **4.** Él se disculpó y ella admitió su error.

_________ **5.** Nunca volverán a dejar de hablarse.

SCORE ____ /5

B Complete the conversation by writing the correct form of the verb in parentheses to express **probability** in the **future.**

David ¡Oye! Ayer vi a Mónica y ella no me quiso hablar. ¿Qué le pasa?

Mateo ¿Mónica? (**6**) _____________ (estar) resentida por la pelea que tuvo con Andrés hace dos días.

David A lo mejor es eso. Pero, ¿por qué pelearon?

Mateo No estoy seguro, (**7**) _____________ (ser) que a Andrés se le olvidó el cumpleaños de Mónica.

David ¡Mira! Es Andrés, cruzando la calle. ¿Adónde (**8**) _____________ (ir) con esas rosas?

Mateo No sé. Se las (**9**) _____________ (querer) dar.

David Pero, Mónica es alérgica a las rosas. Creo que él no lo sabe.

Mateo Bueno, ¡ellos (**10**) _____________ (saber) entenderse!

SCORE ____ /10

PRUEBA: GRAMÁTICA 2

C Complete the following statements, using the **conditional.**

11. En tu lugar, yo ____________ (admitir) mi error.

12. En mi lugar, ¿tú ____________ (dejar) de salir con Rosaura por infiel?

13. En una situación como la de ellos, tú y yo ____________ (saber) resolver nuestros problemas y hacer las paces.

14. Chucho y Álvaro creen que nunca ____________ (poder) ser escogidos para el equipo de tenis.

15. Román me dijo que no sabe lo que él ____________ (hacer) en tu lugar.

SCORE ____ /5

D The following students are talking about their plans for tomorrow. Fill in the blanks with the correct word in parentheses to find out what will happen and what the students will or would do.

16. Mañana ____________ (habrá / habría) un concierto en la universidad. ¿Te gustaría ir conmigo?

17. Si tuviera dinero, ____________ (iría / iré) contigo.

18. Yo que tú, ____________ (le pediría / le pediré) dinero a tu padre. Es un concierto formidable.

19. No está en casa y no ____________ (vendrá / vendría) hasta la semana que viene.

20. ¡Qué lástima! Yo te ____________ (invitaré / invitaría), pero tampoco tengo dinero.

SCORE ____ /15

TOTAL SCORE ____ /35

Nombre ______________________ Clase ______________ Fecha ______________

Aplicación 2

Escuchemos

A Listen to Marcos explain what happened between him and his friend Adriana. Then, read the statements below and choose **a**) for **cierto** or **b**) for **falso.**

_____ **1.** Marcos piensa que ofendió a Adriana.

_____ **2.** Marcos y Adriana discutieron y Adriana dejó de hablarle a Marcos.

_____ **3.** Adriana le pidió perdón a Marcos.

_____ **4.** Adriana no quiso la flor que le trajo Marcos.

_____ **5.** Marcos no piensa reconciliarse con Adriana porque está resentido con ella.

SCORE /10

Leamos

B Read Carmen's message to Olga and the statements that follow. Then, choose **a**) for **cierto** or **b**) for **falso.** On the next page, you will read Olga's reply in which she gives advice to Carmen about how to solve her problem. Read the statements and write **sí** if Olga would agree, and **no** if Olga would not agree.

Hola Olga:
Tengo un problema y necesito tu ayuda. Ayer, mi amigo Julio y yo tuvimos una discusión muy fea y desde entonces Julio me ha dejado de hablar. No me dice ni una sola palabra. Creo que le ofendí mucho con algo que le dije. La verdad es que la discusión fue el resultado de un gran malentendido entre nosotros. Yo sé que tengo razón y por eso no le he pedido perdón todavía. Sin embargo, Julio es un amigo de verdad y no quiero que esté resentido conmigo para siempre. ¿Qué harías en mi lugar? Tu amiga, Carmen

_____ **6.** Carmen y Julio tuvieron una discusión.

_____ **7.** Julio dejó de hablarle a Carmen.

_____ **8.** Carmen y Julio discutieron porque Carmen es terca.

_____ **9.** Carmen dice que Julio tiene razón.

_____ **10.** Carmen no quiere que Julio esté resentido con ella.

PRUEBA: APLICACIÓN 2

Hola Carmen:
Parece que te sientes mal por la discusión que tuviste con tu amigo. Yo que tú, trataría de reconciliarme con él y pronto. Primero, debes admitir tu error y pedirle perdón a tu amigo. Ya sé que tú piensas que tienes la razón, pero no te conviene ser tan terca. Para eso existe la comunicación. ¿Has pensado en comprarle un regalo para hacer las paces? Si estuviera en tu lugar, yo haría eso. Bueno amiga, me despido. Hablaremos después. ¡Suerte!
Olga

_____ **11.** Debes reconciliarte con tu amigo.

_____ **12.** Tienes que admitir tu error y pedirle perdón.

_____ **13.** Debes insistir en tu punto de vista.

_____ **14.** Debes comunicar tus ideas.

_____ **15.** Comprarle un regalo a tu amigo no te ayudará.

SCORE /10

Escribamos

C You had an argument with a friend and you insulted him/her. Write a note admitting the error of your ways and apologizing to your friend. State that you did not mean to hurt his or her feelings and that you will not do it again. Ask him or her to forgive you.

SCORE /15 TOTAL SCORE /35

Nombre ______________________ Clase ______________ Fecha ______________

Lectura

A Read Nadia's letter. Then, match the paraphrase from the right column to the phrases that Nadia used in her letter in the left column.

Querida Camila:

¿Cómo estás? Yo estoy desesperada. Desde que me caí del alazán de papá y me fracturé la tibia y el peroné, estoy en cama. Mi abuela me cuida mucho, pero no me deja hacer nada, ni siquiera andar con las muletas. Ella se enfadó conmigo porque piensa que una señorita no debe montar a caballo. Yo creo que es un prejuicio de ella porque en su juventud las muchachas no podían ser jinetas. Imagínate que yo quiero ser amazona, después de esto, nunca va a permitir que yo practique equitación, con lo terca que es. ¡Ayúdame, por favor!

Nadia

____ **1.** caerse del alazán

____ **2.** fracturarse la tibia y el peroné

____ **3.** andar con muletas

____ **4.** una jineta

____ **5.** la equitación

a. mujer que monta a caballo
b. caminar con la ayuda de dos palos de madera
c. lastimarse la pierna
d. caerse de un animal
e. el deporte de montar a caballo

SCORE ____ /10

B Read the following statements, and choose **a)** for **cierto** or **b)** for **falso.**

____ **6.** Nadia está muy feliz porque se cayó de un caballo.

____ **7.** La abuelita de Nadia no la deja caminar con las muletas.

____ **8.** La abuelita de Nadia montaba a caballo en su juventud.

____ **9.** Nadia quiere ser amazona, pues le encanta la equitación.

____ **10.** Nadia se cayó del caballo de su hermano.

SCORE ____ /10

C In your own words, tell why Nadia's grandmother was angry with her. Do you think she had a reason to be angry with Nadia?

____

____

SCORE ____ /15 TOTAL SCORE ____ /35

Escritura

A Alicia just started a new year of boarding school and is having problems adjusting. It's hard to make friends, the schedule is different, and she isn't doing all that well in some of her courses. Write a letter from her to her parents, explaining how hard her new life is. She tells her parents she knows they'll disagree, but she really feels like she can't take it anymore!

SCORE /15

B Write a response to Alicia from her parents giving her advice for easing her course load and for finding activities where she can make new friends. Have them talk about what it was like when they were in school, and say what they would do in a similar situation. They should say that it's not good for her to be so upset, and suggest some solutions.

SCORE /20

TOTAL SCORE /35

Nombre ______________________ Clase ____________ Fecha ____________

CAPÍTULO 3

Geocultura

PRUEBA

A Match each letter on the map of El Caribe with the name of the place or area it represents.

____ **1.** Puerto Rico

____ **2.** Cuba

____ **3.** Haití

____ **4.** La República Dominicana

____ **5.** Jamaica

SCORE ____ /5

B In the blank, write the letter of the word that does not belong with the other two.

____ **6. a.** Santo Domingo **b.** Arecibo **c.** La Habana

____ **7. a.** la piña **b.** el equipo médico **c.** el plátano

____ **8. a.** Santo Domingo **b.** Regimiento 65 **c.** Primera Guerra Mundial

____ **9. a.** La vieja Habana **b.** Santo Domingo **c.** el Alcázar de Colón

____ **10. a.** los caribes **b.** los africanos **c.** los taínos

SCORE ____ /5

Nombre ______________________ Clase ______________ Fecha ______________

CAPÍTULO 3

PRUEBA: GEOCULTURA

C Read the following statements, and choose **a**) for **cierto** or **b**) for **falso.**

____ **11.** Los taínos cultivaban la yuca, el maíz, la calabaza y los cacahuetes.

____ **12.** Durante la época precolombina no vivía nadie en el Caribe.

____ **13.** Juan Pablo Duarte logró la independencia de Cuba.

____ **14.** Hoy en día, se ve la influencia de la cultura africana en la música y el arte del Caribe.

____ **15.** La madera no fue usada en la artesanía de los taínos.

SCORE ____ /10

D Write one sentence to tell the historical or cultural significance of the following.

16. el observatorio de Arecibo, Puerto Rico

____

17. Cristóbal Colón

____

18. la Guerra Hispano-norteamericana

____

19. los refugiados cubanos

____

20. los esclavos africanos

____

SCORE ____ /10 TOTAL SCORE ____ /30

Vocabulario 1

A. (5 points)

1. b 2. a 3. c 4. c 5. b

B. (5 points)

6. horario
7. ciencias sociales
8. la universidad
9. prueba
10. aprobar

C. (10 points)

11. impresión equivocada
12. actitud negativa
13. falta de respeto
14. juzgarme
15. estereotipos

D. (10 points) Answers will vary.
Possible answers:

16. No me parece justo que tengamos otra prueba en geometría.
17. ¡Qué va! Eso no es cierto.
18. Esto es el colmo, ¡No aguanto más!
19. Me choca la actitud de Hugo hacia los deportes.
20. A mi parecer, no hay igualdad entre el fútbol y el fútbol americano.

Gramática 1

A. (5 points)

1. a 2. b 3. b 4. a 5. a

B. (10 points) Answers will vary.

C. (10 points)

11. sean
12. tomen
13. aprueben
14. lleguen
15. vaya

D. (10 points) Answers will vary.

16. Tienes que estudiar más para el próximo examen.
17. Debes aprender a tomar apuntes en el cuaderno.
18. Deben insistir en que haya igualdad para mujeres y hombres en el trabajo.
19. Debes pedirle que te permita tomar otra clase.
20. Debes tratar de ayudar a tus padres en casa.

Aplicación 1

A. (10 points)

1. a 2. b 3. b 4. a 5. a

B. (10 points)

6. b 7. a 8. a 9. b 10. a

C. (15 points)

Answers will vary.

Vocabulario 2

A. (5 points)

1. dejó de hablarme

2. La comunicación

3. lo volveré a hacer

4. un detalle

5. le dio un beso

B. (10 points) Answers will vary.

C. (5 points)

11. no lo volveré a hacer

12. heriste

13. estaba pensando

14. cometí un error

15. darme tiempo para pensarlo

D. (10 points) Answers will vary.

Gramática 2

A. (5 points)

1. pasado **2.** futuro **3.** pasado
4. pasado **5.** futuro

B. (10 points)

6. Estará

7. será

8. irá

9. dará

10. sabremos

C. (5 points)

11. admitiría

12. dejarías

13. sabríamos

14. podrían

15. haría

D. (15 points)

16. habrá

17. iría

18. le pediría

19. vendrá

20. invitaría

Aplicación 2

A. (10 points)

1. a **2.** a **3.** b **4.** a **5.** b

B. (10 points)

6. a **7.** a **8.** b **9.** b **10.** a

11. sí **12.** sí **13.** no **14.** sí **15.** no

C. (15 points)

Answers will vary.

Lectura

A. (10 points)

1. d **2.** c **3.** b **4.** a **5.** e

B. (10 points)

6. b

7. a

8. b

9. a

10. b

C. (15 points)

Answers will vary.

Escritura

A. (15 points)

Answers will vary. Possible answers may include the following: ¡No aguanto más!, ¡No me gusta para nada!, ¡Esto es el colmo!

B. (20 points)

Answers will vary. Possible answers may include the following: Yo que tú…, En esa situación…, En tu lugar…, No te olvides de…, Sugiero que…, No te conviene…, ¿Has pensado en…?

Geocultura

A. (5 points)

1. e **2.** a **3.** c **4.** d **5.** b

B. (5 points)

6. b **7.** b **8.** a **9.** c **10.** b

C. (10 points)

11. a **12.** b **13.** b **14.** a **15.** b

D. (10 points)

16. Desde **el observatorio de Arecibo, Puerto Rico,** los científicos han descubierto otros planetas.

17. La llegada de **Cristóbal Colón** a las Américas marcó el principio de la época colonial.

18. La Guerra Hispano-norteamericana puso fin al colonialismo español en las Américas. España perdió las colonias de Cuba y Puerto Rico a los Estados Unidos.

19. Cuando Fidel Castro llegó al poder, **los refugiados cubanos** huyeron a Estados Unidos. Hasta la fecha, la influencia cultural de los cubanos es evidente en ciudades como Miami, Florida.

20. Los esclavos africanos tuvieron una gran influencia en la cultura del Caribe. Hoy en día, su influencia se nota en el arte, la música y la comida del Caribe.

Aplicación 1

Escuchemos

A. Listen to Roció's conversation with her guidance counselor. Then, read the statements that follow and choose **a)** for **cierto** or **b)** for **falso.**

Rocío Buenos días señor Morales.

Consejero Buenos días Rocío. Adelante, siéntate. ¿En qué te puedo ayudar?

Rocío Mire, señor Morales. Quiero ir a la universidad el semestre que viene, y quiero estudiar matemáticas. ¿Qué me sugiere?

Consejero Bueno, vamos a ver tu horario. ¿Aprobaste tus clases de matemáticas en los semestres pasados?

Rocío Sí, aprobé el álgebra y la geometría. Este semestre pienso tomar cálculo.

Consejero Muy bien. Pero también insisto en que tomes física y geografía. Necesitas estas clases para entrar a la universidad.

Rocío Está bien. Puedo tomar esas clases. Pero me da miedo suspender geografía. Es que no soy buena para la geografía.

Consejero No creo que vayas a suspender esa clase. Necesitas estudiar mucho y tomar buenos apuntes. Quiero que estudies mucho, ¿de acuerdo?

Rocío Gracias señor Morales.

Aplicación 2

Escuchemos

A. Listen to Marcos explain what happened between him and his friend Adriana. Then, read the statements below and choose **a)** for **cierto** or **b)** for **falso.**

Me siento mal. Creo que ofendí a mi amiga Adriana. Discutimos ayer por la tarde y pienso que la herí con algo que le dije porque la vi llorando. Y además, me ha dejado de hablar. Cometí un gran error cuando peleé con ella y le debo una disculpa. Le traje una flor y no la quiso. Le pedí perdón y no quiso escucharme. Le dije que no volvería a insultarla, pero está tan resentida conmigo que no me hizo caso. Créeme que lo que le dije fue sin querer. No quise hacerle daño. De hecho voy a intentar reconciliarme con ella ahora. No puede ser que ella todavía no quiera hablar conmigo.

Vocabulario 1

A Read the statements. In the blank, write **a)** if the person is reacting to news, or **b)** if the person is making a statement.

____ **1.** No puedo creer que tu hermana sea una mujer casada.

____ **2.** Es cierto que los hermanos se la pasan peleando.

____ **3.** Fíjate que mi primo Manuel se graduó de la universidad en junio.

____ **4.** Me sorprende que Uds. vayan a una reunión familiar.

____ **5.** ¡Qué pena que su abuelo se haya muerto!

SCORE ____ /5

B Two friends are catching up. Complete their conversation with the appropriate word(s) from the box.

sigue	**nació**	**se comprometió**	**cuñado**	**fíjate**

Lola Hola, Gloria. ¡Hace tiempo que no nos vemos! ¿Cómo está tu familia?

Gloria Pues, (**6**) ______________ que mi hija Laura se acaba de graduar de la universidad y mi hijo, Paco, (**7**) ______________ con su novia.

Lola ¡Qué sorpresa que Paco se haya comprometido!

Gloria ¿Cómo está tu (**8**) ______________? ¿(**9**) ______________ trabajando como abogado?

Lola La verdad es que dejó de trabajar hace poco. Ahora, cuida a su nieta, Isabel, que (**10**) ______________ el mes pasado.

Gloria No puedo creer que sea abuelo. ¡Cómo pasan los años!

SCORE ____ /5

PRUEBA: VOCABULARIO 1

C Complete each sentence by filling in the blank with the vocabulary word for the family member described.

11. La mujer que se casó con tu papá después de que tus padres se divorciaron es tu _______________.

12. Una fiesta con todos tus parientes es una _______________.

13. La esposa de tu hermano es tu _______________.

14. El hijo de tu mamá y tu padrastro es tu _______________.

15. La mamá de tu esposo(a) es tu _______________.

SCORE /10

D Read the following short conversations where someone is giving the latest news. Complete each reaction to the news with a different expression from **¡Exprésate!** based on the cues.

Gustavo ¡Nancy y Aurelio se comprometieron! (surprise)

Fernando ¡(**16**) _______________ se hayan comprometido!

Doña Eva Ayer se murió Don Francisco a los 95 años de edad. (disbelief)

Doña Clara ¡(**17**) _______________ creer!

Elda ¡Esmeralda dio a luz a una niña! (surprise)

Román (**18**) No me _______________ ¡Qué alegría que ahora sea mamá!

Efrén Mis suegros se separaron. (regret)

Gloria (**19**) ¡ _______________ se hayan separado!

Lorenzo ¡Nuestro primo Hernán ha dejado de estudiar y ahora es un jugador de béisbol! (astonishment)

Hugo (**20**) Me has _______________. No puedo creer que haya dejado de estudiar y que esté jugando al béisbol.

SCORE /10 TOTAL SCORE /30

Nombre ______________________ Clase ______________ Fecha ______________

CAPÍTULO 4

Gramática 1

PRUEBA

A Read the statements. In the blank, write **a**) if the action is still happening, or **b**) if it occurred in the past.

_____ **1.** La profesora está dando el examen.

_____ **2.** Mi hermanastro lloró cuando Mamá salió de casa.

_____ **3.** Ellas andan diciendo que ya no somos amigas.

_____ **4.** El señor Pérez está leyendo la novela.

_____ **5.** Mi esposa y yo nos divorciamos el mes pasado.

SCORE _____ /5

B At this year's family reunion, Ricardo overhears many conversations. Fill in the blanks with the present perfect subjunctive of the verbs in the box.

ir	**dar a luz**	**separarse**	**morirse**	**comprometerse**

Mamá ¡Ay, Rosa! ¿Te enteraste de que Manolo y Florencia ya no viven juntos?

Tía Rosa No me sorprende que ellos (**6**) ______________________. Se la pasaban peleando.

Tía Lola Abuelita, ¿oíste las buenas noticias? ¡Marta tuvo un bebé!

Abuela ¡Me alegra que ella (**7**) ______________________!

Tío Juan Antonio, ¿te enteraste de que el funeral de Don Cristiano fue la semana pasada?

Papá ¡Qué lástima! Pero ya tenía 95 años. Es natural que él (**8**) ______________________.

Primo Ismael ¡Mira, mi equipo acaba de ganar el partido y está participando en la Serie Mundial!

Primo Edwin ¡Es maravilloso que tu equipo (**9**) ______________________ a la Serie Mundial.

Prima Paula ¿Sabías que Ana y Rubén se van a casar?

Hermanita ¡No me digas! ¡Me sorprende que Rubén (**10**) ______________________!

SCORE _____ /10

PRUEBA: GRAMÁTICA 1

C Felipe and Maritza are getting married, but they have fallen behind on their "to-do" list. Find out what still needs to be done by filling in the blanks with the **present perfect** of the verb in parentheses.

11. Tenemos muchas cosas que hacer. Nosotros no ____________________ (rentar) un lugar para la recepción.

12. Pues, tenemos que hacerlo pronto. Todavía, yo no ____________________ (invitar) a tu familia.

13. ¡Ay, Maritza! Ahora me acordé que yo tampoco ____________________ (comprar) los anillos.

14. No te preocupes que yo también estoy atrasada. Todavía no ____________________ (buscar) el vestido de novia.

15. ¡Esto es un desastre! ¿Cómo nos vamos a casar si nosotros no ____________________ (hacer) nada de la lista?

SCORE /10

D Combine the phrases to make sentences that state events in the **present progressive, present perfect indicative,** or **present perfect subjunctive.**

16. yo todavía no / haber / hacer / la tarea para mañana

____

17. nosotros / seguir / estudiar / para el examen de cálculo

____

18. qué / andar / hacer / Roberto

____

19. qué pena que Rolando y María / haber / divorciarse

____

20. los padres / alegrarse / que sus hijos / haber / aprobar / los exámenes

____

SCORE /10 TOTAL SCORE /35

Nombre ______________________ Clase ______________ Fecha __________

CAPÍTULO

Aplicación 1

4

PRUEBA

Escuchemos

A Listen to the conversation between Cristina and Tío José. Then, read the statements below and choose **a**) for **cierto** or **b**) for **falso.**

_____ **1.** Cristina se graduó de la universidad.

_____ **2.** Tío José sigue trabajando como médico.

_____ **3.** Isabel, la prima de Cristina, se casó.

_____ **4.** Cristina no está sorprendida de que su prima Isabel sea mamá.

_____ **5.** Tío José está sorprendido de que el hermano de Cristina no se haya comprometido todavía.

SCORE ____ /10

Leamos

B Read Mamá's note to the family and answer the questions.

¡No aguanto más! Me molesta que ustedes no me ayuden, así que he decidido que harán todo mi trabajo durante esta semana. Juan, aún no has limpiado el baño como me prometiste. Esta semana tienes que hacerlo. Ricardo, no has cocinado ni una vez durante el último año. Esta semana vas a preparar la comida todos los días. Laura, todavía no has lavado tu ropa. Esta semana tienes que lavarla. Roberto, hace más de un mes que no limpias tu cuarto. Durante esta semana tienes que limpiar tu cuarto, la cocina y la sala de estar. Si no cambian su actitud, seguirán haciendo todo el trabajo de la casa. Espero que ustedes hayan aprendido su lección.

6. ¿Qué no ha hecho Juan?

____

7. ¿Qué va a hacer Ricardo durante esta semana? ¿Con qué frecuencia?

____

8. ¿Quién no ha lavado su ropa?

____

9. Además de limpiar su cuarto, ¿qué tiene que hacer Roberto?

____

10. ¿Qué espera Mamá?

____

SCORE ____ /10

Nombre ______________________ Clase ______________ Fecha ____________

PRUEBA: APLICACIÓN 1

Escribamos

C At a family reunion, you are bombarded with information. Read each statement, then write a two-sentence answer in which you react to the news.

11. Tío Pascual te dice que él y su esposa se han divorciado, pero ellos siempre se la pasaban peleando.

____

____

12. Tu abuela te dice que dejó de trabajar como enfermera. Para ti, es bueno que ella pueda descansar.

____

____

13. Tu mamá te dice que doña Margarita, una amiga de la familia, se ha muerto, y tú no lo sabías.

____

____

14. Tía Beatriz te dice que tus primas Amelia y Claudia dieron a luz al mismo tiempo.

____

____

15. Tu papá te informa que tu hermano se ha comprometido con su novia. Pero su novia no te cae bien.

____

____

SCORE [/15] TOTAL SCORE [/35]

Vocabulario 2

A Read the statements. In the blank, write **a**) if the person liked the food, or **b**) if the person did not like the food.

_____ **1.** ¡Está para chuparse los dedos!

_____ **2.** Al pavo le falta sabor, pero no sé qué le falta.

_____ **3.** Se me hace la boca agua.

_____ **4.** A Enrique se le fue la mano con el ajo.

_____ **5.** El arroz está seco y los frijoles no saben a nada.

SCORE /5

B Read the statements and choose the appropriate response.

_____ **6.** El arroz con frijoles que cocinó tu mamá quedó perfecto.
a. ¡Sabe delicioso!
b. El arroz no sabe a nada.

_____ **7.** La carne que pediste en el restaurante está salada.
a. Está para chuparse los dedos.
b. Al cocinero se le fue la mano con la sal.

_____ **8.** Hiciste un bizcocho, pero tu familia dice que le falta azúcar.
a. Se me fue la mano con el azúcar.
b. Es que se me acabó el azúcar.

_____ **9.** Vas a comer cereal frío, pero la leche tiene un olor horrible.
a. La leche está pasada.
b. La leche está picante.

_____ **10.** Ves que tu abuela ha preparado tu comida favorita.
a. La comida no sabe a nada.
b. Se me hace la boca agua.

SCORE /10

PRUEBA: VOCABULARIO 2

C Read the statements and choose **a**) for **cierto** or **b**) for **falso.**

_____ **11.** La ensalada de aguacate es una entrada.

_____ **12.** Cuando está pasada la leche, quiere decir que se puede tomar.

_____ **13.** El apio y la coliflor son vegetales.

_____ **14.** "Está salado" quiere decir que se le olvidó la sal.

_____ **15.** El bizcocho de chocolate es para las personas a dieta.

SCORE ____ /5

D The Muñoz family is dining out. Read the statements about what they like and dislike, then answer the questions, using the menu in the box.

ENTRADAS	PLATOS PRINCIPALES	POSTRES
Ensalada de aguacate	Pavo relleno y chícharos	Dulce de coco
Caldo de pollo	Arroz con frijoles negros	Ensalada de frutas
	Langosta con papas	Bizcocho de chocolate

16. Sonia es vegetariana. ¿Qué puede pedir de plato principal?

____

17. Marcos quiere algo caliente. ¿Qué puede pedir de entrada?

____

18. Laura es alérgica a los mariscos y no le gusta el arroz. ¿Qué puede pedir de plato principal?

____

19. Papá es adicto al chocolate. ¿Qué le gustaría comer de postre?

____

20. Mamá está a dieta, pero quiere comer postre. ¿Qué puede pedir?

____

SCORE ____ /10 TOTAL SCORE ____ /30

Nombre ______________________ Clase ______________ Fecha ______________

Gramática 2

A Read the statements. In the blank, write **a**) if the action was done on purpose, or **b**) if it was an accident.

_____ **1.** Anoche, me comí el último pedazo de bizcocho.

_____ **2.** Se te fue la mano con la sal.

_____ **3.** Cocinamos el pavo con relleno para la fiesta.

_____ **4.** A los niños se les quemó la pizza.

_____ **5.** A Miranda se le olvidó la tarea en casa.

SCORE _____ /5

B Fill in the blank with the correct form of a verb from the box, using the past progressive or the preterite as appropriate. You may use a verb more than once.

sonar	**estar**	**ver**	**caerse**	**abrir**	**entrar**

6. En cuanto ____________ el pollo frito, se le hizo la boca agua.

7. El profesor ____________ dando el examen cuando yo ____________ al salón de clases.

8. Los amigos ____________ practicando cuando ____________ el teléfono.

9. Al ____________ la leche, nos dimos cuenta de que estaba pasada.

10. Alberto y yo ____________ bailando cuando ____________ al suelo.

SCORE _____ /10

Nombre ______________________ Clase ______________ Fecha ____________

CAPÍTULO 4

PRUEBA: GRAMÁTICA 2

C Fill in the blank with **se + indirect object pronoun + the verb** in parentheses to state what happened unintentionally.

11. A Lourdes ____________________ (quedar) las llaves en su casa.

12. A Uds. ____________________ (quemar) la comida.

13. A ellos ____________________ (ir) el autobús.

14. A Mamá y a mí ____________________ (acabar) las fresas para la ensalada.

15. A Nelson ____________________ (caer) los libros de la mano.

SCORE /10

D Complete Alison's report after going out to dinner with her parents. Use the **preterite,** the **past progressive,** or **se + indirect object pronoun.**

Anoche mis padres y yo (**16.** ir) ____________________ al nuevo restaurante llamado El Pollo Dorado, donde se ofrecen comidas latinoamericanas. De entrada, mamá y papá (**17.** pedir) ____________________ la ensalada de aguacate. El aguacate estaba fresco pero al cocinero (**18.** olvidar) ____________________ ponerle sal. Cuando (**19.** llegar) ____________________ la comida, nosotros ya nos (**20.** morir) ____________________ de hambre. Sin embargo, yo no (**21.** poder) ____________________ comer el pavo porque estaba frío. La responsabilidad no fue de la mesera, porque ella (**22.** traer) ____________________ la comida rápidamente. Papá (**23.** pensar) ____________________ en pagar la cuenta y salir temprano cuando él (**24.** saber) ____________________ que no llevaba la cartera. Parece que (**25.** quedar) ____________________ en casa.

SCORE /10 TOTAL SCORE /35

Nombre ______________________ Clase ______________ Fecha ______________

Aplicación 2

Escuchemos

A Listen to Mauricio talk about his birthday dinner. Then, read the statements below and choose **a**) for **cierto** or **b**) for **falso.**

_____ **1.** Los amigos de Mauricio lo invitaron a cenar porque se graduó del colegio.

_____ **2.** Mauricio y sus amigos esperaron una hora para sentarse porque no hicieron una reservación.

_____ **3.** Mauricio no pudo terminar el caldo de pollo porque estaba frío.

_____ **4.** Mauricio tuvo que pedir un bizcocho de chocolate de plato principal.

_____ **5.** La cuenta dejó a Mauricio boquiabierto porque no le cobraron nada.

SCORE ______ /10

Leamos

B Melvin cooked dinner for his family. Read the family's conversation, and answer the questions that follow in complete sentences.

Melvin ¿Qué les pareció la comida que preparé?

Aracelis Perdóname hermanito, pero el puerco asado estaba salado.

Melvin Es que se me fue la mano con la sal.

Papá Y al arroz le faltaba sabor, pero no sé qué le faltaba.

Melvin Tienes razón, papá. Se me acabó la sal por usarla toda en el puerco.

Mamá La verdad es que la ensalada de aguacate estaba picante.

Melvin Pero mamá, así me gusta. Por lo menos les gustó el dulce de leche que hice, ¿no?

Aracelis Hermanito, debes aprender a cocinar. ¡El dulce de leche fue un desastre! ¡Qué asco!

Melvin ¿Cómo puedes decir eso? No me faltó ningún ingrediente.

Papá Hijo, ¿no oliste la leche antes de usarla? ¡Estaba pasada!

Melvin Sólo fue un pequeño error. La próxima vez, la comida estará mucho mejor.

Mamá Gracias por tu oferta, Melvin, pero yo creo que otra persona debe cocinar de ahora en adelante.

PRUEBA: APLICACIÓN 2

6. ¿Por qué no le gustó el puerco asado a Aracelis?

____

7. ¿Qué dijo Melvin acerca del arroz que preparó?

____

8. Según la mamá de Melvin, ¿cuál fue el problema con la ensalada de aguacate?

____

9. ¿Qué detalle se le escapó a Melvin cuando hizo el dulce de leche?

____

10. ¿Cómo reacciona la mamá cuando Melvin dice que va a mejorar la comida la próxima vez?

____

SCORE ____ /15

Escribamos

C Write a review of a Latin American restaurant. Include details about the food you ordered for each course and comment on the taste of the food and the service. Remember to state whether you would recommend the restaurant or not and why. You can write about a good or a bad dining experience.

____

____

____

____

____

____

____

SCORE ____ /10 TOTAL SCORE ____ /35

Lectura

A Read the magazine article about Dominican culinary art. Use the context to explain what the different dishes highlighted in the article consist of.

El plato nacional dominicano es el sancocho, que es un **guisado** variado de carne de cerdo, mariscos, verduras, batatas dulces y yuca. El sancocho prieto lleva siete tipos de carne. El **asopao** es un caldo espeso de carne, arroz y verduras. El arroz con pollo es otro plato muy popular. La **bandera** es un plato preparado con arroz blanco, frijoles rojos y **tostones** o plátanos verdes fritos, acompañado por carnes cocidas y una ensalada. Otros platos más ligeros, son los **chimichurris**, emparedados de carne de cerdo asada, los yaniqueques o panes de maíz, los pastelitos, los quipes, que consisten en carne molida envuelta con trigo quebrado y el dulce de coco rallado.

1. **guisado** ______________
2. **asopao** ______________
3. **bandera** ______________
4. **tostones** ______________
5. **chimichurris** ______________

SCORE /10

B Answer the following questions based on the article.

6. ¿Cuál es el plato nacional dominicano?

____

7. ¿Qué son los yaniqueques?

____

8. ¿Cuáles serán los ingredientes fundamentales del arroz con pollo?

____

SCORE /15

C Answer the following questions based on your opinions.

9. Si tuvieras que preparar el sancocho, ¿qué ingredientes usarías?

____

10. ¿Qué platos de la República Dominicana te gustaría probar? Explica.

____

SCORE /10 TOTAL SCORE /35

Nombre ______________________ Clase ______________ Fecha __________

Escritura

A Mónica is at a family reunion and just ran into her cousin Alfredo, whom she hasn't seen in over a year. Write a conversation between the two cousins in which they take turns asking about the latest news, responding, and reacting.

SCORE /20

B Mónica and Alfredo sit down to eat with the rest of the family. Some of the food is delicious, but some of it is not as good as what Tía Elena usually makes. Write a conversation in which family members comment on the food and Tía Elena explains or gives excuses.

SCORE /15

TOTAL SCORE /35

Nombre ______________________ Clase ______________ Fecha ______________

CAPÍTULO 4

Geocultura

PRUEBA

A Match each letter on the map of **El Caribe** with the name of the place or area it represents.

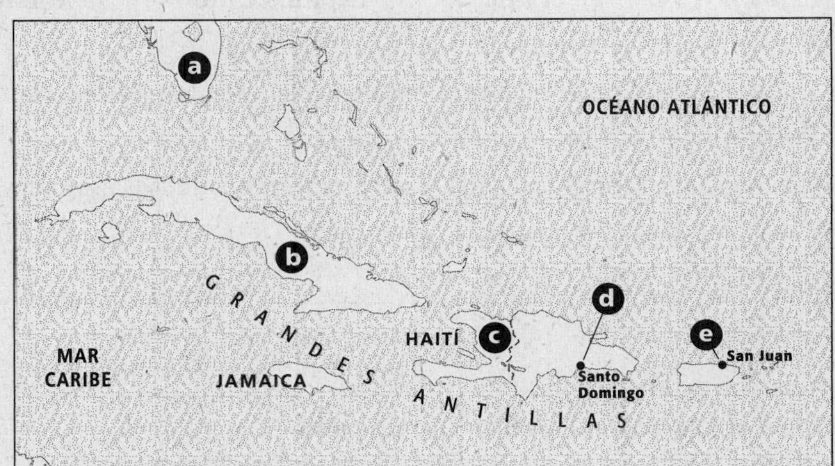

_____ **1.** Es la capital de Puerto Rico.

_____ **2.** Aquí descubrieron la rana más pequeña del hemisferio norte.

_____ **3.** El Alcázar de Colón se construyó aquí.

_____ **4.** Este país luchó contra los dominicanos cuando éstos buscaban su independencia.

_____ **5.** El destino de los 125.000 cubanos que salieron de Mariel.

SCORE ____ /5

B Choose the term from the box that matches each definition.

a. El Velorio	**d.** los caribes
b. Esteban Chartrand	**e.** el Regimiento 65
c. el Alcázar de Colón	**f.** la flotilla de Mariel

_____ **6.** Un grupo que luchó voluntariamente en la Primera Guerra Mundial al lado de los Estados Unidos.

_____ **7.** Una pintura sobre la ceremonia de la muerte de un niño.

_____ **8.** Un grupo de personas que atacó a los taínos.

_____ **9.** Construido en 1509, hoy en día es un museo en Santo Domingo.

_____ **10.** Un pintor que refleja el romanticismo a través de paisajes tropicales.

SCORE ____ /5

PRUEBA: GEOCULTURA

C Complete the sentences with the correct words from the box.

San Salvador	Hispaniola	España	surrealista
joyas	el café	Estados Unidos	abstracto

11. ______________ es el nombre de la isla que comparten Haití y la República Dominicana.
12. En las regiones montañosas del Caribe crecen productos agrícolas como ______________ y el azúcar.
13. Millones de turistas de ______________ y Europa llegan al Caribe cada año.
14. Artefactos de los taínos como muebles y ______________ se encuentran en el Museo del Hombre Dominicano.
15. El arte ______________ contemporáneo del pintor Ramón Oviedo refleja la influencia europea en el arte del Caribe.

SCORE ____ /10

D Answer each question in a complete sentence.

16. ¿Qué grupo étnico tuvo gran influencia en la cultura del Caribe? Da un ejemplo de esa influencia.

    ____

17. ¿Quién fue el líder del grupo la Trinitaria? ¿Qué logró?

    ____

18. ¿Cuáles son algunos peligros de vivir en el Caribe?

    ____

19. ¿Por qué los españoles construyeron fortalezas en el Caribe?

    ____

20. ¿Qué tipo de obras artísticas hacían los taínos? ¿Qué usaban para hacerlas?

    ____

SCORE ____ /10 TOTAL SCORE ____ /30

Vocabulario 1

A. (5 points)

1. a 2. b 3. b 4. a 5. a

B. (5 points)

6. fíjate
7. se comprometió
8. cuñado
9. Sigue
10. nació

C. (10 points)

11. madrastra
12. reunión familiar
13. cuñada
14. medio hermano
15. suegra

D. (10 points)

16. ¡Qué sorpresa que…
17. ¡No lo puedo creer!
18. ¡No me digas!
19. ¡Qué pena que...
20. Me has dejado boquiabierto. / ¡No puedo creer que...

Gramática 1

A. (5 points)

1. a 2. b 3. a 4. a 5. b

B. (10 points)

6. se hayan separado
7. haya dado a luz
8. se haya muerto
9. haya ido
10. se haya comprometido

C. (10 points)

11. hemos rentado
12. he invitado
13. he comprado
14. he buscado
15. hemos hecho

D. (10 points)

16. Yo todavía no he hecho la tarea para mañana.
17. Nosotros seguimos estudiando para el examen de cálculo.
18. ¿Qué anda haciendo Roberto?
19. ¡Qué pena que Rolando y María se hayan divorciado!
20. Los padres se alegran de que sus hijos hayan aprobado los exámenes.

Aplicación 1

A. (10 points)

1. a 2. b 3. b 4. b 5. a

B. (10 points)

6. Juan no ha limpiado el baño como le prometió a Mamá.
7. Ricardo va a cocinar todos los días durante esta semana.
8. Laura no ha lavado su ropa.
9. Además de limpiar su cuarto, Roberto tiene que limpiar la cocina y la sala de estar.
10. Mamá espera que ellos hayan aprendido su lección.

C. (15 points)

Answers will vary. Possible answers:

11. Es natural que Uds. se hayan divorciado. Uds. se la pasaban peleando.
12. Me alegra que Ud. haya dejado de trabajar. Es bueno que pueda descansar.
13. ¡No me digas! ¡Qué pena que doña Margarita se haya muerto!
14. ¡Me has dejado boquiabierto(a)! ¡Qué sorpresa que Amelia y Claudia hayan dado a luz al mismo tiempo!
15. Es horrible que mi hermano se haya comprometido. No me cae bien su novia.

Vocabulario 2

A. (5 points)

1. a 2. b 3. a 4. b 5. b

B. (10 points)

6. a 7. b 8. b 9. a 10. b

C. (5 points)

11. a 12. b 13. a 14. b 15. b

D. (10 points)

16. Sonia puede pedir el arroz con frijoles negros de plato principal.

17. Marcos puede pedir el caldo de pollo de entrada.

18. Laura puede pedir el pavo relleno y chícharos de plato principal.

19. A papá le gustaría comer el bizcocho de chocolate de postre.

20. Mamá puede pedir la ensalada de frutas.

Gramática 2

A. (5 points)

1. a 2. b 3. a 4. b 5. b

B. (10 points)

6. vio

7. estaba, entré

8. estaban, sonó

9. abrir

10. estábamos, nos caímos

C. (10 points)

11. se le quedaron

12. se les quemó

13. se les fue

14. se nos acabaron

15. se le cayeron

D. (10 points) Answers may vary.

16. fuimos

17. pidieron

18. se le olvidó

19. llegó

20. estábamos muriendo

21. pude

22. trajo

23. estaba pensando

24. supo

25. se le quedó

Aplicación 2

A. (10 points)

1. b 2. b 3. a 4. a 5. b

B. (15 points) Answers will vary. Possible answers:

6. A Aracelis no le gustó el puerco asado porque estaba salado.

7. Melvin dijo que le faltaba sal porque la usó toda en el puerco asado.

8. Su mamá dijo que la ensalada de aguacate estaba picante.

9. No olió la leche y estaba pasada.

10. Le da las gracias y dice que alguien más va a cocinar de ahora en adelante.

C. (10 points) Answers will vary.

Lectura

A. (10 points)

1. lleva carnes de cerdo, mariscos, verduras, batatas dulces, y yuca

2. un caldo espeso de carne, arroz y verduras

3. plato preparado con arroz blanco, frijoles rojos y tostones

4. plátanos verdes fritos

5. emparedados de carne de cerdo asada

B. (15 points)

6. El plato nacional dominicano es el sancocho.

7. Los yaniqueques son panes de maíz.

8. Los ingredientes fundamentales serán el arroz y el pollo.

C. (10 points) Answers will vary.

9. Utilizaría diferentes tipos de carnes como carne de res, cerdo, pollo, etc. También le pondría verduras, papas y yuca.

10. Cualquiera de los platos mencionados en el artículo.

Escritura

A. (20 points) Answers will vary.

B. (15 points) Answers will vary.

Geocultura

A. (5 points)

1. e **2.** b **3.** d **4.** c **5.** a

B. (5 points)

6. e **7.** a **8.** d **9.** c **10.** b

C. (10 points)

11. Hispaniola

12. el café

13. Estados Unidos

14. joyas

15. abstracto

D. (10 points) Answers will vary.

Possible answers:

16. Los esclavos africanos influenciaron en la cultura del Caribe. Un ejemplo de su influencia es la bomba puertorriqueña.

17. El líder del grupo la Trinitaria fue Juan Pablo Duarte y logró la independencia de la República Dominicana.

18. Algunos peligros de vivir en el Caribe son las inundaciones, los huracanes y los fallos de electricidad.

19. Los españoles construyeron fortalezas en el Caribe para protegerse de los ataques de Holanda, Inglaterra, Francia y varios grupos de piratas.

20. Los taínos hacían esculturas, muebles, joyas y ollas, y usaban materiales como la madera.

Aplicación 1

Escuchemos

A Listen to the conversation between Cristina and Tío José. Then, read the statements below and choose **a)** for **cierto** or **b)** for **falso.**

Cristina Hola Tío José. Soy su sobrina Cristina.

Tío José ¡No puedo creer que seas Cristina! ¡Cómo has crecido! Dime, ¿cómo van tus estudios?

Cristina El mes pasado, me gradué de la universidad.

Tío José ¡Felicidades!

Cristina Y usted tío, ¿sigue trabajando como médico?

Tío José No. La verdad es que dejé de trabajar hace un par de meses. Ahora quiero dedicarle más tiempo a mi nieto. ¿Te enteraste que tu prima Isabel dio a luz?

Cristina ¡No me diga! ¡No puedo creer que ella sea mamá!

Tío José Bueno, ya lo es. Y tu hermano, ¿qué anda haciendo?

Cristina Según tengo entendido, él se quiere casar. Pero, todavía no se ha comprometido.

Tío José Me sorprende que no se haya comprometido todavía. Pero estoy seguro de que cuando él esté listo para casarse, lo hará.

Cristina Bueno tío, fue un placer verlo. Saludos a su familia de mi parte.

Tío José Igualmente, Cristina. ¡Hasta luego!

Cristina ¡Adiós!

Aplicación 2

Escuchemos

A Listen to Mauricio talk about his birthday dinner. Then, read the statements below and choose **a)** for **cierto** or **b)** for **falso.**

Ayer fue mi cumpleaños. Para celebrar, mis amigos me invitaron a mi restaurante favorito. Normalmente, el servicio es estupendo, pero anoche no fue así. Primero, tuvimos que esperar una hora para sentarnos, aunque teníamos una reservación. Acabábamos de sentarnos cuando el mesero llegó a tomar nuestro pedido. Le pedimos más tiempo, y él se enojó. Cuando regresó el mesero, yo ordené el caldo de pollo de entrada. Cuando llegó, el caldo estaba frío y no pude terminarlo. Pensé que iba a tener suerte con el plato principal, pero cuando llegó el pavo con relleno que había pedido, ¡le faltaba el relleno! También estaba salado, pues al cocinero se le fue la mano con la sal. Le pedí otro plato principal al mesero, pero me dijo que no había. Tenía tanta hambre que ordené el bizcocho de chocolate de plato principal. En vez del bizcocho, el mesero nos trajo la cuenta. La cuenta me dejó boquiabierto. Me cobraron 100 dólares por una cena que no comí. ¡Qué experiencia tan horrible!

Nombre ______________________ Clase ______________ Fecha ______________

Vocabulario 1

PRUEBA

A Match each definition with the vocabulary word it describes.

_____ **1.** un evento que muestra varias obras de arte

_____ **2.** el opuesto de clásico

_____ **3.** un tipo de pintura con colores muy suaves

_____ **4.** el arte de hacer películas

_____ **5.** arte que muestra las cosas como son

a. la acuarela
b. la cinematografía
c. una exposición
d. moderno
e. realista

SCORE ____ /5

B Your friend Francisca can always count on you for good advice. Choose an appropriate answer based on what she likes.

_____ **6.** Admiro mucho las obras modernas.
- **a.** Vamos al museo de arte contemporáneo.
- **b.** Debemos ir al estudio de cinematografía.

_____ **7.** La pintura es la que más me gusta de las artes plásticas.
- **a.** Visitemos la exposición de acuarelas del museo.
- **b.** Vamos a la galería de escultura.

_____ **8.** Me interesa más la arquitectura clásica que la moderna.
- **a.** Saquemos fotos de las nuevas torres del centro. Son impresionantes.
- **b.** Hagamos un tour de la ciudad vieja.

_____ **9.** Los murales me llaman la atención.
- **a.** Vamos al museo a ver las pinturas.
- **b.** Acaban de pintar uno en el centro. ¿Por qué no vamos a verlo?

_____ **10.** Me gustan más las esculturas contemporáneas que las clásicas.
- **a.** Vamos a la galería. Tienen una colección de esculturas abstractas.
- **b.** Hay una exposición de escultura griega. ¿Me acompañas?

SCORE ____ /5

Nombre ______________________ Clase ______________ Fecha ____________

CAPÍTULO 5

PRUEBA: VOCABULARIO 1

C Complete this review of a famous artist's show with the correct form of the words in the box.

maravilloso	**realista**	**llamar la atención**	**retrato**	**cuál**

Anoche yo asistí a la última exposición de la famosa artista Magda Higuera. Todo me impresionó mucho, pero sobre todo sus acuarelas me (**11**) ______________ . ¡Eran tan (**12**) ______________ que pensé que eran fotografías! ¿A ti (**13**) ______________ te gustan más, sus acuarelas o sus (**14**) ______________ al estilo antiguo? Siempre tiene obras (**15**) ______________ para ofrecer al mundo del arte.

SCORE /5

D Translate the phrases in parentheses and use them as part of your responses to the following conversation.

16. ¿Cuál de las artes plásticas te gusta más? (Actually, I admire…)

____

17. ¿Qué opinas de la arquitectura contemporánea? (I find it to be very…)

____

18. No me gusta el estilo moderno. (What do you think of…)

____

19. ¿Quieres ver una exposición de escultura? (Speaking of sculpture,…)

____

20. Me gustaría ir a un concierto. (By the way, what have you heard about…)

____

SCORE /15 TOTAL SCORE /30

Nombre ______________________ Clase ______________ Fecha ____________

CAPÍTULO **5** PRUEBA

Gramática 1

A Read each sentence. In the blank, write **a**) if the sentence is in the active voice, and **b**) if it is in the passive voice.

____ **1.** La policía encontró los artefactos robados el mes pasado.

____ **2.** Ya se vendieron todas las entradas para la nueva película de Antonio Banderas.

____ **3.** Mi hermano sacó una foto fabulosa de la estatua de La Libertad.

____ **4.** La arquitectura antigua de la ciudad fue descrita por el guía turístico.

____ **5.** Las pinturas de Georgia O'Keeffe fueron compradas por la galería hace un mes.

SCORE ____ /5

B Fill in the blank with the form of the adjective that best fits the context.

6. Las pinturas de Diego Rivera son ______________________ . (las más famosas de / famosísimas)

7. La Torre Sears es ______________________ (altísima / la más alta de) todo el país.

8. Frida Kahlo es ______________________ (la más conocida de / tan conocida como) Diego Rivera en el mundo del arte.

9. El Puente Golden Gate en California es ______________________ . (larguísimo / el más largo de)

10. Pienso que las exposiciones de pintura son ______________________ (las más divertidas de / tan divertidas como) las exposiciones de escultura.

SCORE ____ /5

PRUEBA: GRAMÁTICA 1

C Use comparisons of **equality** and **superlatives** to say the following in Spanish.

11. Santa Fe is one of the oldest cities in the U.S.

____

12. Georgia O'Keefe's paintings are the most beautiful of the exhibit.

____

13. The Río Bravo del Norte is extremely long.

____

14. The Saguaros are as tall as trees.

____

15. The classical portraits (*retratos*) are as imaginative as the modern ones.

____

SCORE ____ /10

D Combine the phrases to make sentences using the impersonal **se,** the passive voice with **se,** or the passive voice with **ser.**

16. en el colegio / ofrecer / clases de pintura, escultura y dibujo

____

17. este retrato / pintar / por Frida Kahlo en 1932

____

18. en mi casa / ver / televisión hasta las diez de la noche

____

19. dónde / vender / los boletos para la nueva película

____

20. la *Mona Lisa* / exhibir / por el museo Le Louvre el mes pasado

____

SCORE ____ /15 TOTAL SCORE ____ /35

Aplicación 1

Escuchemos

A Graciela is talking about a recent visit to an art gallery. Listen to what she says, read the following statements, and choose **a)** for **cierto** or **b)** for **falso.**

_____ **1.** Se construyó sólo un nuevo salón.

_____ **2.** Los salones nuevos fueron diseñados por un arquitecto conocido.

_____ **3.** Se hacen exposiciones de artes plásticas en la galería.

_____ **4.** A Graciela no le gustaron las estatuas.

_____ **5.** Graciela piensa que la colección de obras de la galería es pequeñísima.

SCORE ____ /10

Leamos

B Read Patricia's conversation with Rodrigo at the art museum. Then read the statements that follow, and choose **a)** for **cierto** or **b)** for **falso.**

Patricia ¿Qué te parece esta pintura de Juan Gris?

Rodrigo A decir verdad, no me gusta mucho. Me parece muy poco original.

Patricia ¿De verdad? Pues me llama la atención su uso de las formas geométricas. Me hace pensar en el arte de Picasso.

Rodrigo Hablando de Picasso, ¿viste el programa sobre el arte español anoche?

Patricia ¡Sí! Me encantó. ¿Qué pintor te gusta más, Velázquez o El Greco?

Rodrigo Creo que los dos son maravillosos. Pero en realidad, admiro más a Goya. Su trabajo me parece formidable. Nunca se ha hecho una exposición de Goya en este museo, ¿verdad?

Patricia Sí, se hizo una exposición de Goya aquí el mes pasado.

Rodrigo ¡Qué lástima! No la vi.

_____ **6.** A Rodrigo le gusta mucho la pintura de Juan Gris.

_____ **7.** A Patricia le llama la atención el uso de las formas geométricas.

_____ **8.** Patricia vio el programa sobre el arte español.

_____ **9.** A Rodrigo le gusta más el arte de Velázquez que el arte de El Greco.

_____ **10.** Nunca se ha hecho una exposición del arte de Goya en el museo.

SCORE ____ /10

PRUEBA: APLICACIÓN 1

Escribamos

C Write an interview with an art critic about an art exhibit in your community. Include your questions and the critic's answers. The critic changes the subject at least once and compares the different pieces of art in the exhibit.

Entrevistador(a) ____

____

Crítico(a) ____

____

Entrevistador(a) ____

____

Crítico(a) ____

____

Entrevistador(a) ____

____

Crítico(a) ____

____

SCORE /15 TOTAL SCORE /35

Nombre ______________________ Clase ______________ Fecha ______________

CAPÍTULO **5**

Vocabulario 2

PRUEBA

A Your friend Ángela doesn't know much about the arts. Help her out by answering her questions.

____ **1.** A mí me encanta reír. ¿Qué me recomiendas?
a. la comedia **b.** la tragedia **c.** el drama

____ **2.** Si me gusta bailar, ¿qué tipo de clases debo tomar?
a. ballet **b.** drama **c.** dibujo

____ **3.** ¿Qué parte de una canción es tu favorita?
a. la reseña **b.** la orquesta **c.** la letra

____ **4.** ¿Por qué te pareció pésima la comedia? ¿La encontraste…?
a. formidable **b.** estridente **c.** melodiosa

____ **5.** ¿Qué hace el público en una función de teatro?
a. Desempeña los papeles. **b.** Va al ensayo. **c.** Ve y escucha.

SCORE ____ /5

B Read each statement or question and choose the best response.

____ **6.** No me gustan las artes dramáticas.
a. Entonces es mejor que no veas la ópera.
b. Lo encuentro bastante superficial.

____ **7.** ¿Qué tal estuvo la obra de teatro?
a. Pienso que fue de muy mal gusto.
b. La sinfónica tocó muy bien.

____ **8.** Oye, van a presentar una comedia esta semana.
a. Para mí los dramas son incomprensibles.
b. Ya lo sé; mi hermana ayudó a montar el escenario.

____ **9.** ¡Esa película fue formidable!
a. No, gracias. Ya tengo otro compromiso.
b. ¿De veras? Yo leí unas reseñas negativas en el periódico.

____ **10.** El ritmo de esta canción es hermoso, pero la letra es incomprensible.
a. ¿Y qué piensas de la melodía?
b. Pienso tomar clases de ballet.

SCORE ____ /5

Nombre ________________ Clase ________________ Fecha ________________

PRUEBA: VOCABULARIO 2

C Complete this conversation with the correct form of the words from the box.

entretenido	**drama**	**de mal gusto**	**la orquesta**	**creativo**

Isabel ¿Qué te pareció el (**11**) ________________ que presentaron el martes? Van a tener otra función el jueves y quiero saber si vale la pena.

Antón Pues, yo lo encontré (**12**) ________________. No era muy sofisticado, y las ideas no eran muy originales. En mi opinión, fue muy poco (**13**) ________________. Sería buena idea quedarse en casa.

Isabel ¡Qué pena! Sólo quería ver algo (**14**) ________________, como una comedia. ¿Qué me dices del concierto de (**15**) ________________?

Antón Ése sí que vale la pena.

Isabel ¡Genial! ¿Me acompañas?

SCORE ____ /10

D Write what you would say in Spanish in the following situations.

16. Tell someone that you played an important role in a play last year.

____

17. Explain that the crowd was terrible but that the performance was great.

____

18. Tell someone that it would be a good idea to put on a Greek tragedy this year.

____

19. Then ask someone if he or she is interested in assembling the scenery.

____

20. Suggest putting it off until tomorrow because you have practice tonight.

____

SCORE ____ /10 TOTAL SCORE ____ /30

Nombre ______________________ Clase ______________ Fecha ____________

CAPÍTULO 5

Gramática 2

PRUEBA

A Flor writes an advice column for her school newspaper. Read the advice Flor has given to students, and choose the correct form of the verb to complete each sentence.

____ **1.** Te recomiendo que ____ para el equipo de béisbol de nuestro colegio.
a. juegues **b.** juegas

____ **2.** Si te gusta el teatro, ____ participar en el club de drama.
a. puedas **b.** puedes

____ **3.** Te sugiero que ____ gimnasia todos los días.
a. haces **b.** hagas

____ **4.** Es una buena idea que ____ la nueva película de acción.
a. veas **b.** ves

____ **5.** Para saber más de los edificios, ____ ir a la exposición de arquitectura moderna.
a. debas **b.** debes

SCORE ____ /5

B Read the beginning of each sentence, and choose an appropriate match for each.

____ **6.** El profesor sugiere que…

____ **7.** Esta mañana, Alfonso…

____ **8.** Comimos en el restaurante…

____ **9.** Debes acompañar…

____ **10.** Necesito que ustedes…

a. a tu madre a la ópera.

b. nos sugirió un lugar para sacar fotos de la ciudad.

c. que nos había recomendado el guía turístico ayer.

d. practiquen su actuación para la presentación del drama.

e. estudiemos más para el examen.

SCORE ____ /5

Nombre ______________________ Clase ______________ Fecha ______________

CAPÍTULO 5

PRUEBA: GRAMÁTICA 2

C Complete Josué's letter to Samuel by using the **past perfect indicative** or the **present subjunctive** of the verbs in the box.

funcionar **entrar** **ser** **salir** **vender**

¡Ay, Samuel!

¡Hoy fue el día más horrible de mi vida! Esta mañana me desperté tarde y supe que mi despertador no (**11**) ______________________. Cuando llegó el autobús, todavía no había terminado de vestirme. Por eso, fui a la escuela sin arreglarme el pelo. Aún no (**12**) ______________________ a la clase cuando el profesor comenzó con el examen. ¡Yo no había estudiado para el examen! Esta noche, pasé por Raquel porque habíamos quedado en ir al cine. Cuando toqué a su puerta, ella ya (**13**) ______________________. Al llegar al cine, ya se (**14**) ______________________ todas las entradas. No tuve más remedio que regresar a casa. ¡Qué día tan terrible! Espero que mañana (**15**) ______________________ mejor.

Tu amigo,

Josué

SCORE /10

D Combine the phrases to form sentences that show what activity each member of the Rodríguez family wants to do this weekend.

16. Ernesto / querer / todos / ir / al concierto de Thalía

____

17. Sofía / preferir / nosotros / ver / la nueva película de Salma Hayek

____

18. Mamá / querer / ver el ballet / pero Papá / preferir / ver una comedia

____

19. Papá / recomendar / todos / acompañarlos / a la comedia

____

20. Yo / proponer / nosotros / no salir de casa

____

SCORE /15 TOTAL SCORE /35

Aplicación 2

Escuchemos

A Several people are talking about events they attended recently. After listening to each person, choose the appropriate event from the box.

el ensayo de la banda	**la tragedia**	**la comedia**
el concierto	**el baile**	

1. ______________________ **4.** ______________________

2. ______________________ **5.** ______________________

3. ______________________

SCORE ____ /10

Leamos

B Read the conversation between Marta and Rosa and answer the questions.

Marta ¿Quieres ir al ballet el viernes?

Rosa Gracias por invitarme, pero ya lo vi. ¿Por qué no vamos a la nueva obra de teatro el sábado? Fui ayer, pero llegué tarde y ya había empezado. Perdí casi toda la obra.

Marta Lo siento, pero ya tengo otro compromiso el sábado.

Rosa Bueno. Pues, debemos salir el viernes entonces. Mi hermano recomienda que vayamos al concierto de la sinfónica. ¿Te interesa?

Marta ¡Sí! Me encantaría ir. ¡Hasta el viernes!

6. ¿Qué sugiere Marta que hagan el viernes?

____

7. ¿Por qué no quiere ir Rosa?

____

8. ¿Qué pasó cuando Rosa fue al teatro ayer?

____

9. ¿Puede ir Marta al teatro el sábado? Explica.

____

10. ¿Qué recomienda el hermano de Rosa?

____

SCORE ____ /10

PRUEBA: APLICACIÓN 2

Escribamos

C Last night you went to see the senior play and loved it. Write an article for your school paper reviewing the play and recommending that students go to see it. Include comments on the set, the actors, and the incidental music.

SCORE /15 TOTAL SCORE /35

Nombre ______________________ Clase ______________ Fecha ____________

CAPÍTULO 5 PRUEBA

Lectura

A Read the poem and choose the phrase you think describes the theme of the poem.

de ***Versos sencillos*** por José Martí

Yo soy un hombre sincero
de donde crece la palma,
y antes de morirme, quiero
echar mis versos del alma.

Yo vengo de todas partes,
y hacia todas partes voy:
arte soy entre las artes,
en los montes, monte soy.

Yo sé los nombres extraños
de las yerbas y las flores,
y de mortales engaños,
y de sublimes dolores.

Yo he visto en la noche oscura
llover sobre mi cabeza
los rayos de lumbre pura
de la divina belleza.

____ El tema es ____.
a. el paisaje tropical **b.** el hombre y la naturaleza **c.** una historia de amor

SCORE /5

B Choose the phrase that best completes each statement about the poem.

____ **1.** En la línea 2, *de donde crece la palma* se refiere a ____.
a. un país tropical como Cuba
b. un campo donde se cultivan *(are grown)* palmas

____ **2.** *Arte soy entre las artes, en los montes monte soy* quiere decir que el poeta ____.
a. es artista **b.** ha vivido en la ciudad y en el campo

____ **3.** El poeta sabe todos los nombres de las yerbas y las flores porque ____.
a. tiene mucha experiencia del mundo **b.** es botánico

____ **4.** En la línea 15, la palabra *lumbre* probablemente quiere decir ____.
a. luz **b.** ilusión

____ **5.** Los rayos de lumbre pura pueden representar ____.
a. la muerte **b.** los ideales del poeta

SCORE /15

C Write two sentences explaining your interpretation of the poem.

____

____

SCORE /15 TOTAL SCORE /35

Escritura

A Ana has just returned home from a trip to Europe. Her friends Paulo and Fernanda have never traveled to Europe, and are curious about the architecture, museums, and other arts-related activities. Write a conversation where Paulo and Fernanda ask Ana about the things she saw.

Ana ______________________________

Paulo ______________________________

Fernanda ______________________________

Ana ______________________________

Paulo ______________________________

Fernanda ______________________________

Ana ______________________________

Paulo ______________________________

Fernanda ______________________________

Ana ______________________________

SCORE /20

B Write a brief review for the arts column of a newspaper about a classical play you recently attended. Tell the readers your opinion of the acting, directing, etc., and compare the play to others you've seen. Make suggestions and recommendations about attending the play and inviting others to go along.

____

____

____

____

____

____

____

____

____

____

SCORE /15 TOTAL SCORE /35

Nombre ______________________ Clase ______________ Fecha ______________

CAPÍTULO 5

Geocultura

PRUEBA

A Match each letter on the map of **El Suroeste y el Norte de México** with the name of the place or area it represents.

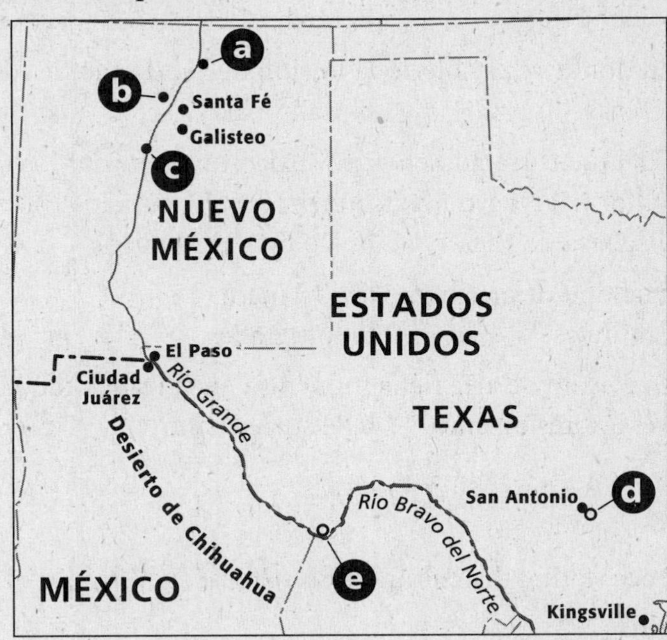

_____ **1.** Lugar donde se encuentran las montañas Chisos.

_____ **2.** Lugar donde se encuentra el Laboratorio Nacional de Los Álamos.

_____ **3.** Lugar en que el general Santa Anna derrotó a los tejanos en 1836.

_____ **4.** En esta ciudad tiene lugar la Fiesta Internacional de Globos.

_____ **5.** Este pueblo ha cambiado poco desde que lo descubrieron los españoles en 1540.

SCORE /5

B Read the following statements and choose **a**) for **cierto** or **b**) for **falso.**

_____ **6.** El desierto de Sonora se extiende desde México hasta el norte de California.

_____ **7.** Tijuana es una ciudad mexicana ubicada en la frontera entre México y Estados Unidos.

_____ **8.** Las alfombras tejidas por los artistas návajos del suroeste son famosas por su técnica tradicional.

_____ **9.** Ellen Ochoa de California fue la primera astronauta femenina latina.

_____ **10.** La primera bomba nuclear fue producida en México.

SCORE /5

PRUEBA: GEOCULTURA

C Choose the correct answer to each of the following questions.

_____ **11.** ¿Qué usaban los grupos indígenas en la región de Santa Fé y Taos para construir sus casas?
a. adobe **b.** madera **c.** piedra

_____ **12.** ¿En dónde se estableció la misión de San Diego de Alcalá en 1769?
a. Texas **b.** California **c.** Arizona

_____ **13.** ¿Cuál fue el tratado en que México tuvo que dar los territorios de California, Nuevo México, Arizona y Texas a los Estados Unidos?
a. Cabeza de Vaca **b.** Dolores Huerta **c.** Guadalupe Hidalgo

_____ **14.** ¿Qué tipo de arte hace David Tineo?
a. murales **b.** fotografías **c.** pinturas

_____ **15.** ¿Qué estilo de arte tiene influencia en el trabajo de Mario Torero?
a. el impresionismo **b.** el surrealismo **c.** el cubismo

SCORE /5

D Write a sentence stating the cultural or historical significance of each of the following people.

16. Álvar Núñez Cabeza de Vaca

____

17. Miguel Hidalgo

____

18. Jerónimo

____

19. César Chávez

____

20. Georgia O'Keeffe

____

SCORE /15 TOTAL SCORE /30

ANSWER KEY: PRUEBAS

Vocabulario 1

A. (5 points)

1. c **2.** d **3.** a **4.** b **5.** e

B. (5 points)

6. a **7.** a **8.** b **9.** b **10.** a

C. (5 points)

11. llamaron la atención

12. realistas

13. cuáles

14. retratos

15. maravillosas

D. (15 points) Answers will vary.

16. En realidad, admiro mucho la pintura.

17. La encuentro muy interesante.

18. ¿Qué te parece el nuevo museo?

19. Hablando de escultura, ¿qué me cuentas de…?

20. A propósito, ¿qué has oído del concierto de la sinfónica?

Gramática 1

A. (5 points)

1. a **2.** b **3.** a **4.** b **5.** b

B. (5 points)

6. famosísimas

7. la más alta de

8. tan conocida como

9. larguísimo

10. tan divertidas como

C. (10 points)

11. Santa Fe es una de las ciudades más antiguas/viejas de los EE.UU.

12. Los cuadros de Georgia O'Keefe son los más bellos de la exhibición.

13. El Río Bravo del Norte es larguísimo.

14. Los saguaros son tan altos como árboles.

15. Los retratos clásicos son tan imaginativos como los modernos.

D. (15 points)

16. En el colegio se ofrecen clases de pintura, escultura y dibujo.

17. Este retrato fue pintado por Frida Kahlo en 1932.

18. En mi casa se ve la televisión hasta las diez de la noche.

19. ¿Dónde se venden los boletos para la nueva película?

20. La *Mona Lisa* fue exhibida por el museo Le Louvre el mes pasado.

Aplicación 1

A. (10 points)

1. b

2. a

3. a

4. b

5. b

B. (10 points)

6. b

7. a

8. a

9. b

10. b

C. (15 points)

Answers will vary.

Vocabulario 2

A. (5 points)

1. a **2.** a **3.** c **4.** b **5.** c

B. (5 points)

6. a **7.** a **8.** b **9.** b **10.** a

C. (10 points)

11. drama

12. de mal gusto

13. creativo

14. entretenido

15. la orquesta

D. (10 points)

Answers will vary. Possible answers:

16. El año pasado, desempeñé un papel importante en la obra de teatro.

17. El público estuvo pésimo, pero la función fue formidable.

18. Sería una buena idea presentar una tragedia griega este año.

19. ¿Te interesa ayudarnos a montar el escenario?

20. Esta noche tengo un ensayo. ¿Por qué no lo dejamos para mañana?

Gramática 2

A. (5 points)

1. a **2.** b **3.** b **4.** a **5.** b

B. (5 points)

6. e **7.** b **8.** c **9.** a **10.** d

C. (10 points)

11. había funcionado

12. había entrado

13. había salido

14. habían vendido

15. sea

D. (15 points)

16. Ernesto quiere que todos vayan al concierto de Thalía.

17. Sofía prefiere que nosotros veamos la nueva película de Salma Hayek.

18. Mamá quiere ver el ballet pero papá prefiere ver una comedia.

19. Papá recomienda que todos los acompañen a la comedia.

20. Yo propongo que nosotros no salgamos de casa.

Aplicación 2

A. (10 points)

1. el baile

2. la comedia

3. el concierto

4. la tragedia

5. el ensayo de la banda

B. (10 points)

6. Sugiere que vayan al ballet.

7. Rosa no quiere ir porque ya lo vio.

8. Rosa llegó tarde y la obra ya había empezado.

9. No, no puede ir porque tiene otro compromiso.

10. Él recomienda que vayan al concierto de la sinfónica.

C. (15 points)

Answers will vary.

ANSWER KEY: PRUEBAS

Lectura

A. (5 points)
b. el hombre y la naturaleza

B. (15 points)
Answers will vary.
1. a
2. b
3. a
4. a
5. b

C. (15 points)
Answers will vary. Possible answer: El poema trata de la relación del hombre con la naturaleza y su conocimiento del mundo en que vive. Dice que sabe todo sobre el bien (la naturaleza, lo bello) y sobre el mal (los engaños, los dolores y los conflictos de su gente).

Escritura

(20 points)

A. Answers will vary. Answers may include: la arquitectura, impresionante, antiguo, moderno, galerías, llamar la atención, el puente, la torre, una exposición, la acuarela, la escultura, el concierto, la orquesta, estridente, hermoso(a), las artes dramáticas, formidable, artísticas, ¿Qué opinas de…?, A decir verdad,…, Lo/La encuentro muy…, En realidad, admiro…, A propósito, ¿qué has oído de…, Hablando de…, ¿qué me cuentas de…?, Eso me hace pensar en…

B. Answers will vary. Answers may include: esta obra es tan creativa como …, es la más entretenida de…, es buenísima/formidable/pésima, se vendieron muchos boletos, la obra fue dirigida por..., les aconsejo /recomiendo que…, no se olviden de invitar a…, es mejor que…, es una buena idea que..., les aconsejo/les sugiero que los niños los acompañen...), cuando llegué al teatro, aún/todavía no había…, and vocabulary such as de buen/mal gusto, el drama, la función, presentar, el público, la tragedia…

Geocultura

A. (5 points)
1. e **2.** b **3.** d **4.** c **5.** a

B. (5 points)
6. b
7. a
8. a
9. a
10. b

C. (5 points)
11. a **12.** b **13.** c **14.** a **15.** b

D. (15 points)

16. Álvar Núñez Cabeza de Vaca fue uno de los primeros exploradores europeos en explorar el suroeste de Estados Unidos.

17. Miguel Hidalgo fue uno de los padres de la lucha por la independencia de México.

18. Jerónimo fue el último líder indígena de la nación apache.

19. César Chávez fundó la Asociación Nacional de Campesinos en 1962 y promovió la identidad chicana.

20. Georgia O'Keeffe pintó las bellezas naturales del suroeste de Estados Unidos.

Aplicación 1

Escuchemos

Graciela is talking about a recent visit to an art gallery. Listen to what she says, read the following statements, and choose **a)** for **cierto** or **b)** for **falso.**

A. Mi última visita a la galería de arte contemporáneo me dejó impresionada. Para empezar, se construyeron varios salones nuevos recientemente y son muy modernos. Los nuevos salones fueron diseñados por un arquitecto conocido. En estos salones se hacen exposiciones de artes plásticas. En un salón, tenían una impresionante colección de acuarelas. Luego, vi la colección de pinturas y dibujos. Algunas obras las encontré muy creativas, pero otras eran las menos originales que he visto. Después entré al salón de las esculturas. Las estatuas talladas en madera me llamaron mucho la atención por la mezcla de estilos clásico y contemporáneo. A decir verdad, si te interesa el arte, una visita a esa galería vale la pena. Esta colección de obras es grandísima. No hay otra tan completa como ésta.

Aplicación 2

Escuchemos

Several people are talking about events they attended recently. After listening to each person, choose the appropriate event from the box.

A.
1. Anoche vimos una presentación de las danzas folclóricas de Tamaulipas. Fue formidable.
2. La obra estuvo muy entretenida. No pude parar de reírme durante toda la obra.
3. La orquesta tocó canciones hermosas. La melodía de la música me impresionó.
4. Todo el público quedó boquiabierto cuando la protagonista de la obra sufrió un terrible accidente.
5. Vamos a practicar esta canción otra vez la semana que viene. Creo que ya sabemos la letra y el ritmo.

Nombre ______________________ Clase ______________ Fecha ______________

CAPÍTULO

Vocabulario 1

PRUEBA

A Read each statement. In the blank, write **a**) if the statement expresses **certainty,** or **b**) if it expresses **doubt.**

_____ **1.** Estoy seguro que la contaminación causa la crisis ambiental.

_____ **2.** Dudo que Adán esté bien informado sobre la crisis económica.

_____ **3.** Claro que nosotros leemos el periódico todos los días.

_____ **4.** Los científicos creen que hay vida en el planeta Marte.

_____ **5.** No creo que los noticieros sean parciales.

SCORE ____ /5

B Fill in the blanks with the phrases that best complete each sentence.

_____ **6.** Es muy importante ___ las noticias.
a. pasar por alto **b.** estar al tanto de

_____ **7.** Los noticieros deben ___ al dar sus informes.
a. ser imparciales **b.** ser parciales

_____ **8.** Nosotros usamos ___ para estar bien informados por Internet.
a. la radio **b.** las noticias en línea

_____ **9.** Todo el mundo sabe que ___ son programas informativos.
a. las telenovelas **b.** los documentales

_____ **10.** ___ los concursos de belleza sean populares.
a. Parece mentira que **b.** Es evidente que

SCORE ____ /5

PRUEBA: VOCABULARIO 1

C Complete the conversation by filling in the blanks with the correct word or phrase.

Luisa Ayer vi un documental sobre la (**11**) ______________ ambiental que me impresionó mucho.

Gabriel ¿Lo viste en el (**12**) ______________ de televisión pública, el 16?

Luisa Sí, y me parece que los locutores hicieron un (**13**) ______________ muy imparcial y muy detallado.

Gabriel ¿De veras? A mí me parece que presentan sus programas de un (**14**) ______________ bastante parcial.

Luisa Pues a mí el programa que vi ayer me (**15**) ______________ mucha confianza.

SCORE /10

D Answer the following questions in your opinion.

16. ¿Qué prefieres leer, las noticias en línea o el periódico? ¿Por qué?

____

17. ¿Estás convencido(a) de que los reporteros sean fiables? Explica.

____

18. ¿Ves alguna que otra telenovela? ¿Por qué?

____

19. ¿Qué tipo de música escuchas a través de tu emisora de radio favorita?

____

20. ¿Te consideras bien informado(a) sobre la política? ¿Por qué?

____

SCORE /10 TOTAL SCORE /30

Nombre ______________________ Clase ______________ Fecha ______________

Gramática 1

A In the blank, write **a**) if the statement expresses **certainty,** or **b**) if it expresses **doubt.**

____ **1.** Claro que conozco a Juan; él es mi hermano.

____ **2.** Es imposible que el reportero haya dicho algo así.

____ **3.** Estamos convencidos de que los reporteros son imparciales.

____ **4.** Ellos no están seguros de que haya una crisis ambiental.

____ **5.** Todo el mundo sabe que los documentales son educativos.

SCORE ____ /5

B Complete the conversation with the **indicative** or **subjunctive** form of the verb in parentheses.

Milagros ¿Viste las noticias del Canal 7 esta mañana?

Joel Por supuesto que las (**6**) ______________ (ver). ¿Qué te pareció el informe?

Milagros Yo creo que faltaron muchos detalles. Me molesta que el reportero no (**7**) ______________ (haber) tratado el tema muy a fondo.

Joel Estoy seguro de que ese reportero no (**8**) ______________ (estar) bien informado. La semana pasada dicen que (**9**) ______________ (hacer) un reportaje sobre lo último en tecnología. Él dio el informe de modo parcial y dejó pasar por alto muchos detalles importantes.

Milagros Parece mentira que él (**10**) ______________ (ser) uno de los reporteros más respetados del país.

SCORE ____ /10

PRUEBA: GRAMÁTICA 1

C Combine the phrases to make sentences using different forms of **haber.**

11. hoy en día / haber / una crisis ambiental por la contaminación

____

12. haber / una tormenta tropical el verano pasado

____

13. es dudoso que los Tigres / haber / ganar / el campeonato

____

14. haber / mucha gente en la fiesta cuando los chicos llegaron

____

15. anoche / haber / varios documentales en la televisión

____

SCORE /10

D Read the newspaper headlines. Write a sentence using the **present perfect indicative** or the **present perfect subjunctive** plus an expression from the box to state that you *believe* or *doubt* it happened.

No cabe duda que	**Estoy convencido(a) de que**	**No puedo creer que**
Por supuesto que	**Estoy seguro(a) (de) que**	**(No) es cierto que**
Es increíble que	**Es dudoso que**	**Dudo que**

16. "Presidente viaja en una nave espacial"

____

17. "Niño de tres años se gradúa de la universidad"

____

18. "La contaminación causa la crisis ambiental"

____

19. "Mujer de 90 años da a luz a gemelos"

____

20. "Hombre pierde boleto de lotería que vale $10 millones"

____

SCORE /10 TOTAL SCORE /35

Nombre ______________________ Clase ______________ Fecha ______________

CAPÍTULO 6

PRUEBA

Aplicación 1

Escuchemos

A Listen to the following statements. In the blank, write **a**) if the speaker expresses **certainty,** or **b**) if the speaker expresses **doubt.**

1. ____
2. ____
3. ____
4. ____
5. ____

SCORE ____ /5

Leamos

B Read the conversation and the statements that follow. Decide who would say each statement. Write **a**) for **Adán** or **b**) for **Bárbara.**

Adán Anoche, hubo un informe sobre la crisis ambiental. Estoy convencido de que debemos hacer algo para mejorar la situación.

Bárbara Dudo que haya una crisis ambiental. Me parece que los reporteros tratan los temas de modo parcial.

Adán Bárbara, es evidente que no estás bien informada. Debes ver los documentales para estar al tanto de las noticias.

Bárbara Todo el mundo sabe que los documentales son muy aburridos. Mejor veo las telenovelas para divertirme.

Adán Parece mentira que seas tan ignorante. Está claro que todos contribuimos a la crisis ambiental. La ignorancia sólo empeora la situación.

Bárbara ¡No puedo creer que me hayas llamado ignorante! No sé mucho de la crisis ambiental, pero estoy segura de que no eres un buen amigo.

PRUEBA: APLICACIÓN 1

_____ 6. Es obvio que hay una crisis ambiental y que debemos hacer algo para mejorar la situación.

_____ 7. Es cierto que los reporteros tratan los temas de modo parcial.

_____ 8. Me parece que los documentales son muy aburridos; por eso veo las telenovelas.

_____ 9. Es increíble que seas tan ignorante.

_____ 10. No creo que seas un buen amigo.

SCORE /10

Escribamos

C Read the newspaper headlines. Write a few sentences stating whether you believe each headline or not and explain why. Remember to use expressions of certainty or doubt.

11. "Hay telenovelas educativas"

____

____

12. "Anoche, hubo un terremoto en el estado de Kansas"

____

____

13. "Científicos encuentran la cura para el cáncer"

____

____

14. "Ayer, agentes del FBI descubrieron una nave espacial en la Casa Blanca"

____

____

15. "Concursos de belleza ayudan a las chicas a ir a la universidad"

____

____

SCORE /20 TOTAL SCORE /35

Vocabulario 2

A Complete the following sentences with the correct word or phrase from the box.

la sección deportiva	**los anuncios clasificados**	**suscribimos**
la sección financiera	**con enfoque mundial**	

1. Leí en ______________ que la economía está mejorando.
2. Si necesitas un apartamento debes leer ______________ .
3. Nos ______________ al periódico para estar al tanto de las noticias.
4. En ______________ puedes saber el resultado del partido.
5. Para informarte sobre España, debes leer las noticias ______________ .

SCORE ____ /5

B Read the conversation and the statements that follow, and decide who would say each one. Write **a**) for **Camila** or **b**) for **Santos.**

Santos Pásame la sección deportiva. Quiero saber el resultado del partido.
Camila Debes leer la sección financiera que estoy leyendo.
Santos Es que no entiendo ni jota de los asuntos financieros. Prefiero leer las noticias deportivas porque sé algo de deportes.
Camila ¿Por qué no estás al tanto de las noticias con enfoque nacional?
Santos No creo que esas noticias sean necesarias.
Camila Pero Santos, ¿no andabas buscando trabajo?
Santos ¿Qué tiene que ver eso con las noticias?
Camila En la primera plana, hay un informe sobre la economía. Los expertos esperan más desempleo *(unemployment).*
Santos Es mejor estar mal informado que saber las malas noticias.

_____ 6. No sé nada de los asuntos financieros.
_____ 7. Me gusta leer la sección financiera.
_____ 8. Las noticias con enfoque nacional no son importantes.
_____ 9. Leí en la primera plana un informe sobre la economía.
_____ 10. Sólo me interesan las buenas noticias.

SCORE ____ /5

PRUEBA: VOCABULARIO 2

C Read each statement, and choose an appropriate response from the box.

Debes leer la sección de moda para saber de los nuevos estilos. Debe leer los anuncios clasificados para no pagar mucho dinero. Debes leer las tiras cómicas para divertirte. Debemos leer la sección de cocina para aprender nuevas recetas. Deben leer las noticias con enfoque mundial para estar bien informados.

11. Nosotros: Nos gusta cocinar.

____

12. Mercedes: Quiero ser diseñadora de ropa.

____

13. Eliezer: Mi hermano busca un carro barato.

____

14. Esteban y Francisca: Trabajamos en una compañía internacional.

____

15. Manuelito: Tengo sólo ocho años.

____

SCORE ____ /10

D Answer the questions with your opinion using words from **Vocabulario.**

16. ¿Qué sección del periódico prefieres leer? ¿Por qué?

____

17. ¿En qué sección del periódico te gustaría (o no) ver tu nombre? ¿Por qué?

____

18. ¿Te interesan los editoriales? ¿Con qué frecuencia los lees?

____

19. ¿Por qué lees la sección de ocio?

____

20. ¿Hay alguien en tu familia que sólo lee los titulares? ¿Por qué?

____

SCORE ____ /10 TOTAL SCORE ____ /30

Nombre ______________________ Clase ______________ Fecha ____________

CAPÍTULO 6

Gramática 2

PRUEBA

A Complete the sentences with the correct word from the box.

ni	algunas	nada	alguien	ningún

1. La verdad es que no sé ____________ de los deportes porque nunca leo la sección deportiva.
2. Jorge no tiene ____________ amigo porque no es nada sociable.
3. Nosotros no somos ni ricos ____________ pobres.
4. ____________ debe saber la respuesta.
5. ____________ chicas leen la sección de moda del periódico. Saben muy bien lo que está de moda.

SCORE /5

B Complete the following paragraph with the appropriate definite article: **el, la, los,** or **las.**

En (**6**) ________ documental de ciencias que escuchamos en (**7**) ________ radio, los científicos dicen que posiblemente hayan encontrado la cura para (**8**) ________ enfermedad más peligrosa del mundo. Ayer en (**9**) ________ Canal 24, hubo un informe de los científicos sobre los detalles del descubrimiento. Emilio Gutiérrez, uno de (**10**) ________ periodistas que ayudó con (**11**) ________ reportaje, afirma que (**12**) ________ tema es de particular interés porque es muy difícil identificar las plantas de las cuales se puede obtener la medicina. Parece que ocurre en (**13**) ________ calabacín y en otras plantas relacionadas, pero en cantidades insuficientes para ser procesada. Ésta es (**14**) ________ razón por la cual tienen que buscar otras plantas que puedan servir de recurso. Los científicos dicen que (**15**) ________ mañana de la medicina depende mucho de las selvas tropicales con su increíble diversidad de especies botánicas.

SCORE /10

PRUEBA: GRAMÁTICA 2

C Mamá and Papá are discussing the news. Complete their conversation by filling in the blanks with the correct form of the verbs in parentheses.

Papá Pásame la sección deportiva. Quiero saber si mi equipo ganó el partido.

Mamá ¿Por qué no lees las noticias? Mira, en la primera plana dice que la economía (**16**) ______________ (estar) decayendo.

Papá Creo que ese periodista no está bien informado. Ayer, los expertos anunciaron que (**17**) ______________ (haber) menos desempleo ahora. Pero dudo que la economía esté mejorando.

Mamá Parece que tú (**18**) ______________ (saber) un poco de la economía. Pero dudo que (**19**) ______________ (saber) algo de la política. Por ejemplo, ¿sabes cuándo son las próximas elecciones?

Papá ¡Ésa no es una pregunta justa! Todo el mundo sabe que yo no (**20**) ______________ (entender) ni jota de política.

SCORE /10

D Write the expressions you would use in the following situations.

21. Ask a friend if he or she thinks TV reporters are impartial.

____

22. Tell someone you are not convinced the economic crisis is finished.

____

23. Ask someone if he or she doubts there is intelligent life on Earth.

____

24. Tell someone it's hard to believe there are insects that live at the North Pole.

____

25. Tell a friend you are sure that there is no test tomorrow in any of your classes.

____

SCORE /10 TOTAL SCORE /35

Aplicación 2

Escuchemos

A Listen to the following radio broadcast of the morning news. Read the statements below, and choose **a)** for **cierto** or **b)** for **falso.**

____ **1.** El jefe de policía tiene una nueva pista en el caso de varios robos que ha habido en la ciudad.

____ **2.** No hay ninguna crisis económica en el país.

____ **3.** La actriz Laura Figueroa se va a casar con un economista.

____ **4.** Los científicos piensan que han encontrado una cura para muchas enfermedades.

____ **5.** Édgar Rodríguez dará las noticias a las cinco de la tarde.

SCORE ____ /5

Leamos

B Read the conversation. Then, choose the phrase that best completes each statement.

Jorge ¿Te enteraste del resultado del partido? ¡Los Red Sox les ganaron a los Yankees!

Benjamín Lo leí en la sección deportiva. Y tú, ¿cómo lo supiste?

Jorge Anoche vi el partido por televisión. Creo que nunca he visto un partido tan emocionante como ése.

Benjamín Ayer un periodista anunció que Los Red Sox iban a perder. Estoy convencido de que ese periodista no sabe nada de béisbol.

Jorge Dudo que él esté bien informado. La semana pasada declaró que los entrenamientos de béisbol se llevarían a cabo en Canadá.

Benjamín ¿En Canadá? Pero, todo el mundo sabe que los entrenamientos siempre se hacen en el sur. Me parece que deben buscar alguien que sepa algo de deportes.

PRUEBA: APLICACIÓN 2

____ **6.** Jorge se enteró del resultado del partido ___.
a. en la sección deportiva **b.** por televisión

____ **7.** Jorge ___ un partido tan emocionante.
a. nunca ha visto **b.** duda que haya sido

____ **8.** Benjamín y Jorge no están seguros que el periodista ___.
a. esté mal informado **b.** sepa algo de béisbol

____ **9.** El periodista dijo que los entrenamientos ___ a cabo en Canadá.
a. no se llevarían **b.** se llevarían

____ **10.** A Benjamín le parece que deben buscar un reportero ___.
a. bien informado **b.** menos parcial

SCORE ____ /10

Escribamos

C Mónica and Carolina are talking about current events that they read in the newspaper. Mónica mentions some news that Carolina does not believe and asks her where she read about it. Then, Mónica and Carolina talk about what they know and do not know about the news. Use expressions of certainty, doubt, and disbelief, and expressions from **¡Exprésate!**

Mónica ______________________________

Carolina ______________________________

Mónica ______________________________

Carolina ______________________________

Mónica ______________________________

Carolina ______________________________

Mónica ______________________________

Carolina ______________________________

Mónica ______________________________

Carolina ______________________________

Mónica ______________________________

Carolina ______________________________

SCORE ____ /20 TOTAL SCORE ____ /35

CAPÍTULO 6

Lectura

PRUEBA

A Read the following news broadcast. As you read, look for words that indicate the chronological order of events and write them on the line below.

El mes pasado el supertanquero *(super tanker) Lincoln* chocó con otro barco cerca de la costa de Veracruz. Más tarde se observaron manchas de petróleo sobre la superficie del agua. Dos semanas después aparecieron varios peces muertos en una playa de Cancún. Luego un equipo de buzos *(divers)* revisó el tanquero y descubrió un escape *(leak)* del combustible. Hoy nuestro corresponsal del mar nos informa que las autoridades le han dicho que primero hay que controlar el escape de petróleo y segundo, hay que asegurar que la carga llegue a su destino la próxima semana sin contaminar más el medio ambiente.

____

____

SCORE ____ /5

B Read each statement and choose **a)** for **cierto** or **b)** for **falso.**

____ **1.** El *Lincoln* chocó con una roca.

____ **2.** Se observaron manchas de petróleo en la superficie del agua.

____ **3.** Encontraron peces muertos en las playas de Galveston, Texas.

____ **4.** El equipo de buzos no encontró ningún problema con el *Lincoln.*

____ **5.** Las autoridades dijeron que la carga no llegaría a su destino.

SCORE ____ /10

C Answer the following questions in complete sentences.

6. ¿Dónde ocurrió el accidente del tanquero *Lincoln?*

____

7. En tu opinión, ¿por qué aparecieron peces muertos en la playa?

____

8. ¿Qué causó el escape del petróleo del *Lincoln?*

____

9. ¿Por qué crees que las autoridades están preocupadas por el medio ambiente?

____

SCORE ____ /20 TOTAL SCORE ____ /35

Nombre ______________________ Clase ______________ Fecha ____________

CAPÍTULO 6 PRUEBA

Escritura

A Imagine that you are interviewing two presidential candidates about their views on a particular issue such as the environment, the economy, or any other controversial topic. Write a conversation in which you ask them a question, they give their answers, and agree or disagree with each other's opinions.

SCORE /15

B Write an essay about a reporter (real or imaginary) that you like or dislike. Talk about his or her knowledge of a particular issue, how well a particular news story was covered, and give your opinion of his or her reporting abilities.

SCORE /20

TOTAL SCORE /35

Nombre ______________________ Clase ______________ Fecha ______________

CAPÍTULO 6

Geocultura

PRUEBA

A Match each letter on the map of **el Suroeste y el Norte de México** with the name of the place or area it represents.

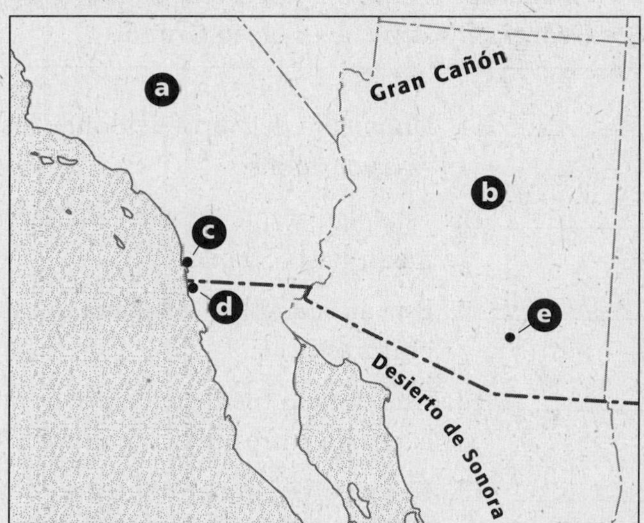

_____ **1.** La ciudad fronteriza de Tijuana.

_____ **2.** Uno de los territorios cedidos a los Estados Unidos mediante el tratado de Guadalupe Hidalgo.

_____ **3.** Lugar de origen de la astronauta latina Ellen Ochoa.

_____ **4.** Lugar donde se encuentra la Misión San Xavier del Bac.

_____ **5.** Lugar de origen del artista y activista Mario Torero.

SCORE ____ /5

B Choose the option that best completes each sentence.

_____ **6.** La zoofarmacognosía es el estudio de ___.
a. cómo las plantas y animales se curan **b.** el cactus Saguaro del desierto de Sonora

_____ **7.** La bomba nuclear fue creada en ___.
a. las montañas Chisos **b.** Nuevo México

_____ **8.** ___ de Carmen Lomas Garza refleja(n) su niñez.
a. Los murales **b.** El arte narrativo

_____ **9.** Los españoles ___ en el suroeste durante los siglos XVIII y XIX.
a. construyeron misiones **b.** encontraron oro y plata

_____ **10.** Mario Torero y ___ se expresan a través de los murales.
a. David Tineo **b.** Georgia O'Keeffe

SCORE ____ /5

Nombre ______________________ Clase ______________ Fecha ____________

CAPÍTULO 6

PRUEBA: GEOCULTURA

C Choose an item from the box that best fits each description and write it on the line next to the description.

Guadalupe Hidalgo	**el cactus Saguaro**	**Taos**
Georgia O'Keeffe	**el río Grande**	

__________ **11.** Un pueblo del Suroeste donde los indígenas vivían en casas de adobe.

__________ **12.** Esta planta, que crece en el desierto de Sonora, puede medir hasta 50 pies.

__________ **13.** Esta artista refleja la belleza del suroeste en sus pinturas.

__________ **14.** Este tratado fue firmado por Santa Anna y puso fin a la guerra entre México y Estados Unidos.

__________ **15.** Es una división natural entre México y Estados Unidos que llega hasta el Golfo de México.

SCORE /10

D Write a sentence stating the cultural or historical significance of the following:

16. Eloy Rodríguez

____

17. los návajos

____

18. el Álamo

____

19. el arte narrativo

____

20. Dolores Huerta

____

SCORE /10 TOTAL SCORE /30

Vocabulario 1

A. (5 points)

1. a **2.** b **3.** a **4.** a **5.** b

B. (5 points)

6. b **7.** a **8.** b **9.** b **10.** a

C. (10 points)

11. crisis

12. canal

13. reportaje

14. modo

15. inspiró

D. (10 points) Answers will vary.

Possible answers:

16. Prefiero leer las noticias en línea porque no me suscribo al periódico.

17. En mi opinión, los reporteros son más o menos imparciales pero no siempre están bien informados.

18. Sí, veo alguna que otra telenovela. Este tipo de programa me hace reír.

19. Yo escucho la música pop a través de mi emisora de radio favorita.

20. Sí, estoy bien informado sobre la política porque leo el periódico.

Gramática 1

A. (5 points)

1. a **2.** b **3.** a **4.** b **5.** a

B. (10 points)

6. vi

7. haya

8. está

9. hizo

10. sea

C. (10 points)

11. Hoy en día hay una crisis ambiental por la contaminación.

12. Hubo una tormenta tropical el verano pasado.

13. Es dudoso que los Tigres hayan ganado el campeonato.

14. Había mucha gente en la fiesta cuando los chicos llegaron.

15. Anoche hubo varios documentales en la televisión.

D. (10 points) Phrases in parentheses will vary.

16. (Dudo que) el presidente (haya) viajado en una nave espacial.

17. (No puedo creer que) un niño de tres años se (haya) graduado de la universidad.

18. (Estoy convencido de que) la contaminación (ha) causado la crisis ambiental.

19. (Es increíble que) una mujer de 90 años (haya) dado a luz a gemelos.

20. (Es cierto que) un hombre (ha) perdido un boleto de lotería que vale $10 millones.

Aplicación 1

A. (5 points)

1. a **2.** b **3.** b **4.** a **5.** a

B. (10 points)

6. a **7.** b **8.** b **9.** a **10.** b

C. (20 points) Answers will vary.

11. (Dudo que haya) telenovelas educativas porque...

12. (Estoy convencida de que) anoche (hubo) un terremoto en Kansas porque...

13. (No creo que) los científicos (hayan) encontrado la cura para el cáncer porque...

14. (No puedo creer que) los agentes del FBI (hayan) descubierto una nave espacial en la Casa Blanca porque...

15. (Es evidente que) los concursos de belleza… los concursos de belleza (ayudan) a las chicas a ir a la universidad porque...

Vocabulario 2

A. (5 points)

1. la sección financiera

2. los anuncios clasificados

3. suscribimos

4. la sección deportiva

5. con enfoque mundial

B. (5 points)

6. b **7.** a **8.** b **9.** a **10.** b

C. (10 points)

11. Debemos leer la sección de cocina para aprender nuevas recetas.

12. Debes leer la sección de moda para saber de los nuevos estilos.

13. Debe leer los anuncios clasificados para no pagar mucho dinero.

14. Deben leer las noticias con enfoque mundial para estar bien informados.

15. Debes leer las tiras cómicas para divertirte.

D. (10 points) Answers will vary. Possible answers:

16. Prefiero leer los editoriales para saber lo que opina la gente.

17. Me gustaría ver mi nombre en la sección de moda porque quiero ser diseñadora. / No me gustaría ver mi nombre en la sección de... porque...

18. No me interesan los editoriales. Nunca los leo.

19. Leo la sección de ocio para enterarme de las nuevas películas.

20. Mi papá sólo lee los titulares porque nunca tiene tiempo para leer los artículos.

Gramática 2

A. (5 points)

1. nada

2. ningún

3. ni

4. Alguien

5. Algunas

B. (10 points)

6. el

7. la

8. la

9. el

10. los

11. el

12. el

13. el

14. la

15. el

C. (10 points)

16. está

17. hay

18. sabes

19. sepas

20. entiendo

D. (10 points) Answers will vary. Possible answers:

21. ¿Crees que los reporteros de la televisión son imparciales?

22. No estoy convencido(a) de que la crisis económica haya terminado.

23. ¿Dudas que haya vida inteligente en la Tierra?

24. Es increíble que haya insectos que viven en el Polo del Norte.

25. Estoy seguro(a) de que no hay examen en ninguna de nuestras clases mañana.

Aplicación 2

A. (5 points)

1. a **2.** b **3.** b **4.** a **5.** a

B. (10 points)

6. b **7.** a **8.** b **9.** b **10.** a

C. (20 points) Answers will vary.

Lectura

A. (5 points)

el mes pasado, más tarde, dos semanas después, luego, hoy, primero, segundo, la próxima semana

B. (10 points)

1. b

2. a

3. b

4. b

5. b

C. (20 points) Answers will vary. Possible answers:

6. El accidente ocurrió en la costa de Veracruz.

7. Los peces murieron porque el petróleo que escapó del tanquero contaminó el agua.

8. El petróleo escapó del tanquero como resultado del accidente.

9. Están preocupadas porque el petróleo hace mucho daño al medio ambiente.

Escritura

A. (15 points) Answers will vary.

Answers should include: controversial topics (el medio ambiente, la economía, etc.), expressions of certainty/doubt (Dudo que... Es cierto que... etc.), uses of **haber** (Hay una crisis ambiental, económica..., etc.)

B. (20 points) Answers will vary.

Answers should include: vocabulary (tratar los temas a fondo, estar bien informado, el reportero, el periodista, el reportaje, etc.), expressions of certainty/doubt (Me parece que... Está claro que... etc.), uses of **haber** (Hubo un reportaje..., etc.)

Geocultura

A. (5 points)

1. d **2.** b **3.** a **4.** e **5.** c

B. (5 points)

6. a **7.** b **8.** b **9.** a **10.** a

C. (10 points)

11. Taos

12. el cactus Saguaro

13. Georgia O'Keeffe

14. Guadalupe Hidalgo

15. el río Grande

D. (10 points) Answers will vary. Possible answers:

16. Eloy Rodríguez inventó un nuevo campo científico llamado la zoofarmacognosía.

17. Los návajos hacen alfombras tradicionales a mano con la misma técnica desde hace siglos.

18. El Álamo es el lugar donde las tropas de Santa Anna derrotaron a los tejanos. Ahora es un museo.

19. El arte narrativo cuenta una historia y refleja la vida cotidiana y la cultura.

20. Dolores Huerta ayudó a fundar la Asociación Nacional de Campesinos para unir a los obreros chicanos.

Aplicación 1

Escuchemos

A Listen to the following statements. In the blank, write **a**) if the speaker expresses **certainty**, or **b**) if the speaker expresses **doubt.**

1. No cabe duda de que el reportero del Canal 6 está mal informado.
2. Parece mentira que las telenovelas sean tan populares.
3. Es increíble que Esteban no esté al tanto de las noticias.
4. Por supuesto que la contaminación ha causado la crisis ambiental.
5. Estamos convencidos de que las noticias en línea tratan los temas a fondo.

Aplicación 2

Escuchemos

A Listen to the following radio broadcast of the morning news. Read the statements below, and choose **a)** for **cierto** or **b)** for **falso.**

Buenos días señores. Les informa Édgar Rodríguez esta mañana con los titulares de hoy. Anoche el jefe de policía de la ciudad anunció que tiene nuevas pistas en el caso de los robos que ha habido en las tiendas de la ciudad en la última semana. Hace dos días hubo otro robo en una tienda de artículos electrónicos. Los ladrones se llevaron varias computadoras, televisores y muchos artículos más. Una mujer afirma que vio a dos hombres entrar a la tienda. El jefe de policía piensa seguir con su investigación. Él cree que los hombres tienen algo que ver con los robos de la semana pasada.

En las noticias nacionales, los economistas informaron que la crisis económica del país ha resultado en muchos problemas. Alfonso Reyes dice que hay mucha gente sin trabajo, pero no hay ningún empleo en la ciudad.

En los titulares de sociedad, la prensa anunció la boda de la actriz Laura Figueroa con el futbolista Juan Bezares. Pueden encontrar todos los detalles en la sección de sociedad en el periódico del día de hoy.

Y finalmente, los científicos se enteraron recientemente de que puede haber una cura para muchas enfermedades en los bosques de Brasil. Un científico descubrió un árbol misterioso y todavía no tiene idea alguna cuántas enfermedades puede curar este árbol.

Éstas son las noticias de esta mañana. Espero que tengan un buen día y les estaré informando de nuevo esta tarde a las cinco.

Nombre ______________________ Clase ______________ Fecha ______________

CAPÍTULO 7

Vocabulario 1

PRUEBA

A Read the statements. Decide what the speaker is talking about, and write **a**) for **desafío** or **b**) for **éxito.**

____ **1.** Tuve que enfrentar muchos obstáculos cuando me mudé a otra ciudad.

____ **2.** Gracias al apoyo de mis padres, logré mi sueño de ir a la universidad.

____ **3.** Mis abuelos tuvieron que hacer muchos sacrificios al llegar a este país.

____ **4.** A Enrique le costó mucho trabajo aprender inglés.

____ **5.** Poco a poco se adaptaron a la nueva cultura.

SCORE /5

B Complete the following statements with the correct phrase.

____ **6.** Emilio es de ascendencia quechua, un ___ de Perú.
a. grupo étnico **b.** modo de ser

____ **7.** Para mí, es ___ ser puertorriqueña.
a. una herencia **b.** un orgullo

____ **8.** Es importante ___ de nuestra cultura.
a. tener éxito **b.** mantener las tradiciones

____ **9.** Podemos tener éxito si ___ .
a. trabajamos duro **b.** estamos agradecidos

____ **10.** Los grupos étnicos ___ a la cultura de un lugar.
a. contribuyen con sus costumbres **b.** superan

SCORE /5

PRUEBA: VOCABULARIO 1

C Fill in each blank with the correct form of a word or phrase from the box.

discriminaba a	pude	
encajaban	me crié	hicieron un gran esfuerzo

Hola, me llamo Samuel. Mis padres son dominicanos, pero yo (**11**) ______________ en un barrio pobre de Nueva York. Cuando mis padres llegaron a este país, enfrentaron muchos obstáculos. Ellos se sentían muy diferentes; les parecía que no (**12**) ______________ en ningún grupo porque no hablaban inglés. Además, había gente que (**13**) ______________ los hispanos. Pero mis padres siempre han sabido trabajar duro, así que (**14**) ______________ para tener éxito en su nueva situación. Finalmente ellos asimilaron el nuevo estilo de vida. Con el tiempo, gracias a su apoyo, yo (**15**) ______________ aprovechar las muchas oportunidades que ofrece este país.

SCORE /10

D Imagine that you're preparing for an interview with Señora Paredes. Write the questions you would ask to find out...

16. if she is of Latino descent.

____

17. if her ancestors spoke Aymara and Spanish.

____

18. if she believes her ethnic group contributed something important to society.

____

19. if it was a big challenge for her to learn English.

____

20. if she has her roots in the U.S. or in Peru.

____

SCORE /10 TOTAL SCORE /30

Nombre ______________________ Clase ______________ Fecha ______________

CAPÍTULO

Gramática 1

PRUEBA

A Complete the following sentences with **lo** or **lo que.**

1. __________ importante en mantener tus costumbres es no olvidar tus raíces.
2. __________ cuesta mucho trabajo es cambiar un estilo de vida por otro.
3. El apoyo de los padres y los profesores es __________ se necesita para tener éxito en el colegio.
4. __________ difícil de mudarse a otro país es que se tiene que asimilar un nuevo estilo de vida.
5. __________ único que se necesita para tener éxito es hacer un esfuerzo.

SCORE /5

B Complete the sentences with the correct form of the verbs in parentheses.

6. Nosotros ______________ (estuvimos / estábamos) en Madrid por diez días.
7. Luisa sabía que ______________ (pudo / podía) hacer un aporte al equipo de natación.
8. Marta y Germán ______________ (tuvieron / tenían) que hacer el proyecto, pero no sé si lo hicieron.
9. Tú ______________ (conociste / conocías) a Gilberto por primera vez cuando se mudó a Houston, ¿verdad?
10. El atleta ______________ (tenía / tuvo) mucho éxito en los Juegos Olímpicos del año pasado.

SCORE /5

PRUEBA: GRAMÁTICA 1

C Complete the paragraph with the correct form of the verbs from the box.

mudarse	**divorciarse**	**acostumbrarse**	**criarse**	**burlarse**

Hola, me llamo Juan y soy puertorriqueño. Mis hermanos y yo (**11**) ______________ en Arecibo, un pueblo en el norte de Puerto Rico. Vivíamos en una finca donde montábamos a caballo y criábamos muchos animales. Cuando tenía diez años, mis padres (**12**) ______________ . Mi mamá, mis hermanos y yo (**13**) ______________ a Nueva York para estar cerca de la familia de mi mamá. Me costó mucho trabajo aprender inglés. Había gente que discriminaba a los hispanos y (**14**) ______________ de mi acento. Poco a poco, yo (**15**) ______________ al estilo de vida de la ciudad. Pude superar todos los obstáculos y ahora tengo muchas oportunidades porque soy bilingüe.

SCORE [/10]

D Combine the phrases to make complete sentences. Be sure to use the correct forms of the **preterite** and **imperfect** as needed.

16. nosotros / querer mantener nuestras costumbres / pero no poder

____

17. ayer, mis hermanos / tener que limpiar sus cuartos / pero no querer hacerlo

____

18. Patricia / estar / estudiando en la Universidad de Madrid por seis meses

____

19. ellos / saber / poder tener éxito con el apoyo de sus padres

____

20. la semana pasada / saber (yo) / mi hermana / ir a tener / un bebé

____

SCORE [/15] TOTAL SCORE [/35]

Nombre ______________________ Clase ______________ Fecha ______________

CAPÍTULO 7

Aplicación 1

PRUEBA

Escuchemos

A Listen to the statements and decide what each speaker is talking about. In the blank, write **a**) for **desafío** or **b**) for **éxito.**

1. ____
2. ____
3. ____
4. ____
5. ____

SCORE ____ /10

Leamos

B Read Pablo's essay about his experiences as a Mexican-American in the United States. Read the statements that follow and choose **a**) for **cierto** or **b**) for **falso.**

Hola, me llamo Pablo. Soy chicano y me crié en Nevada. Mis antepasados son de México. Hace muchos años se mudaron a este país. Mi bisabuelo ayudó a construir el *Hoover Dam* y muchos miembros de mi familia a través del tiempo han llegado a ser personas de éxito, reconocidas por su aporte a la comunidad. Pero aún hay gente que me discrimina porque es evidente que soy de ascendencia mexicana. Piensan que no hablo inglés o que estoy en el país ilegalmente. No dejo que la gente ignorante me moleste porque estoy muy orgulloso de mi herencia cultural. He mantenido las tradiciones y costumbres mexicanas, pero también he asimilado el estilo de vida de este país. Sé que en el futuro voy a tener muchas oportunidades porque puedo expresarme en inglés y en español. A los chicos en la misma situación, les recomiendo que hagan un gran esfuerzo, aunque haya muchos desafíos. Si se esfuerzan, podrán superar cualquier obstáculo.

____ **6.** Pablo se crió en el centro de México y se mudó a Nevada cuando era pequeño.

____ **7.** El bisabuelo de Pablo trabajó en la construcción del *Hoover Dam.*

____ **8.** La gente discrimina a pesar de que la familia de Pablo ha contribuido a la cultura estadounidense.

____ **9.** Pablo no ha mantenido las tradiciones de sus antepasados porque no está orgulloso de su herencia mexicana.

____ **10.** Pablo les recomienda a los inmigrantes que no hagan un esfuerzo porque hay muchos desafíos.

SCORE ____ /10

PRUEBA: APLICACIÓN 1

Escribamos

C Use words from **Vocabulario** to answer the following questions in your opinion.

11. ¿Crees que se debe discriminar a los grupos étnicos? Explica.

____

____

12. ¿Qué es lo bueno de mantener las costumbres de tus antepasados? Explica.

____

____

13. ¿En dónde te criaste? ¿Te has mudado a otro país alguna vez? ¿De dónde son tus antepasados?

____

____

14. ¿Tuviste que enfrentar un obstáculo el año pasado? ¿Qué pasó?

____

____

15. ¿Cuál es tu ascendencia? ¿Aprendiste alguna tradición de tus padres o de tus abuelos?

____

____

SCORE [/15] TOTAL SCORE [/35]

Vocabulario 2

A Choose **a)** if the words in each pair have similar meanings, or **b)** if their meanings are different.

_____ **1.** realizar un sueño / darse por vencido

_____ **2.** meta / iniciativa

_____ **3.** tan pronto como / así que

_____ **4.** objetivo / intención

_____ **5.** por consiguiente / por lo tanto

SCORE ______ /5

B Choose the word or phrase that best completes each statement.

_____ **6.** ___ ser médica y estoy segura que lo lograré si me enfoco en los estudios.
a. Llego a **b.** Sueño con

_____ **7.** Siempre debes ___ aunque haya muchos obstáculos.
a. seguir adelante **b.** criarte

_____ **8.** ___ nuestros derechos y ahora la discriminación es ilegal.
a. Luchamos por **b.** Contribuimos con

_____ **9.** Adrián desayuna con su familia ___ se levanta por la mañana.
a. antes de que **b.** tan pronto como

_____ **10.** Espero que no sea difícil ___ al estilo de vida en España.
a. acostumbrarme **b.** llegar a ser

SCORE ______ /5

PRUEBA: VOCABULARIO 2

C Match each numbered statement with the correct conversational response from the lettered list.

a. ¿Pero no te gustaría triunfar en algo en el futuro?
b. Debes esforzarte en aprender mucho sobre la economía.
c. ¿Entonces vas a la Escuela "Diego Quispe Tito" con la idea de enfocarte en el arte?
d. Sería bueno tomar la iniciativa y llamarle por teléfono.
e. Tienes que empeñarte en seguir tus estudios.

_____ **11.** Sueño con ser pintora.

_____ **12.** Me gusta una chica, pero nunca hemos hablado.

_____ **13.** No tengo ninguna aspiración.

_____ **14.** Estoy frustrado porque no recibí una beca (*scholarship*) para la universidad.

_____ **15.** Quiero tener mi propia compañía algún día.

SCORE /10

D Answer the following questions with your opinion.

16. ¿Qué piensas hacer en cuanto cumplas los dieciocho años?

____

17. ¿Qué quieres hacer antes de que empiecen las clases en septiembre?

____

18. ¿Crees que es importante triunfar en la escuela? ¿Por qué?

____

19. ¿Qué quieres hacer cuando seas mayor?

____

20. ¿Qué haces tan pronto como te levantas por las mañanas?

____

SCORE /10 TOTAL SCORE /30

Gramática 2

A Read each statement. Then, write **a)** for **pasado, b)** for **futuro,** or **c)** for **habitual.**

____ **1.** Tan pronto como me levanto por las mañanas, me baño, me arreglo y desayuno.

____ **2.** Iremos a la fiesta con tal de que podamos regresar tarde a casa.

____ **3.** Cuando mis padres llegaron a este país, no hablaban inglés.

____ **4.** A menos de que Jacinto me invite al cine, me quedaré estudiando en casa.

____ **5.** Siempre tengo práctica de natación después de que salgo del colegio.

SCORE ____ /5

B Complete the statements with the correct form of the words from the box.

lograr	**comer**	**levantarse**	**hablar**	**llegar**

6. Usualmente, llego a casa antes de las dos de la tarde. En cuanto ____________ algo, empiezo mi tarea.

7. Los domingos por la mañana vemos televisión. Tan pronto como ____________ , prendemos el televisor para ver nuestro programa favorito.

8. Todos los veranos, Martín y Felícita visitan a sus abuelos en México. Cuando ellos ____________ a la casa de sus abuelos, pueden oler la comida rica que su abuela ha preparado.

9. Algunos me dicen terco, pero yo siempre sigo luchando hasta que ____________ mis metas.

10. Meche y yo hicimos las paces después de que ____________ honestamente del tema.

SCORE ____ /5

PRUEBA: GRAMÁTICA 2

C Complete Janet's interview with her classmates with the correct form of the verbs in parentheses.

Janet ¿Qué planes tienes para después de la graduación?

Arturo Después de que nosotros (**11**) ________________ (salir) de la graduación, mi familia y yo vamos a celebrar una fiesta familiar.

Janet Y tú, Josefina, ¿vas a la universidad en cuanto te gradúes?

Josefina No. En cuanto (**12**) ________________ (graduarse), viajaré por Europa.

Janet Creo que haré lo mismo cuando (**13**) ________________ (tener) dinero. ¿Seguirás estudiando después de terminar la universidad?

Úrsula Sí, seguiré estudiando hasta que (**14**) ________________ (terminar) mi doctorado. Para lograrlo necesito estudiar por cuatro años más.

Janet Luis, ¿tienes algunas aspiraciones para el futuro?

Luis Claro que sí. Tan pronto como (**15**) ________________ (ganar) la lotería, pienso retirarme para no tener que trabajar más.

SCORE /10

D Combine the phrases to make sentences. Be sure to use the correct form of the verb(s).

16. a menos de que Ramón / haber / estudiado, él no / aprobar / el examen

____

17. mis hermanos siempre me / ayudar / sin que yo les / pedir / ayuda

____

18. Nora, por favor / llamar / a Luisa antes de que ella / salir / de su casa

____

19. tú deber / enfocarte en tus estudios para que / poder / lograr tus sueños

____

20. nosotros / ir / al concierto con tal de que papá / comprar / las entradas

____

SCORE /15 TOTAL SCORE /35

Nombre ______________________ Clase ______________ Fecha ____________

Aplicación 2

CAPÍTULO 7 PRUEBA

Escuchemos

A Listen carefully to each statement. Choose **a)** for **pasado** or **b)** for **futuro.**

1. ____
2. ____
3. ____
4. ____
5. ____

SCORE ____ /10

Leamos

B Read Jessica and Sergio's conversation. Read the statements that follow, and choose **a)** for **cierto** or **b)** for **falso.**

Jessica ¿Cómo te fue en las vacaciones de verano?

Sergio Lo pasé bien. Visité a mis abuelos en Florida como siempre.

Jessica ¿Qué haces con tus abuelos durante las vacaciones?

Sergio Tan pronto como llego a su casa, mi abuela me prepara mi plato favorito. Después de comer, mi abuelo me lleva a pescar. Cuando terminamos de pescar, regresamos a su casa y nos relajamos frente al televisor.

Jessica Me parece que tus vacaciones fueron muy aburridas. Yo sólo visito a mis abuelos con tal de que ellos me lleven a pasear.

Sergio Y tú, ¿hiciste algo más interesante durante las vacaciones?

Jessica La verdad es que pensaba ir a Río de Janeiro. Pero cuando empezaron las vacaciones, no tenía el dinero para el pasaje. Por eso, busqué un trabajo. Voy a seguir trabajando hasta que tenga el dinero para viajar a Brasil.

Sergio A menos que gane un millón de dólares, nunca podré viajar a Brasil.

PRUEBA: APLICACIÓN 2

_____ **6.** Sergio pasó las vacaciones de verano con sus abuelos en Florida.

_____ **7.** Sergio estuvo muy aburrido durante sus vacaciones.

_____ **8.** Jessica no visita a sus abuelos a menos que ellos la lleven a pasear.

_____ **9.** Jessica trabajará hasta que tenga dinero para visitar a sus abuelos.

_____ **10.** Sergio puede ir a Brasil sin que gane un millón de dólares.

SCORE ____ /10

Escribamos

C Write about a goal you have for the near future. Explain why you set that goal, when you want to achieve it, what you must do in order to achieve your goal, and what obstacles you must overcome.

____

____

____

____

____

____

____

____

____

____

SCORE ____ /15 TOTAL SCORE ____ /35

Nombre ______________________ Clase ______________ Fecha ______________

Lectura

A Read the following story about a boy from Perú. What can you infer about the **hombre español loco** by reading "between the lines"? Write the words or phrases that helped you make your inference.

Historia de un niño peruano

Nací en la isla Tequile del Lago Titicaca. Desde pequeño mi padre me enseñó los secretos de la pesca en el lago, como habían hecho todos mis antepasados con sus sucesores; pero siempre supe que yo sería el último eslabón *(link)* de la cadena y que no viviría para siempre en aquella desolada isla. Siempre quise saber qué había fuera del lago. De un hombre español loco que vivió en mi aldea *(village)* por un tiempo, estudiando todo tipo de animal, aprendí el castellano y muchas cosas de su mundo. Me gustó tanto su mundo, que hoy soy jefe del departamento de zoología en la Universidad de los Andes.

Your inferences: ____

____

SCORE ____ /10

B Read the statements and choose **a)** for **cierto** or **b)** for **falso.**

____ **1.** El narrador nació en una isla de la costa peruana.

____ **2.** El padre del narrador le enseñó a pescar cuando él era pequeño.

____ **3.** El abuelo del narrador le enseñó el castellano.

____ **4.** Desde pequeño, el narrador se interesó por saber qué había en el mundo fuera de su aldea.

____ **5.** El narrador es actualmente profesor de zoología en la universidad.

SCORE ____ /10

C Answer the following questions.

6. ¿Crees que el narrador realizó el sueño de su vida? Explica.

____

____

7. ¿Cómo crees que se sentirán los padres del narrador? Explica.

____

____

SCORE ____ /15 TOTAL SCORE ____ /35

Escritura

A Imagine that you are interviewing a student who has just moved to the United States from a Latin American country. Write an interview in which you ask the student about the obstacles that he or she has overcome and his or her goals for the future. Ask to what factors the student owes his or her present success.

Entrevistador ______________________________

____

Estudiante ______________________________

____

Entrevistador ______________________________

____

Estudiante ______________________________

____

Entrevistador ______________________________

____

Estudiante ______________________________

SCORE /20

B María has graduated in business administration and dreams of having her own business. A while ago, she wrote to her grandfather to ask him about his success in his family business. Write her grandfather's reply and explain how he has managed to succeed and why.

____

____

____

____

____

____

____

____

____

____

SCORE /15 TOTAL SCORE /35

Nombre ______________________ Clase ______________ Fecha ______________

Geocultura

A Match each letter on the map of **los Andes** with the name of the place or area it represents.

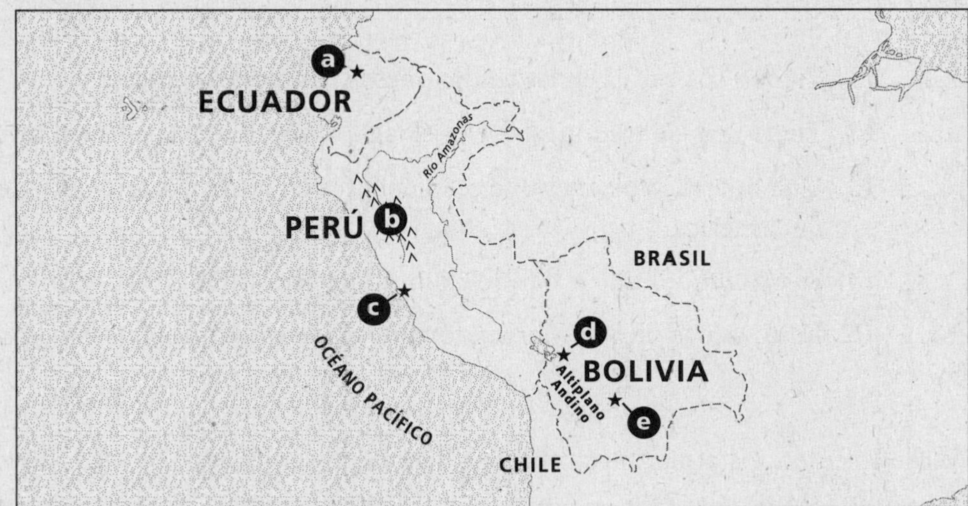

_____ **1.** Sucre

_____ **2.** Quito

_____ **3.** La Paz

_____ **4.** Lima

_____ **5.** Machu Picchu

SCORE ____ /5

B Fill in the blank with the phrase that best completes each statement.

_____ **6.** El Huascarán es ___ de Perú.
a. la montaña más alta **b.** el cañón más profundo

_____ **7.** La ciudad de ___ era el centro del imperio inca.
a. Quito **b.** Cuzco

_____ **8.** Francisco Pizarro traicionó a los incas y mató a ___ .
a. Atahualpa **b.** José de San Martín

_____ **9.** Los españoles llevaron a Europa ___ que los andinos cultivaban.
a. la yuca **b.** la papa y el maíz

_____ **10.** La ciudad de ___ no fue descubierta hasta 1911, pero atrae a miles de turistas todos los años.
a. Sucre, Bolivia **b.** Machu Picchu

SCORE ____ /5

PRUEBA: GEOCULTURA

C Write the letter of the word(s) from the box that correspond(s) to each statement.

a. Titicaca	**b.** el imperio inca	**c.** los trajes folclóricos andinos
d. el Cinturón de Fuego		**e.** Simón Bolívar

____ **11.** Tienen sus raíces en las tradiciones españolas e incaicas.

____ **12.** Tiene más de treinta islas y es el lago navegable más alto del mundo.

____ **13.** Una línea de volcanes que se encuentra en la costa occidental de Sudamérica.

____ **14.** Se extendió desde el sur de Colombia hasta Chile.

____ **15.** Junto a José de San Martín, formó la Gran Colombia.

SCORE ____ /10

D Write a sentence stating the cultural or historical significance of the following:

16. la encomienda

____

____

17. la provincia de Tarapaca

____

____

18. Atahualpa

____

____

19. el estilo indigenista

____

____

20. Jaime Roldós

____

____

SCORE ____ /10 TOTAL SCORE ____ /30

Vocabulario 1

A. (5 points)

1. a **2.** b **3.** a **4.** a **5.** b

B. (5 points)

6. a **7.** b **8.** b **9.** a **10.** a

C. (10 points)

11. me crié

12. encajaban

13. discriminaba a

14. hicieron un gran esfuerzo

15. pude

D. (10 points)

16. ¿Es Ud. de ascendencia latina?

17. ¿Hablaban sus antepasados aymara y español?

18. ¿Cree Ud. que su grupo étnico contribuyó con algo importante a la sociedad?

19. ¿Fue un gran desafío para Ud. aprender inglés?

20. ¿Tiene Ud. sus raíces en Estados Unidos o en Perú?

Gramática 1

A. (5 points)

1. Lo **2.** Lo que **3.** lo que **4.** Lo **5.** Lo

B. (5 points)

6. estuvimos

7. podía

8. tenían

9. conociste

10. tuvo

C. (10 points)

11. nos criamos

12. se divorciaron

13. nos mudamos

14. se burlaba

15. me acostumbré

D. (15 points)

16. Nosotros queríamos mantener nuestras costumbres, pero no pudimos.

17. Ayer, mis hermanos tenían que limpiar sus cuartos, pero no quisieron hacerlo.

18. Patricia estuvo estudiando en la Universidad de Madrid por seis meses.

19. Ellos sabían que podían tener éxito con el apoyo de sus padres.

20. La semana pasada supe que mi hermana iba a tener un bebé.

Aplicación 1

A. (10 points)

1. b **2.** a **3.** a **4.** b **5.** b

B. (10 points)

6. b **7.** a **8.** a **9.** b **10.** b

C. (15 points) Answers will vary. Possible answers:

11. Creo que no se debe discriminar a los grupos étnicos porque cada grupo hace su aporte a la sociedad.

12. Lo bueno de mantener las costumbres de mis antepasados es que nunca olvidaré mis raíces.

13. Me crié en Massachusetts y nunca me he mudado a otro país. Mis antepasados son de Venezuela.

14. El año pasado tuve que enfrentar un obstáculo. No entendía las matemáticas para nada, pero me esforcé mucho en mis estudios y aprobé la clase.

15. Soy de ascendencia hawaiana. Una tradición que aprendí de mi abuela y mi mamá es bailar la hula.

Vocabulario 2

A. (5 points)

1. b **2.** b **3.** b **4.** a **5.** a

B. (5 points)

6. b **7.** a **8.** a **9.** b **10.** a

C. (10 points)

11. c

12. d

13. a

14. e

15. b

D. (10 points) Answers will vary. Possible answers:

16. En cuanto cumpla los dieciocho años, pienso trabajar para poder tener independencia.

17. Antes de que empiecen las clases en septiembre, quiero viajar con mis amigos a Perú.

18. Sí, creo que es importante triunfar en la escuela para poder tener éxito en la universidad.

19. Quiero ser profesora cuando sea mayor.

20. Tan pronto como me levanto por las mañanas, me lavo los dientes y desayuno.

Gramática 2

A. (5 points)

1. c **2.** b **3.** a **4.** b **5.** c

B. (5 points)

6. como

7. nos levantamos

8. entran

9. logro

10. hablamos

C. (10 points)

11. salgamos

12. me gradúe

13. tenga

14. termine

15. gane

D. (15 points)

16. A menos de que Ramón haya estudiado, él no aprobará el examen.

17. Mis hermanos siempre me ayudan sin que yo les pida ayuda.

18. Nora, por favor llama a Luisa antes de que ella salga de su casa.

19. Tú debes enfocarte en tus estudios para que puedas lograr tus sueños.

20. Nosotros vamos al concierto con tal de que papá compre las entradas.

Aplicación 2

A. (10 points)

1. b **2.** a **3.** b **4.** a **5.** a

B. (10 points)

6. a **7.** b **8.** a **9.** b **10.** b

C. (15 points)

Answers will vary. Answers should include: vocabulario (sueño con…, metas), grammatical reflexives (graduarme, esforzarme), subjunctive with future actions (Estudiaré hasta que obtenga mi título.), indicative with adverbial conjunctions (Estudio hasta que me viene el sueño.)

Lectura

A. (10 points)

Answers will vary. Possible answers:

El hombre español no está loco, es un zoólogo. Me basé en "estudiando todo tipo de animal" y "Me gustó … tanto que ahora soy …"

B. (10 points)

1. b **2.** a **3.** b **4.** a **5.** a

C. (15 points) Answers will vary. Possible answers:

6. Creo que sí realizó el sueño de su vida porque logró salir de su aldea y hacerse profesor de la universidad.

7. Creo que sus padres se sentirán decepcionados porque rompió con la tradición familiar.

Escritura

A. (20 points)

Answers will vary. Answers should include: vocabulario (enfrentar obstáculos...), grammatical reflexives (esforzarme...), preterite and imperfect with stative verbs, (lo bueno, lo que...), subjunctive with future actions (Estudiaré hasta que sea doctor.), preterite (tuve que...), imperfect (sabía que podía...), indicative with habitual past actions (Cuando llegamos, no hablaba inglés.) (Mi éxito se debe a...)

B. (15 points)

Answers will vary. Possible answers may include: Preterite and imperfect of stative verbs: estaba agradecido por..., pude lograr mi sueño de…, me esforcé en..., no me quejé de..., lo bueno es que llegué a ser..., lo malo es que tuve que hacer un gran esfuerzo para..., lo que no debes hacer es darte por vencido, gracias al apoyo de..., he podido superar..., por fin, logré..., nos esforzamos en..., concentrate en tu objetivo…, con tal de que se haga realidad, mi éxito en... se debe a..., no estudié, así que...

Geocultura

A. (5 points)

1. e **2.** a **3.** d **4.** c **5.** b

B. (5 points)

6. a **7.** b **8.** a **9.** b **10.** b

C. (10 points)

11. c **12.** a **13.** d **14.** b **15.** e

D. (10 points)

16. La encomienda fue un sistema de esclavitud en el cual los indígenas tenían que trabajar los campos para los españoles.

17. La provincia de Tarapaca contiene valiosos minerales y causó la Guerra del Pacífico entre Chile, Perú y Bolivia.

18. Atahualpa fue el último emperador de los incas y fue asesinado por Francisco Pizarro.

19. El estilo indigenista fue fundado por José Sabogal y es un estilo de arte con el propósito de resaltar al indígena.

20. Jaime Roldós fue el primer presidente de una democracia latinoamericana y fue elegido por el voto popular en Ecuador.

Aplicación 1

Escuchemos

A. Listen to the statements and decide what each speaker is talking about. In the blank, write **a**) for **desafío** or **b**) for **éxito.**

1. Ana María tuvo que esforzarse mucho en la universidad para poder ser reportera. El año pasado, empezó a trabajar para una emisora de televisión.
2. Mis padres tuvieron que enfrentar muchos obstáculos cuando llegaron a Estados Unidos por primera vez. No hablaban inglés y había gente que discriminaba a los hispanos.
3. Cuando yo llegué a este colegio, no encajaba en ningún grupo. No tenía amigos y me la pasaba solo.
4. Judith y Virginia trabajaron duro y por eso, hoy son dueñas de una compañía de moda. Como jefas de la compañía, ganan mucho dinero y no necesitan trabajar mucho.
5. Adán pudo mantener sus tradiciones y asimilar el estilo de vida de este país. Ahora tiene muchas oportunidades porque habla dos idiomas.

Aplicación 2

Escuchemos

A. Listen carefully to each statement. Choose **a**) for **pasado** or **b**) for **futuro.**

1. En cuanto cumpla los dieciocho años, iré a la universidad para estudiar medicina. Sueño con ser médico algún día.
2. Cuando Rogelio y Patricia llegaron a este país, creían que todo el mundo era rico porque en su país no había las mismas oportunidades.
3. Después de que Filomena se gradúe, va a trabajar como editora de un periódico. Cuando tenga suficiente dinero, irá al Caribe de vacaciones.
4. Mi tío Pedro no se acostumbró a la vida en Australia hasta que dejó de hacerles caso a las personas que tenían prejuicios sobre las personas de Estados Unidos.
5. Mis padres estudiaron inglés antes de mudarse a este país. Por eso, asimilaron rápidamente el nuevo estilo de vida.

Nombre ______________________ Clase ______________ Fecha ______________

Vocabulario 1

A Read each statement and choose **a)** for **cierto** or **b)** for **falso.**

_____ **1.** Un hombre de negocios trabaja con los enfermos en un hospital.

_____ **2.** Cuando alguien tiene talento para algo, quiere decir que no logra entenderlo.

_____ **3.** Los adelantos tecnológicos han mejorado la vida diaria.

_____ **4.** El teléfono celular y las agendas electrónicas son adelantos tecnológicos muy comunes.

_____ **5.** Una desventaja de los adelantos en la medicina es que la gente vive más tiempo.

SCORE ____ /5

B Read each sentence and choose the appropriate response.

_____ **6.** Ahora que Olga tiene un ___, ya no tiene que preocuparse de organizar su oficina ella misma.
a. robot **b.** teléfono celular **c.** auxiliar administrativo

_____ **7.** Con este adelanto tecnológico, no necesito estar en casa cuando mis amigos me llaman por teléfono.
a. el contestador automático **b.** el robot **c.** la computadora

_____ **8.** Si tienes que compartir un documento con tus compañeros de trabajo, debes utilizar este adelanto tecnológico.
a. la agenda electrónica **b.** la fotocopiadora **c.** el robot

_____ **9.** Es fácil hacer las invitaciones para una fiesta porque con este adelanto tecnológico puedes cambiar el texto en un santiamén.
a. el teléfono **b.** la agenda electrónica **c.** la computadora

_____ **10.** En el futuro, las amas de casa *(housewives)* no tendrán nada que hacer gracias a este adelanto tecnológico.
a. el robot **b.** el teléfono celular **c.** la fotocopiadora

SCORE ____ /5

PRUEBA: VOCABULARIO 1

C Read each sentence, and choose the most appropriate response from the box.

No, él es capaz de hacer dos cosas a la vez.
Mira, Tulio, trata de concentrarte más en los estudios y menos en las chicas.
Lo puedo hacer porque siempre he tenido talento para las computadoras.
No me cabe en la cabeza que el álgebra sea tan fácil para ti.
Al contrario, creemos que pueden facilitar la vida diaria.

11. No sé por qué no logras entender la lección de matemáticas.

____

12. ¿A Juan le es difícil ver televisión y hacer la tarea al mismo tiempo?

____

13. ¿Creen que los robots nos harán perezosos?

____

14. Buscamos alguien que sepa utilizar este programa de diseño.

____

15. Cuando Nina me dijo que me ayudaría con la tarea, me decidí a aceptar inmediatamente.

____

SCORE ____ /10

D Write the question or statement you would use in each situation.

16. Tell a friend that if she works hard, nothing is outside her reach.

____

17. Ask a friend if there is something he doesn't quite grasp.

____

18. Say that these days technological advances change our daily life right away.

____

19. Ask a panel of experts if they think technology makes our social problems worse.

____

20. Say that you're capable of using a computer but it takes a lot of work for you.

____

SCORE ____ /10 TOTAL SCORE ____ /30

Nombre ______________________ Clase ______________ Fecha ____________

CAPÍTULO **8** PRUEBA

Gramática 1

A Decide how **se** is used in each statement and choose **a**) for **no intencional, b**) for **voz pasiva, c**) for **impersonal,** or **d**) for **reflexivo.**

____ **1.** A José se le olvidó que tenía que pasar por Laura.

____ **2.** Se dice que todos tendremos robots competentes en el futuro.

____ **3.** La auxiliar administrativa se compró una agenda electrónica para no olvidarse de todas sus reuniones.

____ **4.** Se presentaron muchos adelantos tecnológicos en la última Feria Internacional.

____ **5.** Se nos quemó la comida mientras hablábamos por teléfono.

SCORE ____ /5

B Complete the sentences with the correct **indirect object pronoun.**

6. A Selma ____________ resulta difícil utilizar el programa de computadora porque no logra entender las nuevas tecnologías.

7. ____________ costó trabajo establecerse, pero al fin, Tina y Marta llegaron a ser mujeres de negocios.

8. A nosotros ____________ molesta que no podamos llegar tarde a casa.

9. ¿Cómo ____________ fue a Uds. en sus vacaciones?

10. ____________ resultó fácil el examen de cálculo porque estudié mucho anoche.

SCORE ____ /5

Nombre ______________________ Clase ______________ Fecha ______________

PRUEBA: GRAMATICA 1

C Choose the verb that best completes each sentence.

____ **11.** ¡Me estoy ___ loca con la agenda electrónica! Nunca me funciona.
a. volviendo **b.** llegando **c.** haciendo

____ **12.** Samuel siempre tuvo talento para el debate, por eso se ___ abogado.
a. quedó **b.** puso **c.** hizo

____ **13.** Nos ___ boquiabiertos cuando oímos la sorprendente noticia.
a. convertimos **b.** quedamos **c.** pusimos

____ **14.** ¿Viste la nueva película de terror? El hombre se ___ en un vampiro.
a. pone **b.** convierte **c.** queda

____ **15.** Ellas se ___ felices cuando les dimos el contestador automático.
a. pusieron **b.** volvieron **c.** hicieron

SCORE ____ /10

D Combine the phrases to make sentences using **reflexive verbs** and/or **indirect object pronouns.**

16. a mí / costar trabajo / usar la fotocopiadora

____

____

17. hoy en día, el teléfono celular / facilitar / la vida diaria a la gente

____

____

18. Carmelo y yo / graduarse / del colegio el mes pasado

____

____

19. a Uds. / resultar / bastante difícil encontrar trabajo

____

____

20. el chico travieso / convertirse / en un hombre de negocios muy competente

____

____

SCORE ____ /15 TOTAL SCORE ____ /35

Nombre ______________________ Clase ______________ Fecha ____________

Aplicación 1

Escuchemos

A Listen to the speakers. Read the statements that follow, and choose **a**) for **cierto** or **b**) for **falso.**

_____ **1.** Katerina no trabajó duro y por eso no logró ser mujer de negocios.

_____ **2.** A Cristina le gustaría trabajar para una compañía de computadoras después de que se gradúe de la universidad.

_____ **3.** La narradora se volvió loca de alegría porque le dieron el puesto de gerente.

_____ **4.** Nuestros compañeros de trabajo se pusieron contentos y lo celebraron cuando nosotros nos fuimos de la compañía.

_____ **5.** El narrador está seguro que los robots empeorarán la vida diaria.

SCORE ____ /10

Leamos

B Elena is interviewing her brother Andrés for the school paper. Read the interview. Then, choose the phrases that best complete the statements.

Elena ¿Por qué te interesa la tecnología? Y, ¿cómo te mantienes al tanto de los adelantos tecnológicos?

Andrés Siempre he tenido talento para la tecnología; por eso, pude arreglarte la computadora. Me mantengo al tanto leyendo artículos sobre el tema. Además, me gusta ver programas sobre la tecnología. Por ejemplo, anoche vi un programa sobre un implante electrónico que les devuelve la audición a las personas que no pueden oír. Me interesa cómo las nuevas tecnologías mejoran la vida diaria.

Elena ¿En qué campo te gustaría trabajar? ¿Cómo lograrás tus sueños?

Andrés Me encantaría trabajar en el campo de ingeniería electrónica. Necesito estudiar mucho porque sueño con asistir a un instituto de tecnología prestigioso. Si me aceptan en alguno, me decido a ir en un santiamén.

Elena ¿Crees que los robots nos facilitarán el trabajo en el futuro?

Andrés Claro que sí. Pero una desventaja de ese adelanto tecnológico es que nos haremos más perezosos. Los adelantos como la computadora y la tele nos han mostrado eso.

PRUEBA: APLICACIÓN 1

_____ **6.** Andrés pudo arreglarle la computadora a Elena porque ___ .
a. leyó artículos sobre cómo hacerlo
b. tiene talento para la tecnología

_____ **7.** El programa que Andrés vio se trataba de ___ .
a. un implante electrónico
b. la tecnología en la vida diaria

_____ **8.** Si lo aceptan, Andrés ___ .
a. estudiará en un instituto tecnológico
b. llegará a ser un médico especializado en implantes

_____ **9.** Para Andrés, ___ de tener robots es que la gente se volvería perezosa.
a. una ventaja
b. una desventaja

_____ **10.** Andrés afirma que ___ ya han demostrado que los adelantos tecnológicos también tienen desventajas.
a. la computadora y la tele
b. los robots

SCORE ____ /10

Escribamos

C Write an essay about technology in your daily life. Explain how technology aids or impedes you in daily tasks and any advantages or disadvantages you have seen with the use of technology.

____
____
____
____
____
____
____
____
____

SCORE ____ /15 TOTAL SCORE ____ /35

Nombre ______________________ Clase ______________ Fecha ______________

Vocabulario 2

A Complete the statements with the correct word or phrase.

_____ **1.** Victoria tiene un empleo de ___ ; por eso trabaja 40 horas a la semana.
a. medio tiempo **b.** tiempo completo **c.** voluntaria

_____ **2.** Adjunté mi ___ a la carta de solicitud.
a. currículum vitae **b.** seguro médico **c.** entrevista

_____ **3.** La compañía ofrece ___ como el seguro médico y dos semanas de vacaciones.
a. empresas **b.** salarios **c.** beneficios

_____ **4.** Reinaldo ___ . Por esa razón, él no cobra dinero por su trabajo.
a. requiere un salario **b.** no tiene carrera **c.** dona su tiempo

_____ **5.** ___ ingeniería eléctrica para ser un ingeniero en una compañía grande.
a. Siempre he querido ser **b.** Me gustaría estudiar **c.** Si pudiera

SCORE /5

B Match each want ad with the appropriate candidate.

_____ **6.** Revista internacional busca editor(a) que sepa dirigir a varios empleados.

_____ **7.** Solicitamos profesor(a) de álgebra. Requisitos: título universitario y referencias.

_____ **8.** Programa después de clases busca profesor(a) de arte para niños. No se requiere experiencia.

_____ **9.** La Cruz Roja solicita voluntarios para organizar clases nocturnas de primeros auxilios. Horario flexible.

_____ **10.** Se busca gerente con conocimientos actualizados del rol de la tecnología en la ingeniería mecánica. Se requieren 10 años de experiencia.

a. Soy banquero pero quiero cambiar de carrera. Tengo títulos universitarios en economía y computación.

b. Soy bilingüe. Trabajé en una revista donde supervisé a un equipo de cinco personas.

c. Soy enfermera en un hospital local. Sólo puedo trabajar a medio tiempo. No necesito salario.

d. Busco trabajo a medio tiempo. Tengo talento para dibujar y trabajé en un centro infantil.

e. Llevo 20 años con una compañía que construye puentes. Usábamos robots para parte de la construcción.

SCORE /10

PRUEBA: VOCABULARIO 2

C Complete the following letter with the correct word(s) from the box.

atentamente	**estimado**	**adjunto**	**de la presente**	**carrera**

(**11**) ____________________ Sr. Velázquez:

Por medio (**12**) ____________________ , quisiera solicitar el puesto de tiempo completo como gerente del departamento de ventas de su empresa. Actualmente, soy supervisor de empleados en una compañía de computadoras. Mi (**13**) ____________________ profesional incluye cinco años de experiencia como auxiliar administrativo en una agencia de publicidad y tengo un título universitario en administración. Le (**14**) ____________________ mi currículum vitae a esta carta. Le agradecería que se comunicara conmigo sobre las posibilidades de empleo en su compañía. Puedo reunirme con Ud. a la hora que le sea conveniente.

Muy (**15**) ____________________ ,

Manolo Acosta

SCORE /5

D Answer the following questions with your opinion.

16. Si tuvieras la oportunidad de viajar, ¿adónde irías?

____

17. ¿Qué te gustaría estudiar? ¿Por qué?

____

18. ¿Prefieres trabajar en una empresa o en tu propio negocio?

____

19. ¿Qué tipo de trabajo te interesaría conseguir después de graduarte? Explica.

____

20. ¿Tienes un empleo de medio tiempo? ¿Por qué?

____

SCORE /10 TOTAL SCORE /30

Gramática 2

A Read the statements. In the blank, write **a)** for **pasado** or **b)** for **presente.**

_____ **1.** Le recordé a mi amiga que adjuntara una copia de su currículum vitae a la jefa de la empresa.

_____ **2.** A Emilio le gustaría donar tiempo a una causa, pero está muy ocupado.

_____ **3.** Luisa nos pidió que la ayudáramos a preparar su presentación.

_____ **4.** Sus padres preferían que fuera médico, pero se hizo músico en una banda de rock.

_____ **5.** El ambiente de trabajo es muy relajado; por eso puedo usar vaqueros todos los días.

SCORE ____ /5

B Complete the job interview with the correct verbs from the box.

fuera	**actualizaría**	**estuvieran**	**podría**	**haría**

Sr. Castro Srta. Machado, tengo entendido que está interesada en el puesto de gerente de artes visuales en el departamento de publicidad. ¿Qué contribución (**6**) ____________ a nuestra compañía?

Lidia Creo que (**7**) ____________ contribuir muchísimo a su compañía. Tengo cinco años de experiencia en este campo y un título universitario en artes visuales. Además, me mantengo al tanto de los adelantos tecnológicos.

Sr. Castro Si (**8**) ____________ gerente, ¿qué cambios haría en el departamento y por qué?

Lidia Primero, (**9**) ____________ su página Web y su programa de diseño. Creo que la página Web es bastante difícil de navegar y el programa de diseño es muy antiguo. En mi último puesto, ofrecí clases de diseño gráfico a los empleados para que ellos (**10**) ____________ al tanto de los adelantos tecnológicos.

Sr. Castro Estoy seguro de que sería una gerente espléndida. Estaremos en contacto con Ud. tan pronto como tomemos una decisión.

SCORE ____ /5

Nombre ______________________ Clase ______________ Fecha ____________

CAPÍTULO **8**

PRUEBA: GRAMÁTICA 2

C Combine the phrases to make complete sentences using the **conditional** tense of the verbs and your opinion.

11. Esteban y Marcos / querer / un puesto con...

____

12. me / gustar / encontrar empleo de tiempo completo para...

____

13. Silvia no / enviar / una carta de solicitud a esa empresa porque...

____

14. ser / las once de la noche cuando...

____

15. nosotros / viajar / a Buenos Aires pero...

____

SCORE ____ /10

D Use a word or phrase from each column to write hypothetical statements about what you *would* or *would not do* given a certain situation. Make sure to use the **conditional** or **past subjunctive** if necessary.

tener	rico(a)	donar a una causa
poder	oportunidad	ir a Chile
ser	tiempo	conocer a un actor
	viajar	llegar a ser famoso(a)
	talento	tomar unas vacaciones
	hablar francés	estudiar en Francia
		tocar en una banda
		comprar una mansión
		trabajar en un banco

16. ____

17. ____

18. ____

19. ____

20. ____

SCORE ____ /15 TOTAL SCORE ____ /35

Nombre ______________________ Clase ______________ Fecha ____________

CAPÍTULO

PRUEBA

Aplicación 2

Escuchemos

A Listen to the speakers, and choose the best answer to the questions.

____ **1.** Para Carmela, hacerse jefa de su propia compañía ____.
a. estuvo fuera de su alcance **b.** no le fue nada fácil

____ **2.** ¿Por qué no trabajaría como voluntario para la Cruz Roja?
a. Sus padres no lo dejarían. **b.** No le gustaría.

____ **3.** ¿Qué necesita hacer para poder viajar a Europa?
a. Ver muchas cosas. **b.** Tener dinero.

____ **4.** ¡Pobre Reina! Ella ____.
a. no sabe por qué fracasó **b.** por fin captó la idea de prepararse bien

____ **5.** ¿Con qué sueña el narrador?
a. Ser auxiliar administrativo. **b.** Hacer trabajo difícil.

SCORE ____ /10

Leamos

B Read the want ad and the candidate's response. Then, read the statements that follow and choose **a)** for **cierto** or **b)** for **falso.**

SE BUSCA
Trabajador(a) social con cinco años de experiencia para empleo de tiempo completo trabajando con niños discapacitados. Requisitos: título universitario en trabajo social o psicología, conocimiento de computadoras y español. Beneficios incluyen seguro médico, plan de retiro y dos semanas de vacaciones. Por favor, dirija su carta de solicitud al Sr. Muñoz, Avenida San Cristóbal, Santa Fe, NM.

Estimado Sr. Muñoz:

Por medio de la presente, quisiera solicitar el puesto de tiempo completo como trabajadora social. Actualmente, soy estudiante en la Universidad de Nuevo México y espero recibir un título en psicología infantil a fines del mes. Tengo cinco años de experiencia trabajando con niños que sufren de autismo. Además, estudié francés durante los últimos ocho años y he trabajado con varios sistemas computadorizados. Le adjunto mi currículum vitae a esta carta. Puedo reunirme con Ud. para una entrevista a la hora que le sea conveniente.

Reciba un cordial saludo,
Roselia Domínguez

PRUEBA: APLICACIÓN 2

_____ **6.** El anuncio es para un empleo de tiempo completo y se busca un(a) psicólogo(a) para niños discapacitados.

_____ **7.** En la actualidad, Roselia estudia en la Universidad de Nuevo México.

_____ **8.** Roselia cumple con todos los requisitos para el puesto.

_____ **9.** El Sr. Muñoz le dará el puesto de trabajadora social porque Roselia sabe francés.

_____ **10.** Roselia iría a una entrevista a la hora que le fuera conveniente al Sr. Muñoz.

SCORE /10

Escribamos

C Write about the job of your dreams. Explain what position you would hold, what your job requirements would be, and any benefits you would have. Then write a brief description of a career you would not like to have and why.

____

____

____

____

____

____

____

____

____

SCORE /15 TOTAL SCORE /35

Lectura

A Read the following story. While you read, think about the author's reasons for writing the story. Then, write down at least two of them.

Somos bolivianas. Mis padres emigraron a Texas buscando un futuro mejor para nosotras. Cuando llegamos, no hablábamos inglés, pero lo aprendimos muy rápido porque éramos muy pequeñas. Mi hermana se llama Leticia y es muy inteligente y estudiosa. Sólo tiene veintiún años y ya se graduó de ingeniería cibernética y trabaja en una compañía que desarrolla y construye robots. También tiene muchas habilidades manuales y cada vez que un aparato deja de funcionar en casa, ella lo arregla. Ahora, está estudiando mecánica automotriz y ya arregla todos los carros de la familia. ¡Qué suerte tener una hermana así!

____

____

SCORE /10

B Answer the following questions based on the reading.

1. ¿De qué país son las protagonistas de esta historia?

____

2. ¿Por qué dice la narradora que aprendieron inglés rápidamente?

____

3. ¿Qué hace la compañía donde trabaja Leticia?

____

4. ¿Por qué Leticia puede arreglar cualquier aparato que se rompa?

____

5. ¿Qué está estudiando ahora Leticia?

____

SCORE /15

C Answer the following questions.

6. ¿Crees que la narradora admira a su hermana? Explica.

____

7. ¿Crees que Leticia llegará a ser una buena mecánica? Explica.

____

SCORE /10 TOTAL SCORE /35

Escritura

A Write about an activity or job in which you excel. Explain what you do to maintain your abilities and how you would like to use those abilities in a future career.

SCORE /15

B Write about what you would do if you had $10 million. Explain how your life *would* or *would not* change, how you would spend your time, what you would do with the money, and any advantages or disadvantages you would have. Be sure to use the conditional and past subjunctive in your answer.

SCORE /20 TOTAL SCORE /35

Nombre ______________________ Clase ______________ Fecha ____________

CAPÍTULO

Geocultura

PRUEBA

A Match each letter on the map of **los Andes** with the name of the place or area it represents.

_____ **1.** El volcán activo más alto del mundo está en este país.

_____ **2.** Machu Picchu se encuentra en este país.

_____ **3.** Es la ciudad andina de origen aymara más importante.

_____ **4.** La Iglesia de San Francisco está en esta ciudad.

_____ **5.** La antigua Estación de Desamparados se encuentra en esta ciudad.

SCORE _____ /5

B Fill in the blanks with the word or phrase that best completes the statements.

_____ **6.** En 1979 ____ fue el primer país latinoamericano en elegir a un presidente por voto popular después de una dictadura.
a. Perú **b.** Ecuador

_____ **7.** Los chimú contribuyeron ____ a la cultura de los incas.
a. la artesanía de oro y plata **b.** el estilo indigenista

_____ **8.** La fachada de ____ es una reproducción del palacio de El Escorial de España.
a. la Escuela Cuzqueña **b.** la Iglesia de San Francisco

_____ **9.** En la batalla de Iquique, Perú perdió ____ y cedió control de la costa a Chile.
a. la nave *Independencia* **b.** el emperador Atahualpa

_____ **10.** El propósito de la Escuela de Tejidos es ____ .
a. resaltar al indígena **b.** conservar las tradiciones textiles

SCORE _____ /5

Nombre ______________________ Clase ______________ Fecha ______________

CAPÍTULO **8**

PRUEBA: GEOCULTURA

C Write the letter of the words from the box that match the definitions below.

a. estilo indigenista	**b. *El Grito***	**c. Gran Colombia**
d. Miguel Andrango	**e. Ecuador**	

____ **11.** Formada por Simón Bolívar y José de San Martín. Incluía Ecuador, Venezuela y Colombia.

____ **12.** País latinoamericano que mantuvo conflictos armados con Perú por disputas fronterizas.

____ **13.** Fundado por José Sabogal, tiene como meta resaltar al indígena.

____ **14.** Fundó la Escuela de Tejidos.

____ **15.** Refleja el dolor y la miseria sufrida por la humanidad.

SCORE ____ /10

D Write a sentence stating the cultural or historical significance of the following:

16. Simón Bolívar

____

____

17. los chimú

____

____

18. el imperio inca

____

____

19. Juan de la Cruz Machicado

____

____

20. la antigua Estación de Desamparados

____

____

SCORE ____ /10 TOTAL SCORE ____ /30

Vocabulario 1

A. (5 points)

1. b **2.** b **3.** a **4.** a **5.** b

B. (5 points)

6. c **7.** a **8.** b **9.** c **10.** a

C. (10 points)

11. No me cabe en la cabeza que el álgebra sea tan fácil para ti.

12. No, él es capaz de hacer dos cosas a la vez.

13. Al contrario, creemos que pueden facilitar la vida diaria.

14. Lo puedo hacer porque siempre he tenido talento para las computadoras.

15. Mira, Tulio, trata de concentrarte más en los estudios y menos en las chicas.

D. (10 points) Answers will vary. Possible answers:

16. Si trabajas duro, nada está fuera de tu alcance.

17. ¿Hay algo que se te escapa? / ¿Hay algo que no logras entender?

18. Hoy en día los adelantos tecnológicos cambian la vida diaria enseguida.

19. ¿Creen Uds. que la tecnología empeora nuestros problemas sociales?

20. Soy capaz de utilizar una computadora pero me cuesta mucho trabajo.

Gramática 1

A. (5 points)

1. a **2.** c **3.** d **4.** b **5.** a

B. (5 points)

6. le

7. Les

8. nos

9. les

10. Me

C. (10 points)

11. a **12.** c **13.** b **14.** b **15.** a

D. (15 points)

16. A mí me cuesta trabajo usar la fotocopiadora.

17. Hoy en día, el teléfono celular le facilita la vida diaria a la gente.

18. Carmelo y yo nos graduamos del colegio el mes pasado.

19. A Uds. les resulta bastante difícil encontrar trabajo.

20. El chico travieso se convirtió en un hombre de negocios muy competente.

Aplicación 1

A. (10 points)

1. b **2.** a **3.** a **4.** b **5.** b

B. (10 points)

6. b **7.** a **8.** a **9.** b **10.** a

C. (15 points)

Answers will vary. Answers should include: **Vocabulario** expressions (utilizo las nuevas tecnologías...), indirect object pronouns (Los adelantos tecnológicos me facilitan la vida diaria.), uses of *se* (El teléfono celular se puede usar en cualquier sitio. Se puede escuchar mensajes en el contestador automático.)

Vocabulario 2

A. (5 points)

1. b **2.** a **3.** c **4.** c **5.** b

B. (10 points)

6. b **7.** a **8.** d **9.** c **10.** e

C. (5 points)

11. Estimado

12. de la presente

13. carrera

14. adjunto

15. atentamente

D. (10 points) Answers will vary. Possible answers:

16. Si tuviera la oportunidad de viajar, iría a París.

17. Me gustaría estudiar arte porque siempre he querido ser artista.

18. Preferiría trabajar en una empresa porque quiero buenos beneficios.

19. Me gustaría conseguir un puesto de voluntario(a) con la Cruz Roja.

20. No tengo un empleo de medio tiempo porque el estudio no me lo permite.

Gramática 2

A. (5 points)

1. a **2.** b **3.** a **4.** a **5.** b

B. (5 points)

6. haría

7. podría

8. fuera

9. actualizaría

10. estuvieran

C. (10 points) Answers will vary. Possible answers:

11. Esteban y Marcos querrían un puesto con mejores beneficios.

12. Me gustaría encontrar empleo de tiempo completo para ganar dinero.

13. Silvia no enviaría una carta de solicitud a esa empresa porque no ofrecen puestos de medio tiempo.

14. Serían las once de la noche cuando me dejaron el mensaje en el contestador automático.

15. Nosotros viajaríamos a Buenos Aires pero no tenemos ni tiempo ni dinero.

D. (15 points) Answers will vary. Possible answers:

16. Si fuera rico, donaría mucho dinero a una causa.

17. Si tuviera la oportunidad, trabajaría en un banco.

18. Si pudiera hablar francés, no estudiaría en Francia.

19. Si tuviera talento, llegaría a ser famosa.

20. Si tuviera tiempo, tomaría unas vacaciones.

Aplicación 2

A. (10 points)

1. b **2.** a **3.** b **4.** b **5.** a

B. (10 points)

6. b **7.** a **8.** b **9.** b **10.** a

C. (15 points) Answers will vary. Answers should include: conditional (Me gustaría ganar mucho dinero.), subjunctive with hypothetical statements (Si pudiera, trabajaría como corresponsal de deportes para un canal de televisión.)

Lectura

A. (10 points) Answers will vary. Possible answers: La narradora está orgullosa de su hermana y quiere contar su historia. La narradora quiere demostrar que los latinos también pueden triunfar en Estados Unidos.

B. (15 points)

1. Son de Bolivia.

2. Porque eran muy pequeñas cuando llegaron a Estados Unidos.

3. Desarrolla y construye robots.

4. Porque tiene muchas habilidades manuales.

5. Ahora está estudiando mecánica automotriz.

C. (10 points) Answers will vary. Possible answers:

6. Creo que sí porque dice que es "muy inteligente y estudiosa", que "tiene muchas habilidades manuales" y que "es una suerte tener una hermana así".

7. Creo que sí porque tiene habilidades manuales y eso es algo importante para esa profesión.

Escritura

A. (15 points) Answers will vary. Answers should include: **Vocabulario** expressions (tengo talento para...), indirect object pronouns (me resulta fácil...), verbs "to become" (me vuelvo loco por los deportes, quiero llegar a ser atleta, me pongo triste cuando no puedo practicar, me haré jugador de béisbol...), subjunctive with hypothetical statements (Si los Yankees me escogieran, me decidiría a jugar para ellos en un santiamén.)

B. (20 points) Answers will vary. Answers should include: **Vocabulario** expressions (ventajas, desventajas...), indirect object pronouns (Me resultaría fácil ir a Europa.), verbs "to become" (me volvería loco(a), me pondría triste, me haría gerente de un equipo de béisbol...), subjunctive with hypothetical statements (Si tuviera $10 millones, viajaría por el mundo entero.)

Geocultura

A. (5 points)

1. a **2.** b **3.** d **4.** c **5.** e

B. (5 points)

6. b **7.** a **8.** b **9.** a **10.** b

C. (10 points)

11. c **12.** e **13.** a **14.** d **15.** b

D. (10 points)

16. Simón Bolívar peleó por la independencia de Sudamérica y fundó la Gran Colombia junto a José de San Martín.

17. Los chimú reinaron sobre partes de Perú hasta que fueron conquistados por los incas. Aportaron su artesanía de oro, plata y cobre a la cultura incaica.

18. El imperio inca era sofisticado y se extendía desde el sur de Colombia hasta el norte de Chile.

19. Juan de la Cruz Machicado es un artista peruano que pinta en el estilo abstracto expresionista. Pintó *La Familia Cuzqueña en San Blas.*

20. La antigua Estación de Desamparados es un museo donde se exhiben las obras de artistas indígenas.

Aplicación 1

Escuchemos

A Listen to the speakers. Read the statements that follow, and choose **a**) for **cierto** or **b**) for **falso.**

1. En el colegio, Katerina se la pasaba estudiando. Al terminar la universidad, trabajó duro y llegó a ser una mujer de negocios.
2. A Cristina le gustaría tener un trabajo de medio tiempo hasta que se gradúe de la universidad. Después, tiene planes de trabajar en una empresa donde pueda utilizar su talento para las computadoras.
3. Me volví loca al oír que me habían dado el puesto de gerente. Di un grito, salté de alegría y le di un abrazo al jefe de la empresa.
4. Nuestros compañeros de trabajo se pusieron tristes cuando nos fuimos de la compañía. Algunos lloraron y otros no quisieron decirnos adiós.
5. En el futuro, los robots facilitarán la vida diaria de la gente. Imagínate tener un robot que te lave los dientes, te haga la tarea y te prepare el desayuno. ¡Sería maravilloso!

Aplicación 2

Escuchemos

A Listen to the speakers, and choose the best answer to the questions.

1. Carmela — Siempre trabajé duro y nunca me di por vencida. Ahora, soy jefa de mi propia compañía y gano mucho dinero.
2. Alberto — Si pudiera, trabajaría como voluntario para la Cruz Roja, pero no lo creo posible porque mis padres no me dejarían.
3. Gladys — Si tuviera el dinero, viajaría a Europa. Quisiera ver la Torre Eiffel en Francia, la Alhambra en España y muchas cosas más.
4. Reina — La entrevista fue fatal. Primero, se me olvidó llevar una copia de mi currículum vitae. Cuando les dije que yo no sé usar ni una fotocopiadora, me sugirieron que buscara otro trabajo.
5. Roberto — Sé que el trabajo es bastante difícil, pero estoy seguro de que sería un auxiliar administrativo fantástico.

Nombre ________________ Clase ________________ Fecha ________________

Vocabulario 1

A Complete each sentence with a vocabulary word from the box.

a. leyendas
b. castigaban
c. palacio
d. fantasma
e. misterioso

____ **1.** El rey y la reina vivían en un hermoso ___.

____ **2.** Las ___ vienen de la realidad y la ficción.

____ **3.** A los niños les dio miedo escuchar la historia del ___.

____ **4.** Nadie sabe de dónde vino el hombre ___.

____ **5.** Los amos ___ a sus esclavos.

SCORE ____ /5

B Read each definition and choose the vocabulary word that best fits each one.

____ **6.** Es una persona con muchos conocimientos.
a. un sabio **b.** un fantasma **c.** una princesa

____ **7.** Es un ser supremo que tiene distintas características según la religión.
a. un príncipe **b.** un hechicero **c.** un dios

____ **8.** En este edificio se celebran ritos religiosos.
a. el mito **b.** el templo **c.** el castigo

____ **9.** Esta persona es infiel a una causa o principio.
a. un enamorado **b.** un traidor **c.** un desconocido

____ **10.** Son habilidades mágicas que tienen los hechiceros.
a. las causas **b.** los hechos **c.** los poderes

SCORE ____ /5

PRUEBA: VOCABULARIO 1

C You are telling a Latin American exchange student about a legend in your country. Write how you would express the following in Spanish.

11. Many years ago,...

____

12. From what we've been told, the villain...

____

13. It's told that all of a sudden...

____

14. In the end, we realized...

____

15. From then on, they lived happily ever after.

____

SCORE /10

D Starting with the phrases you wrote in Activity C, build a complete short story. You can draw on the words from the following box to round your story out.

ahora bien	**tan pronto como**	**enamorarse**	**aunque**
enemigo	**a causa de**	**encantado**	**mágico**

____

____

____

____

____

____

____

____

SCORE /10 TOTAL SCORE /30

Gramática 1

A Laura and Jorge are at the beach. Complete the following sentences with **por** or **para.**

1. Laura lleva jugo frío ______________ tomar cuando tiene sed.
2. Jorge quiere estar al sol ______________ mucho tiempo.
3. Laura y Jorge fueron a la playa ______________ el camino más corto.
4. Salieron muy temprano por la mañana ______________ estar más tiempo en la playa.
5. Pagaron cinco dólares ______________ el estacionamiento.

SCORE ____ /5

B Complete the statements with the **preterite** or **imperfect** form of the verbs in parentheses according to the context.

6. Los padres de Carlos ______________ (fueron / iban) todos los años a España.
7. Me contaron que la tía de Marta ______________ (tuvo / tenía) un hijo.
8. Un día ______________ (llegó / llegaba) una persona desconocida a mi pueblo.
9. Mi abuela ______________ (vio / veía) las telenovelas todas las tardes.
10. La profesora les ______________ (dijo / decía) a los estudiantes la semana pasada que debían estudiar para el examen.

SCORE ____ /10

Nombre ______________________ Clase ______________ Fecha ______________

PRUEBA: GRAMÁTICA 1

C Complete the following story with the correct form of the words from the box.

desaparecer **por** **para** **vivir** **escapar**

Hace muchos años, en un pueblo escondido entre las montañas, (**11**) ______________ un esclavo. Un día, el esclavo (**12**) ______________ y se fue a vivir junto a un río cerca de las montañas. Se cuenta que se bañó una vez en el río, y después de eso, sus heridas (**13**) ______________ enseguida. A partir de entonces, la gente iba con frecuencia a bañarse en ese río (**14**) ______________ curar su piel. A causa de esto, (**15**) ______________ mucho tiempo se pensó que el agua de ese río era mágica.

SCORE /10

D Use the phrases to make complete sentences using the **preterite** or the **imperfect** form of the verbs. Use the **modelo** as a guide.

MODELO hace muchos años / vivir / una princesa / que tener / poderes mágicos
Hace muchos años, vivía una princesa que tenía poderes mágicos.

16. una vez / haber / un rey inteligente

____

17. el rey / ser / alto, fuerte y poderoso

____

18. la reina siempre / ir a / todas partes con el rey

____

19. el rey y la reina / estar / en el palacio cuando / llegar / los malvados

____

20. el rey / no preocuparse / porque saber que / el palacio estar / protegido

____

SCORE /10 TOTAL SCORE /35

Nombre ______________________ Clase ______________ Fecha ______________

Aplicación 1

Escuchemos

A Listen to Raúl talk about myths, legends, and fairy tales. Then, read the statements below and choose **a**) for **cierto** or **b**) for **falso.**

____ **1.** Los mitos tratan de explicar los misterios de la naturaleza.

____ **2.** Todos los pueblos del mundo tienen los mismos mitos.

____ **3.** Las leyendas generalmente se basan en hechos reales.

____ **4.** A menudo en los cuentos de hadas hay reyes, príncipes y princesas.

____ **5.** En los cuentos de hadas no hay elementos de fantasía.

SCORE ____ /5

Leamos

B Read about the creation of man according to the *Popol Vuh.* Then, answer the questions that follow.

En el *Popol Vuh,* el antiguo libro sagrado de los maya, se cuenta que los dioses crearon la tierra y los mares, y luego los llenaron de plantas y animales. Como los animales sólo hacían ruido en vez de adorar a sus creadores, los dioses decidieron crear a los humanos. Los dioses usaron muchos materiales en la creación del ser humano. Primero, usaron el barro, pero no les funcionó. Después, los dioses usaron la madera y tampoco les dio resultado. Los dioses no estuvieron contentos con la creación de este ser hasta que decidieron crearlo usando las plantas de maíz. Esta vez los dioses quedaron contentos con su creación.

PRUEBA: APLICACIÓN 1

6. ¿De qué habla el libro sagrado de los maya?

____

7. ¿Qué crearon primero los dioses?

____

8. ¿Por qué los dioses decidieron crear a los humanos?

____

9. ¿Qué materiales no dieron resultado en la creación del ser humano?

____

10. Al final, ¿de qué material hicieron los dioses a los humanos?

____

SCORE /15

Escribamos

C Write an essay about a legend you know from Latin American countries or from your community. Use expressions from **¡Exprésate!,** the preterite, and the imperfect in your legend.

____

____

____

____

____

____

____

____

____

SCORE /15 TOTAL SCORE /35

Nombre ______________________ Clase ______________ Fecha ______________

CAPÍTULO

Vocabulario 2

PRUEBA

A Choose the word that does not logically fit with the others.

____ **1. a.** independencia **b.** libertad **c.** sufrir

____ **2. a.** cobarde **b.** héroe **c.** valiente

____ **3. a.** el soldado **b.** el dictador **c.** las tropas

____ **4. a.** la derrota **b.** la bandera **c.** la batalla

____ **5. a.** luchar **b.** regocijarse **c.** acordar la paz

SCORE ____ /5

B Match the definitions below with a word from the box that best fits each one.

a. valiente	**b.** acordar la paz	**c.** el imperio
d. la víctima	**e.** el campo de batalla	

____ **6.** Persona que sufre o pierde la vida como consecuencia de una guerra o un desastre natural.

____ **7.** Una manera de terminar la guerra entre dos países.

____ **8.** Una persona que es lo contrario de cobarde.

____ **9.** Extenso territorio que es gobernado por un emperador o un rey.

____ **10.** Lugar donde las tropas van para luchar con el enemigo.

SCORE ____ /5

PRUEBA: VOCABULARIO 2

C Read Pablo's essay on the struggle for independence in Latin America. Complete his essay with the correct form of the words from the box.

tropas	**declarar la guerra**	**honrar**	**vencer**	**explorador**

Cuando los españoles llegaron a las Américas, establecieron un imperio. Los (**11**) ________________ españoles llevaron su bandera y tomaron las Américas en nombre de su rey. España mantuvo control de sus colonias durante más de trescientos años hasta que los países latinoamericanos (**12**) ________________ contra España. Los nuevos países mandaron (**13**) ________________ para luchar por su independencia. Hubo muchas víctimas en estas guerras, pero los soldados latinoamericanos por fin (**14**) ________________ a los españoles. Cuando se acordó la paz después de muchos años de guerra, la gente decidió (**15**) ________________ a sus héroes con un monumento.

SCORE ____ /10

D Using expressions from **Vocabulario** and **¡Exprésate!,** write a complete, original sentence that you would use in each situation. Use your imagination to complete the unfinished part of the sentence.

16. to describe yours or someone else's dream of a lifetime

____

17. to say it's too bad people believe that...

____

18. to tell someone you regret that...

____

19. to say that hopefully your graduation party will be...

____

20. to say your parents had great hopes that...

____

SCORE ____ /10 TOTAL SCORE ____ /30

Nombre ______________________ Clase ______________ Fecha ______________

Gramática 2

A Lorenzo is talking with Carlos about running in a marathon. Complete their conversation with the **indicative** or **subjunctive** of the verb according to the context.

Lorenzo Quiero que nosotros (**1**) ______________ (corremos / corramos) en la próxima carrera de maratón.

Carlos Por supuesto. Yo creo que ya (**2**) ______________ (estamos / estemos) listos para el maratón. Y tú, ¿qué piensas?

Lorenzo No me parece que (**3**) ______________ (estamos / estemos) bien preparados. Debemos entrenarnos más.

Carlos Entonces, sugiero que nos (**4**) ______________ (preparamos / preparemos) juntos. ¿Qué te parece?

Lorenzo Excelente. Estoy seguro que (**5**) ______________ (vamos / vayamos) a cumplir nuestros objetivos.

SCORE /5

B Complete each sentence with the **present** or **past subjunctive** of the verb in parentheses according to the context.

6. El profesor recomienda que ______________ (investigar) hechos importantes de la historia y que ______________ (mantenernos) informados.

7. Él les pidió a Uds. que ______________ (escoger) un evento histórico y que ______________ (escribir) un párrafo sobre el mismo.

8. Él sugirió que Raúl ______________ (entrevistar) a un periodista y que ______________ (buscar) información en la biblioteca.

9. Entrevisté a mi padre y me sorprende que él ______________ (recordar) tantos detalles y que ______________ (saber) tanto de historia.

10. En verdad es necesario que tú ______________ (conocer) bien la historia para que no ______________ (repetir) los errores del pasado.

SCORE /10

PRUEBA: GRAMÁTICA 2

C Read the following sentences. Then rewrite each **subordinate clause** with the correct sequence of tenses according to the verb in the **main clause.**

11. Alejandro sugiere que veamos la película.
Alejandro sugirió ______________________________

12. Pablo dice que invitará a Rosa.
Pablo dijo ______________________________

13. Estamos seguros de que la película será fantástica.
Estábamos seguros ______________________________

14. Ernesto quiere que todos vayamos al estreno.
Ernesto quería ______________________________

15. Roberto va a ir en cuanto llegue su hermano.
Roberto iba a ir ______________________________

SCORE /10

D Complete Rubén's letter with the **subjunctive** or **indicative** form of the verbs from the box. Make sure to base your answers on the verbs in the other clause of each sentence.

recomendar	**honrar**	**terminar**	**pedir**	**escribir**

Querida hermana:

Nuestro profesor de historia nos (**16**) ______________ que hiciéramos un ensayo sobre la lucha por la independencia en Latinoamérica, y quiero que tú me (**17**) ______________ algunos libros sobre ese tema. Nos dijo que (**18**) ______________ sobre las batallas de la independencia porque es importante que nosotros (**19**) ______________ a los héroes que hicieron posible la victoria. Prometo que te mostraré mi ensayo en cuanto lo (**20**) ______________. Sin duda alguna, te sentirás orgullosa de mí.

Tu hermano,

Rubén

SCORE /10 TOTAL SCORE /35

Nombre ______________________ Clase ______________ Fecha ______________

Aplicación 2

Escuchemos

A Listen to part of Paulina's presentation on Latin American history. Then, choose the most appropriate answer to each question.

_____ **1.** ¿En qué año llegaron los exploradores a América?
a. en 1776 **b.** en 1492

_____ **2.** ¿Los españoles crearon un imperio en América?
a. sí **b.** no

_____ **3.** ¿Qué pasó en los países de Latinoamérica después de muchos años sin justicia?
a. la revolución industrial **b.** la guerra de la independencia

_____ **4.** ¿Quiénes lucharon por la libertad?
a. los soldados **b.** los dictadores

_____ **5.** ¿A quiénes honraron los ciudadanos después de la victoria?
a. a los traidores **b.** a los héroes

SCORE /5

Leamos

B Read the conversation and answer the questions that follow.

Alina La verdad es que yo estoy en contra de las guerras.

Fernando Pienso que hay guerras injustas, pero hay otras que son necesarias para lograr la independencia o la justicia.

Alina Sí, la victoria es la cara bonita, pero no se habla mucho de las víctimas civiles y la destrucción que dejan las guerras.

Fernando Pero la gente valiente siempre se ha sacrificado por su país, y hay que reconocerlo.

Alina Bueno, entiendo tu punto de vista. Pero ojalá que algún día se pueda lograr la paz sin perder una sola vida.

PRUEBA: APLICACIÓN 2

6. ¿Está Alina a favor de la guerra? Explica.

____

7. ¿Piensa Fernando que todas las guerras son necesarias? Explica.

____

8. Según Alina, ¿cuál es la cara fea de la guerra?

____

9. ¿Qué dice Fernando que han hecho siempre los valientes?

____

10. ¿Qué quiere Alina que se logre algún día?

____

SCORE ______ /15

Escribamos

C You've been thinking about the different types of war and the need for freedom and justice in the world throughout history. Write a letter explaining to a friend your point of view about war and what has happened in the past. Use words from **Vocabulario** and expressions from **¡Exprésate!** in your letter.

____

____

____

____

____

____

____

____

____

SCORE ______ /15 TOTAL SCORE ______ /35

Nombre ______________________ Clase ______________ Fecha ______________

CAPÍTULO 9

Lectura

PRUEBA

A Read the following paragraph about the legendary origins of **yerba mate.** Then, write the main idea of the paragraph on the lines below.

El origen de la yerba mate se atribuye a diferentes dioses legendarios. En una leyenda, Tupú, el genio del bien, se paseaba por un país desconocido cuando llegó a la casa de un anciano muy pobre. A pesar de su pobreza, el anciano lo dejó entrar a su casa, y le dio de comer y de beber. Para darle las gracias, Tupú le dejó la yerba. En otra leyenda, Yasi y Araí (la Luna y la nube) fueron atacadas por un jaguar en el bosque. Vino un cazador para salvarlas, y ellas como premio le dieron la *caá* (yerba). Una tercera leyenda cuenta que el guerrero Maté descansaba una noche cuando vino la diosa Sumá y le dio un ramo verde de yerba. Le dijo que lo plantara, y que después de secar las hojas, éstas le darían una bebida deliciosa.

Main idea: ____

____

SCORE ____ /10

B Read the statements and choose **a)** for **cierto** or **b)** for **falso,** based on the reading.

____ **1.** Nadie sabe la verdad sobre el origen de la yerba mate.

____ **2.** Una leyenda dice que un anciano le dio la yerba a Tupú, el genio del bien.

____ **3.** Otra leyenda cuenta que Yasi y Araí le dieron la yerba a un cazador.

____ **4.** Según la leyenda de Yasi y Araí, la yerba mate se llama *caá*.

SCORE ____ /10

C Answer the following questions based on the reading.

5. ¿Quién era Tupú y qué le dio al anciano?

____

6. ¿Por qué Yasi y Araí le dieron la yerba a un cazador?

____

7. ¿Qué recibió el guerrero Maté de la diosa?

____

SCORE ____ /15 TOTAL SCORE ____ /35

Escritura

PRUEBA

A María's brother Sergio is in the Army. She is very proud of him, because she considers him a hero. Write a letter from María to Sergio asking about what his hopes were going into the war, and how his opinions have changed. Use expressions from **¡Exprésate!**

____

____

____

____

____

____

____

____

SCORE ____ /15

B Write a response to María from Sergio, answering her questions and telling her about the realities and the ugly face of war. He does not consider himself special, but he is proud of being able to help the victims of war. Use expressions from **¡Exprésate!**

____

____

____

____

____

____

____

____

SCORE ____ /20 TOTAL SCORE ____ /35

Nombre ______________________ Clase ______________ Fecha ______________

Geocultura

A Match each letter on the map of the **Cono Sur** with the name of the place or area it represents.

____ **1.** Argentina

____ **2.** Chile

____ **3.** Brasil

____ **4.** Paraguay

____ **5.** Uruguay

SCORE /5

B Read the following statements and choose **a)** for **cierto** or **b)** for **falso.**

____ **6.** Montevideo está ubicado en la desembocadura del Río de la Plata.

____ **7.** En Chile, hay tradiciones de los maya.

____ **8.** José de San Martín fue el libertador de Argentina, Chile y Perú.

____ **9.** Los chilenos invadieron las Islas Malvinas.

____ **10.** Los veranos en el Gran Chaco son muy calientes.

SCORE /5

Nombre ______________________________ Clase ________________ Fecha ____________

PRUEBA: GEOCULTURA

C Read the following questions and choose the most appropriate response.

____ **11.** ¿Cuál NO es la capital de un país en Latinoamérica?
a. Santiago **b.** Madrid **c.** Buenos Aires

____ **12.** ¿Qué famoso militar acordó la paz con España?
a. Roberto Carlos **b.** José de San Martín **c.** Augusto Pinochet

____ **13.** ¿Dónde se encuentran las Islas Malvinas?
a. en el Océano Pacífico **b.** al sur de Chile **c.** en el Océano Atlántico

____ **14.** ¿Dónde vivían los mapuches cuando llegaron los españoles?
a. en Chile **b.** en palacios **c.** en Asunción

____ **15.** ¿Quién gobernó su país con la doctrina del "Justicialismo"?
a. Bernardo O'Higgins **b.** Augusto Pinochet **c.** Juan Perón

SCORE ____ /10

D Write one sentence to tell the historical importance of each of the following:

16. Juan Manuel de Rosas

____

17. Pedro de Valdivia

____

18. Carlos Federico Reyes

____

19. Augusto Pinochet

____

20. los mapuches o araucanos

____

SCORE ____ /10 TOTAL SCORE ____ /30

Vocabulario 1

A. (5 points)

1. c **2.** a **3.** d **4.** e **5.** b

B. (5 points)

6. a **7.** c **8.** b **9.** b **10.** c

C. (10 points)

11. Hace muchos años...

12. Según nos dicen, el malvado...

13. Se cuenta que de pronto...

14. Al final, nos dimos cuenta de...

15. A partir de entonces, vivieron siempre felices.

D. (10 points) Answers will vary. Answers should include:

vocabulary: expressions for setting the scene of a story and for continuing and ending a story; grammar: use of the preterite and imperfect

Gramática 1

A. (5 points)

1. para **2.** por **3.** por **4.** para **5.** por

B. (10 points)

6. iban

7. tuvo

8. llegó

9. veía

10. dijo

C. (10 points)

11. vivía

12. escapó

13. desaparecieron

14. para

15. por

D. (10 points)

16. Una vez hubo un rey inteligente.

17. El rey era alto, fuerte y poderoso.

18. La reina siempre iba a todas partes con el rey.

19. El rey y la reina estaban en el palacio cuando llegaron los malvados.

20. El rey no se preocupó porque sabía que el palacio estaba protegido.

Aplicación 1

A. (5 points)

1. a **2.** b **3.** a **4.** a **5.** b

B. (15 points)

6. Habla de la creación del mundo.

7. Primero, crearon la tierra y los mares.

8. Porque los animales hacían ruido y no adoraban a sus dioses.

9. Ni el barro ni la madera dieron resultado.

10. Al final, los dioses hicieron a los humanos de las plantas de maíz.

C. (15 points)

Answers will vary.

Vocabulario 2

A. (5 points)

1. c **2.** a **3.** b **4.** b **5.** a

B. (5 points)

6. d **7.** b **8.** a **9.** c **10.** e

C. (10 points)

11. exploradores

12. declararon la guerra

13. tropas

14. vencieron

15. honrar

D. (10 points) Answers will vary. Possible answers:

16. El sueño de mi vida es escalar el cerro Aconcagua en Argentina.

17. Es lamentable que la gente crea que las guerras son necesarias.

18. Me arrepiento de haber abandonado mis clases de guitarra flamenca.

19. Es de esperar que la fiesta de graduación sea divertida para todos.

20. Mis padres tenían muchas esperanzas de regresar a su país de origen.

Gramática 2

A. (5 points)

1. corramos

2. estamos

3. estemos

4. preparemos

5. vamos

B. (10 points)

6. investiguemos / nos mantengamos

7. escogieran / escribieran

8. entrevistara / buscara

9. recuerde / sepa

10. conozcas / repitas

C. (10 points)

11. Alejandro sugirió que viéramos la película.

12. Pablo dijo que invitaría a Rosa.

13. Estábamos seguros que la película sería fantástica.

14. Ernesto quería que todos fuéramos al estreno.

15. Roberto iba a ir en cuanto llegara su hermano.

D. (10 points)

16. pidió

17. recomiendes

18. escribiéramos

19. honremos

20. termine

Aplicación 2

A. (5 points)

1. b **2.** a **3.** b **4.** a **5.** b

B. (15 points)

6. No. Alina está en contra de la guerra.

7. No. Piensa que algunas guerras son necesarias.

8. La cara fea es la destrucción que queda y las víctimas civiles.

9. Los valientes se han sacrificado por sus países.

10. Quiere que algún día se pueda lograr la paz sin perder una sola vida.

C. (15 points)

Answers will vary.

Lectura

A. (10 points) Answers will vary.
Possible answer:

Idea principal: Se presentan diferentes versiones legendarias sobre el origen de la yerba mate. Estas leyendas tienen en común la idea de que el bien con el bien se paga.

B. (10 points)

1. a **2.** b **3.** a **4.** a

C. (15 points)

5. Tupú era el genio de bien y le dio la yerba mate al anciano.

6. Yasi y Araí le dieron la yerba al cazador en agradecimiento por haberles salvado la vida.

7. El guerrero Maté recibió la yerba de la diosa Sumá.

Escritura

A. (15 points)

Answers will vary.

B. (20 points)

Answers will vary.

Geocultura

A. (5 points)

1. e **2.** a **3.** c **4.** b **5.** d

B. (5 points)

6. a **7.** b **8.** a **9.** b **10.** a

C. (10 points)

11. b **12.** b **13.** c **14.** a **15.** c

D. (10 points) Answers will vary.
Possible answers:

16. Juan Manuel de Rosas fue uno de los caudillos más famosos de Argentina y llegó a ser dictador de su país.

17. Pedro de Valdivia luchó contra los araucanos y fundó la ciudad de Santiago de Chile.

18. Carlos Federico Reyes es un artista paraguayo que utiliza un estilo naïf para recrear escenas de su niñez.

19. Augusto Pinochet fue un militar y político chileno quien fue dictador de Chile.

20. Los mapuches o araucanos poblaban gran parte de Chile antes del imperio de los incas y resistieron a los españoles hasta 1883.

Aplicación 1

Escuchemos

A Listen to Raúl talk about myths, legends, and fairy tales. Then, read the statements below and choose **a**) for **cierto** or **b**) for **falso.**

Los mitos, las leyendas y los cuentos de hadas son relatos tradicionales y son diferentes según los pueblos y las culturas.

Los mitos tratan de explicar fenómenos de la naturaleza. Sus personajes muchas veces son dioses poderosos. En muchos mitos de civilizaciones antiguas, las personas construían templos para sus dioses.

Las leyendas se basan en hechos reales que con el tiempo pueden volverse fantásticos. Sus personajes son seres humanos que tienen poderes extraordinarios y misteriosos.

Los reyes y las reinas no solamente son personajes de la vida real, también son personajes de los cuentos de hadas. En estos relatos que tienen elementos de fantasía y de realidad, se cuentan historias de príncipes y princesas que se enamoran y viven siempre felices.

Aplicación 2

Escuchemos

A Listen to part of Paulina's presentation on Latin American history. Then, choose the most appropriate answer to each question.

Los exploradores españoles llegaron al continente americano en el año 1492. Poco después, crearon un imperio en las Américas. Después de muchos años sin libertad política, los países de Latinoamérica comenzaron una guerra de independencia. Muchos soldados lucharon por la libertad de sus países y muchos murieron en el campo de batalla. Pero al final, los países latinoamericanos ganaron la guerra y lograron su objetivo. Después de la victoria, los ciudadanos honraron a los héroes por los sacrificios que éstos hicieron.

Vocabulario 1

A Complete each sentence with the correct vocabulary word from the box.

a. desastre	**b.** descubrimiento	**c.** erupción	**d.** estreno	**e.** pánico

____ **1.** Fuimos al ___ de una nueva película.

____ **2.** Los científicos han hecho un nuevo ___ en el planeta.

____ **3.** La explosión de una bomba provocó el ___ .

____ **4.** El pueblo quedó destruido después de la ___ del volcán.

____ **5.** Los huracanes son un ___ natural.

SCORE ____ /5

B Read each definition and choose the vocabulary word that best fits each one.

____ **6.** Algo nuevo hecho por una persona.
a. el invento **b.** las elecciones **c.** el estreno

____ **7.** Objeto celeste sin luz propia.
a. la nave **b.** el planeta **c.** la bomba

____ **8.** Competencia donde se gana un premio.
a. el campeonato **b.** la manifestación **c.** la cooperación

____ **9.** Evento inesperado, sobre todo negativo.
a. la indiferencia **b.** el acontecimiento **c.** el accidente

____ **10.** Sentimiento de lástima por el mal de otros.
a. la indiferencia **b.** la compasión **c.** la alegría

SCORE ____ /5

PRUEBA: VOCABULARIO 1

C Give an opinion on the following issues using the phrases from the box.

Creo que vale la pena acordarse de...	**Lo que noto es que...**
Aunque estoy de acuerdo, creo que...	**Ten en cuenta que...**
A pesar de que..., por otro lado...	

11. los inmigrantes y la necesidad de aprender otro idioma

____

12. adelantos de la tecnología y sus efectos en la comunicación

____

13. relaciones entre países ricos y pobres: ¿solidaridad o indiferencia?

____

14. el invento del DVD y la popularidad del cine

____

15. la llegada de los refugiados a otros países

____

SCORE /10

D You are telling another student about a natural disaster that you witnessed. Write how you would say the following in Spanish.

16. I remember it like it was yesterday.

____

17. I was home watching television when I heard about the tragic accident.

____

18. No, I don't remember at all.

____

19. There was a lot of destruction and the situation was terrifying.

____

20. But it was moving to see how many people tried to help others.

____

SCORE /10 TOTAL SCORE /30

Nombre ______________________ Clase ______________ Fecha ______________

CAPÍTULO **10** PRUEBA

Gramática 1

A Complete Joaquín's essay on his winter vacation with the correct form of **haber** and the verb in parentheses.

El invierno pasado visité a mi hermano en Canadá. Mis amigos me (**1**) ____________ (invitar) a Florida y me (**2**) ____________ (gustar) ir con ellos, pero mis padres me convencieron de ir a conocer algo nuevo. Lo más emocionante fue ver tanta tierra cubierta de un manto blanco. ¡Yo nunca (**3**) ____________ (ver) la nieve! También me gustó ver las esculturas de hielo, pero caminar sobre el agua congelada en las aceras no fue tan divertido. Todas las tardes cuando llegaba de la calle a la casa de mi hermano, su esposa ya me (**4**) ____________ (preparar) un chocolate caliente. Hasta ahora, ése (**5**) ____________ (ser) el invierno más duro de mi vida.

SCORE ____ /10

B Pedro is telling Alberto the news about an earthquake. Complete the sentences with the correct form of **haber.**

Pedro (**6**) ____________ un terremoto en Asia, ¿no leíste las noticias?

Alberto No, no lo sabía. ¿(**7**) ____________ muchas víctimas?

Pedro Sí, fue un desastre muy grande. (**8**) ____________ mucha gente en la ciudad cuando todo comenzó.

Alberto Es terrible. Ojalá (**9**) ____________ métodos pronto para saber cuándo va a ocurrir un terremoto.

Pedro Sí, es difícil saberlo con exactitud ahora pero en un futuro no muy lejano (**10**) ____________ más precisión y se salvarán muchas más vidas.

SCORE ____ /5

PRUEBA: GRAMÁTICA 1

C Answer the following questions using the phrase in parentheses in the **present** or **past progressive** depending on the context.

11. ¿Qué hacían ellos cuando empezó la película? (seguir hablar)

____

12. ¿Qué deporte estás practicando este año? (seguir practicar béisbol)

____

13. ¿Qué estaba haciendo tu hermana cuando llegaste? (estar leer un libro)

____

14. ¿Qué está haciendo Raúl en la biblioteca? (estar estudiar para el examen)

____

15. ¿Qué anda haciendo Francisco en el estadio? (andar hacer entrevistas)

____

SCORE /10

D For each situation, write the expression you would use to...

16. tell someone how long ago you learned how to (ride a bike, play the guitar...)

____

17. ask someone how long ago the movie started

____

18. tell someone how long you've been listening to this radio station

____

19. ask someone what they did for the first time this year

____

20. tell someone how you feel since you stopped (eating candy, doing aerobics...)

____

SCORE /10 TOTAL SCORE /35

Nombre ______________________ Clase ____________ Fecha __________

CAPÍTULO **10**

Aplicación 1

PRUEBA

Escuchemos

A Listen to Rolando's essay about natural disasters and choose **a**) for **cierto** or **b**) for **falso.**

____ **1.** Rolando compara los huracanes con los terremotos.

____ **2.** Rolando sabe algo de los huracanes porque los ha observado en persona.

____ **3.** Según Rolando, los científicos estudian los huracanes para tratar de aprovecharlos como fuente de energía.

____ **4.** Se forman los equipos de rescate solamente por personas que donan su tiempo.

____ **5.** Para Rolando, es muy posible que haya menos víctimas de los desastres naturales en el futuro.

SCORE ____ /10

Leamos

B Read Armando's letter to his friend and answer the questions that follow.

Querido Luis:

¡Cuánto tiempo sin escribirte! Mucho ha pasado desde la última vez que te escribí. Sobre todo estoy orgulloso porque este año voy a votar por primera vez para elegir al presidente de Estados Unidos. Ése va a ser un momento emocionante para mí porque siento que por fin pertenezco a este país. Hace unos años, mi familia huyó de la situación aterradora en nuestro país. Allá nunca había elecciones, por eso hacíamos manifestaciones y nos perseguían. La gente simplemente no tenía libertad en mi país. En cambio, aquí la gente es libre de hacer o decir lo que quiera sin tener miedo de la persecución. El gobierno de Estados Unidos mostró compasión por nuestra familia cuando nos recibió como refugiados. Todos nosotros creemos que valió la pena venir a vivir aquí. Hemos encontrado un lugar seguro donde vivir en paz.

Tu amigo,

Armando

PRUEBA: APLICACIÓN 1

6. ¿Por qué está Armando orgulloso?

    ____

7. ¿Qué momento va a ser emocionante para Armando? ¿Por qué?

    ____

8. ¿Cómo era la situación política en su país? Explica.

    ____

9. ¿Qué hizo el gobierno de Estados Unidos por la familia de Armando?

    ____

10. ¿Por qué cree Armando que valió la pena venir a Estados Unidos?

    ____

SCORE /10

Escribamos

C Write an essay about a natural disaster. Be sure to include the dangers and consequences of different types of disasters and talk about some of the positive things that people do to help after a disaster occurs.

____

SCORE /15 TOTAL SCORE /35

Vocabulario 2

A Choose the word that does not fit logically with the others.

____ **1. a.** los pesticidas **b.** los productos de cultivo biológico **c.** la contaminación

____ **2. a.** el desempleo **b.** la drogadicción **c.** los recursos naturales

____ **3. a.** el crimen **b.** los combustibles **c.** la fusión nuclear

____ **4. a.** reciclar **b.** conservar **c.** desperdiciar

____ **5. a.** la energía eléctrica **b.** la energía solar **c.** las enfermedades

SCORE ____ /5

B Match each statement about environmental problems with the most appropriate prediction or warning from the box.

a. Me imagino que el gobierno va a crear programas de reciclaje.
b. Calculo que dentro de cinco años, todos los productos se cultivarán sin pesticidas.
c. Te apuesto que en el futuro se va a usar más energía solar.
d. Es muy posible que se implementen leyes contra la contaminación del medio ambiente.
e. Ya verás que van a promover el uso del transporte público.

____ **6.** Se advierte que debemos usar fuentes de energía alternativas.

____ **7.** En las ciudades modernas, el tráfico es cada vez peor.

____ **8.** Los niveles de contaminación están aumentando.

____ **9.** Con el desperdicio de recursos se agotan los recursos no renovables.

____ **10.** Los productos biológicos se cultivan sin pesticidas.

SCORE ____ /5

PRUEBA: VOCABULARIO 2

C Answer the following questions with phrases from **Vocabulario.**

11. ¿Cómo podemos eliminar el hambre?

____

____

12. ¿Cómo afectarán los carros híbridos al medio ambiente?

____

____

13. ¿Cómo podemos desperdiciar menos?

____

____

14. ¿Cómo podemos mejorar la calidad del aire?

____

____

15. ¿Podremos sustituir los combustibles como el petróleo por energía de otro tipo?

____

____

SCORE ____ /10

D Combine expressions from **¡Exprésate!** and the words and phrases from the two columns to write original sentences with your predictions about the environment.

sembrar	**error**
cometer	**fuentes de energía**
promover	**productos**
reciclar	**adelantos**
desarrollar	**programas**

16. ____

17. ____

18. ____

19. ____

20. ____

SCORE ____ /10 TOTAL SCORE ____ /30

Gramática 2

A Carlos and Lucas are collecting bottles in their neighborhood. Complete their conversation with the correct form of the verb in parentheses.

Carlos ¡Vamos! Sólo nos faltan dos casas.

Lucas Creo que (**1**) ____________ (vamos a / fuimos a) recoger más botellas de lo que habíamos pensado.

Carlos Así es, y de esta forma (**2**) ____________ (ayudó / ayudaremos) a proteger el medio ambiente. Supongo que con tantas botellas recicladas, se (**3**) ____________ (utilizarán / utilizaron) menos recursos en la producción de refrescos en el futuro. ¿Cuántas tenemos ya?

Lucas (**4**) ____________ (Voy / Vine) a contarlas.

Carlos Creo que tú (**5**) ____________ (quedaremos / quedaste) en primer lugar.

SCORE ____ /5

B Complete the following sentences with the **indicative** or the **subjunctive** of the verbs in parentheses.

6. Dudo que las leyes contra las drogas ______________ (causar) más problemas de drogadicción.

7. Es cierto que ______________ (haber) leyes a favor de conservar el medio ambiente.

8. Es una lástima que las personas ______________ (desperdiciar) los recursos naturales.

9. Me alegra que los gobiernos ______________ (promover) los programas de reciclaje.

10. Calculo que los científicos ______________ (descubrir) más fuentes de energía alternativas en el futuro.

SCORE ____ /10

PRUEBA: GRAMÁTICA 2

C Complete this letter to the editor with the appropriate phrases from the box.

para que	antes de que	hasta que	a menos que	en cuanto

Estimado editor:

No puedo creer que esto siga ocurriendo. Una vez más, se han cortado hectáreas de bosques indiscriminadamente. Esta realidad es preocupante, y (**11**) ______________ dejemos de hacerlo, muy pronto sufriremos las consecuencias. No dejaremos de luchar (**12**) ______________ se implementen leyes contra la destrucción de los bosques. Es necesario hacer algo por el medio ambiente (**13**) ______________ sea demasiado tarde. En muchos lugares, se demostró que la calidad del aire mejoró (**14**) ______________ decidieron sembrar más árboles. En *Green Peace,* haremos todo lo posible (**15**) ______________ nuestro planeta no deje de ser verde.

Por un planeta más limpio,

Lázaro

SCORE /10

D Complete the following sentences with your own opinions. Make sure to use the **subjunctive** or **indicative** depending on the expression of time and the verb tense used at the beginning of the sentence.

16. En mi colegio empezaremos a reciclar después de que...

____

17. Tan pronto como se cerró el puente en mi ciudad, el tráfico...

____

18. Cuando los carros eléctricos sean más accesibles, habrá...

____

19. Se tendrán que implementar leyes para proteger el medio ambiente en caso de que...

____

20. La gente aceptará el reciclaje cuando...

____

SCORE /10 TOTAL SCORE /35

Nombre ______________________ Clase ______________ Fecha ______________

Aplicación 2

Escuchemos

A Listen to Alicia, Roberto, and the professor talk about air pollution. Then, read the questions and choose the most appropriate answer.

____ **1.** ¿Qué cree Alicia de la calidad del aire?
a. ha empeorado **b.** ha mejorado

____ **2.** ¿Qué dice Roberto del combustible de los carros?
a. contamina el aire **b.** desarrolla el país

____ **3.** ¿Qué alternativa menciona el profesor?
a. los molinos de viento **b.** la energía nuclear

____ **4.** ¿Los carros eléctricos contaminan el aire?
a. sí **b.** no

____ **5.** ¿Sobre qué quiere aprender Roberto?
a. los carros eléctricos **b.** la conservación del medio ambiente

SCORE ____ /10

Leamos

B Rafael and Sara are at the supermarket. Read their conversation and answer the questions that follow.

Rafael ¡Cuántas frutas y vegetales! Esta parte del supermercado es mi preferida. Mira, éstas son manzanas orgánicas. Son más caras; ¿crees que también son más sabrosas?

Sara Tal vez lo sean. Pero lo más importante es que son más saludables. Además, se cultivan sin usar pesticidas y no contaminan el medio ambiente.

Rafael Pero no veo muchos productos biológicos aquí; parece que casi todos son cultivados con la ayuda de pesticidas y otros productos químicos. ¡Qué lástima!

Sara Es cierto. Me imagino que en el futuro habrá leyes contra la venta de los productos de cultivo no biológico.

Rafael A lo mejor. Ya verás cómo bajará la contaminación.

PRUEBA: APLICACIÓN 2

6. ¿Dónde están Rafael y Sara?

____

7. ¿Qué tipo de manzanas vio Rafael?

____

8. ¿Qué dice Sara de las manzanas orgánicas?

____

9. ¿Qué imagina Sara sobre el futuro?

____

10. ¿Qué cree Rafael que pasará con la contaminación?

____

SCORE /10

Escribamos

C You've been thinking about the environment and unemployment. Write a letter to your future grandchildren about the problems of today's world and what you think might happen in the future. Use expressions from **¡Exprésate!** in your letter.

____

SCORE /15 TOTAL SCORE /35

Nombre ______________________ Clase ______________ Fecha ____________

Lectura

A Read the story. Then, write four words you do not know on the lines and guess their meaning based on similar words you have seen in English or Spanish.

El primer día de primavera del año 2573, Jacinto se ajustó su escafandra *(spacesuit)* y decidió salir a estirar las piernas por el corredor de "naturaleza virtual", que se conocía como "Aire Libre". En este espacio, se recreaba el medio ambiente sin contaminación, el cual había dejado de existir hacía tiempo. Hacía casi doscientos años los humanos habían dejado de reciclar, habían talado todos los bosques y habían renunciado a usar fuentes de energía alternativas. Después del inevitable desastre ecológico, los sobrevivientes se refugiaban en una especie de contenedor enterrado en el subsuelo y resistente a la contaminación. Estos contenedores servían como residencia y nadie se atrevía a salir a la superficie sin protección. El planeta se había convertido en un basurero infinito con todo lo que se había desperdiciado en otra época, y los bosques habían desaparecido para siempre.

____

____

SCORE /10

B Based on the reading, match the words on the left with the clues on the right.

____ **1.** contaminación
____ **2.** fuentes de energía alternativas
____ **3.** reciclar
____ **4.** basurero
____ **5.** desperdiciado

a. recipiente para la basura
b. volver a usar los productos
c. mal empleado o mal usado
d. ensuciar el medio ambiente
e. combustibles que no usan petróleo

SCORE /10

C Answer the following questions based on the reading.

6. ¿Qué sucedió en la Tierra según el relato?

____

7. ¿Dónde vivían los sobrevivientes del desastre ecológico? ¿Por qué?

____

8. ¿Piensas que podría ser una historia real? ¿Por qué?

____

SCORE /15 TOTAL SCORE /35

Escritura

A Antonio is interviewing his grandfather for his history class. He asks his grandfather what he remembers about a great event such as a natural disaster, a scientific discovery, or a great moment in sports history. Antonio asks his grandfather what he was doing or where he was at the time. First write Antonio's questions, and then include his grandfather's answers. Include expressions from **¡Exprésate!**

Antonio ____

Abuelo ____

Antonio ____

Abuelo ____

Antonio ____

Abuelo ____

Antonio ____

Abuelo ____

Antonio ____

Abuelo ____

SCORE /15

B Write a letter to an imaginary pen pal from the future. Include your opinion about the environmental problems in the world today, and your predictions about the future. Also include what you think can be done to solve or lessen these problems. Use the future tense and expressions from **¡Exprésate!**

____

____

____

____

____

____

____

____

SCORE /20 TOTAL SCORE /35

Nombre ______________________ Clase ______________ Fecha ______________

CAPÍTULO 10

Geocultura

PRUEBA

A Match each letter on the map of the **Cono Sur** with the name of the place or area it represents.

_____ **1.** ciudad que fundó Pedro de Valdivia en 1541

_____ **2.** océano Pacífico

_____ **3.** Montevideo

_____ **4.** lugar donde se encuentran las Islas Malvinas

_____ **5.** Buenos Aires

SCORE /5

B Read each statement and choose **a**) for **cierto** or **b**) for **falso.**

_____ **6.** Pedro de Valdivia fundó Santiago y murió en la guerra contra los araucanos.

_____ **7.** Los mapuches no ofrecieron resistencia en ningún momento a la dominación hispánica.

_____ **8.** La fachada de la Catedral Basílica de Salta, Argentina, es de estilo italiano clásico.

_____ **9.** Evita fue la voz del pueblo en asuntos sociales en Argentina.

_____ **10.** La guerra entre Argentina y Gran Bretaña duró siete días.

SCORE /5

PRUEBA: GEOCULTURA

C Read the following questions and choose the most appropriate answer.

____ **11.** El argentino Luis Federico Leloir recibió el premio Nobel por sus descubrimientos en el campo de ___.
a. la física **b.** la química **c.** la astronomía

____ **12.** Las tunas son ___.
a. pescados chilenos **b.** grupos teatrales **c.** grupos musicales

____ **13.** Argentina y Gran Bretaña se fueron a la guerra con motivo de ___.
a. el Gran Chaco **b.** las islas Malvinas **c.** las islas Galápagos

____ **14.** ¿Cómo estaban organizados los mapuches antes de la llegada de los incas?
a. en una democracia **b.** en una tribu **c.** en clanes familiares

____ **15.** Roberto Matta (1911-2002) fue uno de los artistas predominantes del Movimiento ___.
a. Surrealista **b.** Impresionista **c.** Naturalista

SCORE /10

D Write one sentence to tell the importance of each of the following:

16. Buenos Aires

____

17. el cerro Aconcagua

____

18. Bernardo O'Higgins

____

19. Salvador Allende

____

20. el desierto de Atacama

____

SCORE /10 TOTAL SCORE /30

Vocabulario 1

A. (5 points)

1. d 2. b 3. e 4. c 5. a

B. (5 points)

6. a 7. b 8. a 9. c 10. b

C. (10 points) Answers will vary.
Possible answers:

11. A pesar de que los inmigrantes quieren mantener su herencia, por otro lado, es importante que se asimilen.

12. Ten en cuenta que los adelantos de la tecnología pueden tener un efecto positivo o negativo en la comunicación.

13. Lo que noto es que hoy en día hay más solidaridad.

14. Aunque estoy de acuerdo que el DVD es un invento genial e innovador, creo que el cine siempre será más popular entre los jóvenes.

15. Creo que vale la pena acordarse de las dificultades que muchos refugiados han tenido que superar antes de llegar a otros países.

D. (10 points)

16. Lo recuerdo como si fuera ayer.

17. Estaba en casa viendo televisión cuando supe del trágico accidente.

18. No, no me acuerdo para nada.

19. Hubo mucha destrucción y la situación fue aterradora.

20. Pero fue conmovedor ver cuánta gente trataba de ayudar a los demás.

Gramática 1

A. (10 points)

1. habían invitado

2. habría/hubiera gustado

3. había visto

4. había preparado

5. ha sido

B. (5 points)

6. Hubo

7. Hubo

8. Había

9. haya

10. habrá

C. (10 points)

11. Ellos seguían hablando.

12. Sigo practicando béisbol.

13. Mi hermana estaba leyendo un libro.

14. Raúl está estudiando para el examen.

15. Francisco anda haciendo entrevistas.

D. (10 points) Answers will vary.
Possible answers:

16. Aprendí a montar en bicicleta hace ocho años.

17. ¿Cuánto tiempo hace que empezó la película?

18. Hace dos años que escucho esta estación de radio.

19. ¿Qué hiciste por primera vez este año?

20. Me siento mejor desde que dejé de comer dulces.

Aplicación 1

A. (10 points)

1. a 2. b 3. b 4. b 5. a

B. (10 points)

6. Está orgulloso porque va a votar por primera vez.

7. Votar por el presidente de Estados Unidos va a ser emocionante porque por fin va a sentirse parte de este país.

8. La situación en su país era aterradora. No había libertad.

9. Recibió a los miembros de su familia como refugiados.

10. Cree que valió la pena porque ha encontrado un lugar seguro donde vivir en paz.

C. (15 points)
Answers will vary.

Vocabulario 2

A. (5 points)

1. b **2.** c **3.** a **4.** c **5.** c

B. (5 points)

6. c **7.** e **8.** d **9.** a **10.** b

C. (10 points) Answers will vary. Possible answers:

11. Podemos eliminar el hambre si desarrollamos programas para sembrar productos más resistentes a los insectos.

12. Si más gente maneja carros híbridos, habrá menos contaminación del aire.

13. Podemos reciclar muchos materiales que la gente tira a la basura.

14. Podemos buscar fuentes de energía alternativas y utilizar los carros con menos frecuencia.

15. Sí, podremos sustituir los combustibles como el petróleo por la energía eléctrica, solar o nuclear.

D. (10 points) Answers will vary. Possible answers:

16. Ya verás que van a seguir sembrando productos genéticamente modificados.

17. Calculo que se cometerán menos errores con respecto a los recursos renovables.

18. A lo mejor se desarrollarán mejores programas para ayudar a la gente sin casa.

19. Me imagino que el gobierno promoverá adelantos en las fuentes de energía alternativas.

20. Es de suponer que para el año 2100 ya no habrá nuevas fuentes de petróleo.

Gramática 2

A. (5 points)

1. vamos a **2.** ayudaremos
3. se utilizarán **4.** Voy **5.** quedaste

B. (10 points)

6. causen

7. hay

8. desperdicien

9. promuevan

10. descubrirán

C. (10 points)

11. a menos que

12. hasta que

13. antes de que

14. en cuanto

15. para que

D. (10 points)

16. …implementemos un programa de reciclaje.

17. …aumentó mucho.

18. …menos contaminación del aire y menos estrés.

19. …la situación empeore.

20. …todos tengamos alimentos saludables.

Aplicación 2

A. (10 points)

1. a **2.** a **3.** a **4.** b **5.** b

B. (10 points)

6. Están en el supermercado.

7. Vio manzanas orgánicas.

8. Que son más saludables y se cultivan sin pesticidas.

9. Que habrá leyes contra la venta de productos que no sean de cultivo biológico.

10. Que bajará el nivel de contaminación.

C. (15 points)

Answers will vary.

Lectura

A. (10 points) Answers will vary.
Possible answers:

se recreaba: de *recrear:* imitar o crear de nuevo

subsuelo: de *sub:* debajo y *suelo:* tierra: debajo de la tierra.

sobrevivientes: *sobre* y *vivir:* Personas que viven después de un evento trágico o un desastre natural.

contenedor: de *contener:* un objeto dentro del cual se puede guardar cosas.

B. (10 points)

1. d **2.** e **3.** b **4.** a **5.** c

C. (15 points)

6. Desapareció el medio ambiente como lo conocemos ahora. Las personas no podían salir a la superficie sin protección.

7. Los sobrevivientes vivían en contenedores enterrados en el subsuelo.

8. Sí, podría ser una historia real porque algo parecido podría pasarle a nuestro medio ambiente.

Escritura

A. (15 points) Answers will vary.

B. (20 points) Answers will vary.

Geocultura

A. (5 points)

1. b **2.** a **3.** c **4.** e **5.** d

B. (5 points)

6. a **7.** b **8.** a **9.** a **10.** b

C. (10 points)

11. b **12.** c **13.** b **14.** c **15.** a

D. (10 points)

16. Buenos Aires es el puerto principal de Argentina y uno de los puertos más importantes del mundo.

17. El cerro Aconcagua es la montaña más alta de las Américas.

18. Bernardo O'Higgins ayudó a José de San Martín a lograr la independencia de Chile.

19. Salvador Allende murió al ser asaltado en el Palacio de la Moneda por las fuerzas militares chilenas.

20. El desierto de Atacama es uno de los lugares más secos del mundo, con lugares donde nunca ha llovido.

Aplicación 1

Escuchemos

A Listen to Rolando's essay about natural disasters and choose **a)** for **cierto** or **b)** for **falso.**

Tanto los huracanes como los terremotos son desastres naturales y por eso no se pueden prevenir. Nunca he vivido una experiencia de éstas, pero sé que estos desastres son espantosos y causan mucha destrucción. Hoy en día, los científicos estudian los desastres naturales y tratan de descubrir formas de evitarlos. Hasta ahora no ha sido posible, pero afortunadamente cuando estos acontecimientos ocurren, se puede contar con equipos de rescate. Estos equipos se forman de trabajadores y otros voluntarios que ofrecen su tiempo para ayudar a las víctimas en estos momentos aterradores. Estoy seguro de que con la ayuda de los adelantos tecnológicos, en el futuro habrá menos muerte por causa de los desastres naturales.

Aplicación 2

Escuchemos

A Listen to Alicia, Roberto, and the professor talk about air pollution. Then, read the questions and choose the most appropriate answer.

Alicia Estoy segura que en los últimos años, la calidad del aire ha empeorado.

Roberto Tienes razón. Es por la contaminación. El combustible de los carros contamina el aire. Y tú sabes, con tantos carros la situación no puede mejorar.

Alicia La verdad es que si no se implementan medidas para disminuir el tráfico, la calidad del aire no va a mejorar. Profesor Aquiles, ¿qué alternativas existen?

Profesor Pues, para empezar, los carros eléctricos no contaminan el aire. Y por supuesto, se pueden considerar otras fuentes de energía que disminuyan la contaminación en general, como la energía solar o la creada por los molinos de viento.

Roberto ¿Los molinos de viento? No lo sabía. Quisiera aprender más acerca de las fuentes de energía alternativas y la conservación del medio ambiente.

Tests

Table of Contents

CHAPTER TESTS

To the Teacher

Evaluating Written Tests and Assignments

Various criteria can be applied to the evaluation of written tests and/or assignments but should include content, comprehensibility, and accuracy.

An evaluation of the student's content means determining to what extent the writer (i.e., the student) uses vocabulary and functional expressions that are appropriate to the topic. The degree to which a student does or does not accomplish this can be given a numeric value that can then form the basis for an overall grade.

In any written assignment, the student's comprehensibility should be measured; that is, the extent to which someone reading the assignment can understand what the writer is trying to communicate.

Accuracy is another criterion that should be included in a written assignment: whether the student uses grammar, spelling, word order, and punctuation correctly.

Written assignments can also be judged on their organization: how well did the student organize his or her thoughts, concepts, and so on? Are they organized in a logical and effective way?

Students very often put a great deal of effort into written assignments, whether on a test, project, or daily homework assignment. That effort can also become a part of the overall grade: how much care and effort did the student put into fulfilling the requirements of the assignment?

The rubric on page 204 reflects these criteria and provides guidelines for assessing each of them on a range of 4 (best) to 1 (worst).

Evaluating Oral Tests and Assignments

The criteria that can be applied to the evaluation of oral tests and/or assignments should include content, both comprehension and comprehensibility, and accuracy.

An evaluation of content in an oral assignment means determining to what extent the speaker (i.e., the student) uses the appropriate functions and functional expressions and vocabulary in order to communicate. The degree to which a student does or does not accomplish this can be given a numeric value that forms the basis for an overall grade.

In any oral assignment, both the student's ability to understand what is said to him or her (as in a conversation), as well as the ability to communicate so that the listener understands, should be evaluated. How well students do or do not accomplish that can be evaluated with the use of a rubric.

Accuracy is another criterion that should be included in an oral assignment: whether the student uses language correctly, including grammar and word order.

A criterion that applies specifically to oral delivery is fluency: does the speaker speak clearly without hesitation? Do the speaker's pronunciation and intonation sound natural?

As with the evaluation of written work, students generally appreciate it if you include as a criterion the effort they put into the test, assignment, or project. It is especially gratifying to students who make a special effort—who include, for example, details that go beyond what is required—to know that their effort is part of the big picture, and that their special effort is recognized.

The rubric on page 204 reflects these criteria and provides guidelines for assessing each of them on a range of 4 (best) to 1 (worst).

Rubric for Evaluating Written and Oral Tests and Assignments

Writing Rubric

CONTENT (inclusion of all required information)	(POOR)	1	2	3	4	(EXCELLENT)
COMPREHENSIBILITY (ability to communicate ideas)	(POOR)	1	2	3	4	(EXCELLENT)
ACCURACY (ability to use structures and vocabulary correctly)	(POOR)	1	2	3	4	(EXCELLENT)
ORGANIZATION (ability to organize information)	(POOR)	1	2	3	4	(EXCELLENT)
EFFORT (inclusion of details beyond the minimum requirements)	(POOR)	1	2	3	4	(EXCELLENT)

Speaking Rubric

COMPREHENSION (ability to understand verbal cues and respond appropriately)	(POOR)	1	2	3	4	(EXCELLENT)
COMPREHENSIBILITY (ability to communicate ideas and be understood)	(POOR)	1	2	3	4	(EXCELLENT)
ACCURACY (ability to use structures and vocabulary correctly)	(POOR)	1	2	3	4	(EXCELLENT)
FLUENCY (ability to communicate clearly and smoothly)	(POOR)	1	2	3	4	(EXCELLENT)
EFFORT (inclusion of details beyond the minimum requirements)	(POOR)	1	2	3	4	(EXCELLENT)

Nombre ______________________ Clase ______________ Fecha ______________

CAPÍTULO **1** EXAMEN

¡Adiós al verano!

Escuchemos

A Listen to the following comments and write the letter of the image that corresponds to each statement.

a.

b.

c.

d.

1. ____ **3.** ____

2. ____ **4.** ____

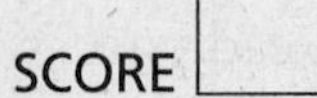

SCORE /8

B Listen to the following conversation between Julio and Adriana. Read the statements below, and choose **a**) for **cierto** or **b**) for **falso.**

____ **5.** Hace dos años que Julio fue a España.

____ **6.** Adriana lo pasó de maravilla el verano pasado.

____ **7.** Julio sugiere que Adriana vaya a Madrid.

____ **8.** Adriana nunca viajaba de niña.

SCORE /8

EXAMEN

Leamos

C Read this interview with an exchange student from Spain. Then, read the statements that follow and write **cierto** or **falso.**

Rosa, ¿puedes hablarnos un poco de ti? Por ejemplo, ¿de dónde eres? ¿cómo es tu hogar? ¿por qué decidiste venir a Estados Unidos?

Soy de Cuenca, un pueblo de Castilla-La Mancha en España. De niña soñaba con viajar y me interesaba conocer Estados Unidos. Así que decidí venir.

¿Cuándo llegaste a Estados Unidos?

Llegué hace un mes, en agosto. Fui a Nueva York y lo pasé de maravilla. También fui a Washington, D.C. Visité los monumentos y me encantaron.

¿Qué planes tienes para este año?

Mi amiga Susana quiere que participe en el club de debate, pero no me interesa. Para mí, los deportes son más divertidos que los clubs.

__________ **9.** Rosa es de España.

__________ **10.** Cuando Rosa era joven, nunca pensaba en viajar.

__________ **11.** Rosa fue a Nueva York y lo encontró muy aburrido.

__________ **12.** A Rosa le gustan los deportes más que los clubs.

SCORE ____ /8

D Read part of Karina's essay about her summer vacation and answer the questions.

En julio acampé con mi familia al lado de un lago en el bosque. Cuando llegamos me pareció un lugar muy solitario. Soy una persona muy sociable y me gusta conversar con mis amigos. Me aburro cuando estoy sola. Además, estaba lloviendo a cántaros cuando llegamos. Decidí sentarme a escribir poemas. Luego salió el sol y hacía calor. Practiqué el esquí acuático y luego di una caminata por el bosque. Me lo pasé muy bien. Les recomiendo que salgan de la ciudad porque es una buena manera de relajarse.

13. ¿Qué hizo Karina durante el verano? ______________________

14. ¿Qué tipo de persona es Karina? ______________________

15. ¿Cómo le pareció el lugar? ______________________

16. ¿Qué hizo Karina para divertirse? ______________________

SCORE ____ /8

Cultura

E Answer the following questions about **Castilla-La Mancha.**

_____ **17.** ¿Qué significa la palabra *Castilla*?
a. casas colgadas **b.** región montañosa **c.** tierra de castillos

_____ **18.** ¿Qué región de Castilla-La Mancha ha sido nombrada "patrimonio de la humanidad"?
a. Guadalajara **b.** Cuenca **c.** Albacete

_____ **19.** ¿Qué río pasa por la ciudad de Toledo?
a. el Tajo **b.** el Consuegra **c.** el Guadalquivir

_____ **20.** ¿De qué animal viene el queso manchego?
a. la cabra **b.** la oveja **c.** la vaca

SCORE /8

Vocabulario

F Choose a term from the box that best matches its description below.

_____ **21.** En esta clase, te enseñan a hablar en público.

_____ **22.** Tienes que hacer esto para grabar tus canciones favoritas en disco.

_____ **23.** Desde este lugar puedes viajar a otra ciudad.

_____ **24.** Estos ejercicios te mantendrán en forma.

_____ **25.** Puedes hacer esta actividad en el bosque.

a. quemar un CD
b. acampar
c. la oratoria
d. la estación de trenes
e. aeróbicos

SCORE /5

Nombre ______________________ Clase ______________ Fecha ______________

CAPÍTULO 1

EXAMEN

Vocabulario

G Román and Martín are talking about what they did last summer. Fill in the blanks with correct expressions from **Vocabulario** and **¡Exprésate!**

Martín Román, ¿(**26**) ______________ el verano pasado?

Román Fui al (**27**) ______________ con mis amigos para hacer el esquí (**28**) ______________ .

Martín ¿Y (**29**) ______________ lo pasaron?

Román Lo pasamos de (**30**) ______________ . Y tú Martín, ¿adónde fuiste?

Martín Yo fui al (**31**) ______________ con mi familia. Acampamos ahí y observamos (**32**) ______________ . Luego, viajé a Albacete.

Román ¿(**33**) ______________ Albacete?

Martín Lo encontré muy interesante, pero cayeron (**34**) ______________ y llovió a cántaros todo el día. Al día siguiente, di (**35**) ______________ por la ciudad.

SCORE ____ /10

H María and Carmen are talking about New Year's resolutions. Complete the conversation in a way that best fits the context.

María (**36**) ¿Qué cambios ______________________________?

Carmen De hoy en adelante voy a cuidar mi cuerpo.

María (**37**) ¿Cómo ______________________________?

Carmen Voy a hacer gimnasia y saltar a la cuerda.

María (**38**) ¿Adónde ______________________________?

Carmen Pienso ir al centro recreativo. ¿Puedes darme algún consejo?

María (**39**) ______________________________.

Carmen ¿Qué más me recomiendas?

María (**40**) ______________________________.

SCORE ____ /5

EXAMEN

Gramática

I Complete each sentence with the correct form of **ser** or **estar.**

41. ¿De dónde ____________?

42. Yo ____________ español. Mis papás son de la ciudad de Granada.

43. ¿Cómo ____________ la ciudad de Granada?

44. La ciudad ____________ cerca del mar y es fantástica para ir de vacaciones.

SCORE /4

J Complete Miguel's description of Jaime with the correct pronoun, and with **más** or **menos.**

45. Jaime, tú y ____________ fuimos muy distintos en la universidad. Tú lo pasabas de película y siempre tenías ____________ ganas que yo de divertirte.

46. A ti ____________ gustaban los deportes, y naturalmente eras ____________ intelectual que yo.

47. Para ____________, siempre fuiste un atleta admirable. A todos ____________ impresionaba tu manera de correr.

48. A mí sólo ____________ interesaba el club de debate pero ahora veo partidos de fútbol por televisión ____________ que nadie. ¡Qué curioso! ¿Verdad?

SCORE /8

K Write the following sentences in Spanish.

49. I became friends with Jaime two years ago.

____

50. He never wants to play golf.

____

51. He has been collecting coins for 6 years.

____

52. But he doesn't have any coins from Spain.

____

SCORE /8

Nombre ______________________ Clase ______________ Fecha ____________

EXAMEN

Escribamos

L Write a paragraph describing several activities you used to like to do when you were five to ten years old. Then explain whether or not you like the same activities now.

____

____

____

____

____

____

____

____

SCORE ____ /10

M Imagine that you are being interviewed. The interviewer wants to know what you are going to do differently this year, what you plan to do in the future, or where you plan to go. Write the questions you think you will be asked and answer them.

____

____

____

____

____

____

____

____

SCORE ____ /10 TOTAL SCORE ____ /100

Nombre ______________________ Clase ______________ Fecha ______________

CAPÍTULO 1

Score Sheet: Examen

Escuchemos

A

1. a b c d
2. a b c d
3. a b c d
4. a b c d

SCORE ____ /8

B

5. a b
6. a b
7. a b
8. a b

SCORE ____ /8

Leamos

C

9. ______________
10. ______________
11. ______________
12. ______________

SCORE ____ /8

D

13. ______________________________
14. ______________________________
15. ______________________________
16. ______________________________

SCORE ____ /8

Cultura

E

17. a b c
18. a b c
19. a b c
20. a b c

SCORE ____ /8

Vocabulario

F

21. a b c d e
22. a b c d e
23. a b c d e
24. a b c d e
25. a b c d e

SCORE ____ /5

G

26. ______________
27. ______________
28. ______________
29. ______________
30. ______________
31. ______________
32. ______________
33. ______________
34. ______________
35. ______________

SCORE ____ /10

H

36. ______________________________
37. ______________________________
38. ______________________________
39. ______________________________
40. ______________________________

SCORE ____ /5

Nombre ______________ Clase ______________ Fecha ______________

CAPÍTULO 1

SCORE SHEET: EXAMEN

Gramática

I

41. ______________
42. ______________
43. ______________
44. ______________

SCORE /4

J

45. ______________
46. ______________
47. ______________
48. ______________

SCORE /8

K

49. ______________
50. ______________
51. ______________
52. ______________

SCORE /8

Escribamos

L

SCORE /10

M

SCORE /10

TOTAL SCORE /100

Answer Key: Examen

CAPÍTULO 1

Escuchemos

A

1. a b c (d)
2. (a) b c d
3. a (b) c d
4. a b (c) d

SCORE /8

B

5. a (b)
6. a (b)
7. (a) b
8. a (b)

SCORE /8

D

13. Karina acampó cerca de un lago, dio una caminata por el bosque y escribió poemas.
14. Es una persona sociable.
15. Le pareció muy solitario.
16. Dio una caminata y practicó el esquí acuático.

SCORE /8

Leamos

C

9. cierto
10. falso
11. falso
12. cierto

SCORE /8

Cultura

E

17. a b (c)
18. a (b) c
19. (a) b c
20. a (b) c

SCORE 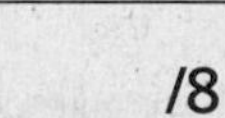 /8

Vocabulario

F

21. a b (c) d e
22. (a) b c d e
23. a b c (d) e
24. a b c d (e)
25. a (b) c d e

SCORE /5

G Answers will vary. Sample answers provided.

26. qué hiciste
27. lago
28. acuático
29. qué tal
30. película
31. bosque
32. la naturaleza
33. Qué te pareció
34. truenos
35. una caminata

SCORE /10

H

36. ¿Qué cambios vas a hacer de hoy en adelante?
37. ¿Cómo vas a mantenerte en forma?
38. ¿Adónde piensas ir?
39. Te aconsejo que sigas una dieta balanceada.
40. Te recomiendo que practiques atletismo.

SCORE /5

Gramática

I

41. eres
42. soy
43. es
44. está

SCORE /4

J

45. yo, más
46. te, menos
47. mí, nos / les
48. me, más

SCORE /8

K

49. Hace dos años, me hice amigo(a) de Jaime.
50. Nunca quiere jugar al golf. / No quiere jugar al golf nunca (jamás).
51. Hace seis años que colecciona monedas.
52. Pero no tiene ninguna moneda de España.

SCORE /8

Escribamos

L

Answers will vary. Answers should include: De niño(a), me gustaba..., Cuando era joven, solía..., De pequeño(a), me lo pasaba bomba..., Cuando tenía diez años, me encantaba..., Siempre disfrutaba de..., pero ahora prefiero..., hoy en día (no) me gusta..., ya no / todavía me gusta..., es más / menos divertido que

SCORE /10

M

Answers will vary. Answers should include: ¿Qué vas a hacer..., ¿Adónde piensas ir...?, ¿Cómo vas a mantenerte en forma?, ¿Qué cambios vas a hacer?, Voy a estudiar..., Pienso ir..., espero..., debo..., mi entrenador(a) recomienda que yo..., hace un año que no...

SCORE /10

TOTAL SCORE /100

Escuchemos

A Listen to the following comments and write the letter of the image that corresponds to each statement.

1. Te recomiendo que viajes por tren. El viaje es mucho más corto y no te vas a aburrir.

2. De niña, me gustaba mucho jugar naipes con mis amigos. Ahora me parece muy aburrido pero ellos se divierten mucho.

3. Mi vida es muy solitaria. Quiero participar en alguna actividad en el colegio, como el club de español, pero soy muy tímida. Debo hacerme amiga de alguien que participe en el club.

4. Me interesan las computadoras y también el arte. Nunca he diseñado páginas Web, pero ahora estoy tomando una clase para aprender a hacerlo.

B Listen to the following conversation between Julio and Adriana. Read the statements below, and choose **a**) for **cierto** or **b**) for **falso.**

Adriana ¡Hola Julio! Hace mucho tiempo que no te veo. ¿Qué hiciste el verano pasado?

Julio Fui a España y regresé hace dos días. Lo pasé de película. Fui a Madrid, Barcelona y Sevilla y a algunos pueblos del campo.

Adriana ¿Qué te pareció Madrid?

Julio La encontré genial, pero me gustaron más los pueblos del campo. Un día montamos a caballo y también acampamos.

Adriana Pues yo me aburrí muchísimo este verano. Quiero planear un viaje, pero creo que iré solamente a una ciudad. ¿Qué me recomiendas?

Julio Si puedes ir solamente a una ciudad, te recomiendo que vayas a Madrid. De allí, puedes tomar un tren hasta Toledo si quieres. Hay una catedral muy bella, y puedes dar una caminata por el río.

Adriana Me parece perfecto. De niña viajaba mucho con mi familia, pero hace años que no voy a ningún lugar.

Nombre ______________________ Clase ______________ Fecha ____________

¡Adiós al verano!

EXAMEN ORAL

Interview

A Respond to the following questions in Spanish.

1. ¿Qué actividades te gustan más durante el verano? Explica.
2. ¿Te gusta ir a la playa? ¿Por qué?
3. ¿Qué hiciste durante tus vacaciones este verano?
4. ¿Qué país visitaste o quieres visitar y por qué?
5. ¿Hace cuánto tiempo no vas a la playa?

Role-Play

B Act out the following situation with a classmate.

Imagine that you and a classmate are students from different towns in Castilla-La Mancha. Take turns asking each other about as many historical attractions of each other's town as you can think of, and why you would or would not recommend seeing each one.

SPEAKING RUBRIC

COMPREHENSION (ability to understand verbal cues and respond appropriately)	(POOR)	1	2	3	4	(EXCELLENT)
COMPREHENSIBILITY (ability to communicate ideas and be understood)	(POOR)	1	2	3	4	(EXCELLENT)
ACCURACY (ability to use structures and vocabulary correctly)	(POOR)	1	2	3	4	(EXCELLENT)
FLUENCY (ability to communicate clearly and smoothly)	(POOR)	1	2	3	4	(EXCELLENT)
EFFORT (inclusion of details beyond the minimum requirements)	(POOR)	1	2	3	4	(EXCELLENT)

Nombre ______________________ Clase ______________ Fecha ______________

CAPÍTULO 2

¡A pasarlo bien!

EXAMEN

Escuchemos

A Listen to Arturo describe the ideal friend. Read the statements below, and choose **a)** for **cierto** or **b)** for **falso.**

____ **1.** Arturo dice que un buen amigo es abierto y amigable.

____ **2.** Una persona chismosa es un buen amigo.

____ **3.** Un buen amigo puede ser terco, pero no debe ser celoso.

____ **4.** Es importante tener mucho en común con un amigo.

SCORE ____ /8

B Listen to the short conversations about sports and activities. Match the letter of the image to the conversation that you hear.

a.

b.

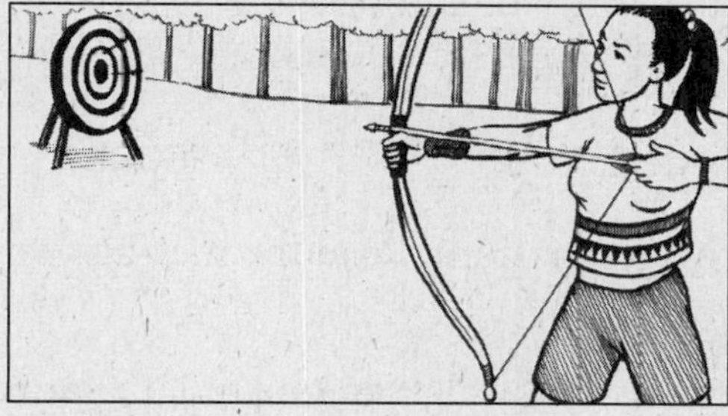

c.

d.

5. ____

6. ____

7. ____

8. ____

SCORE ____ /8

EXAMEN

Leamos

C Read the e-mail that Mateo sent to his friend Lalo. Then, read the statements below and choose **a)** for **cierto** or **b)** for **falso.**

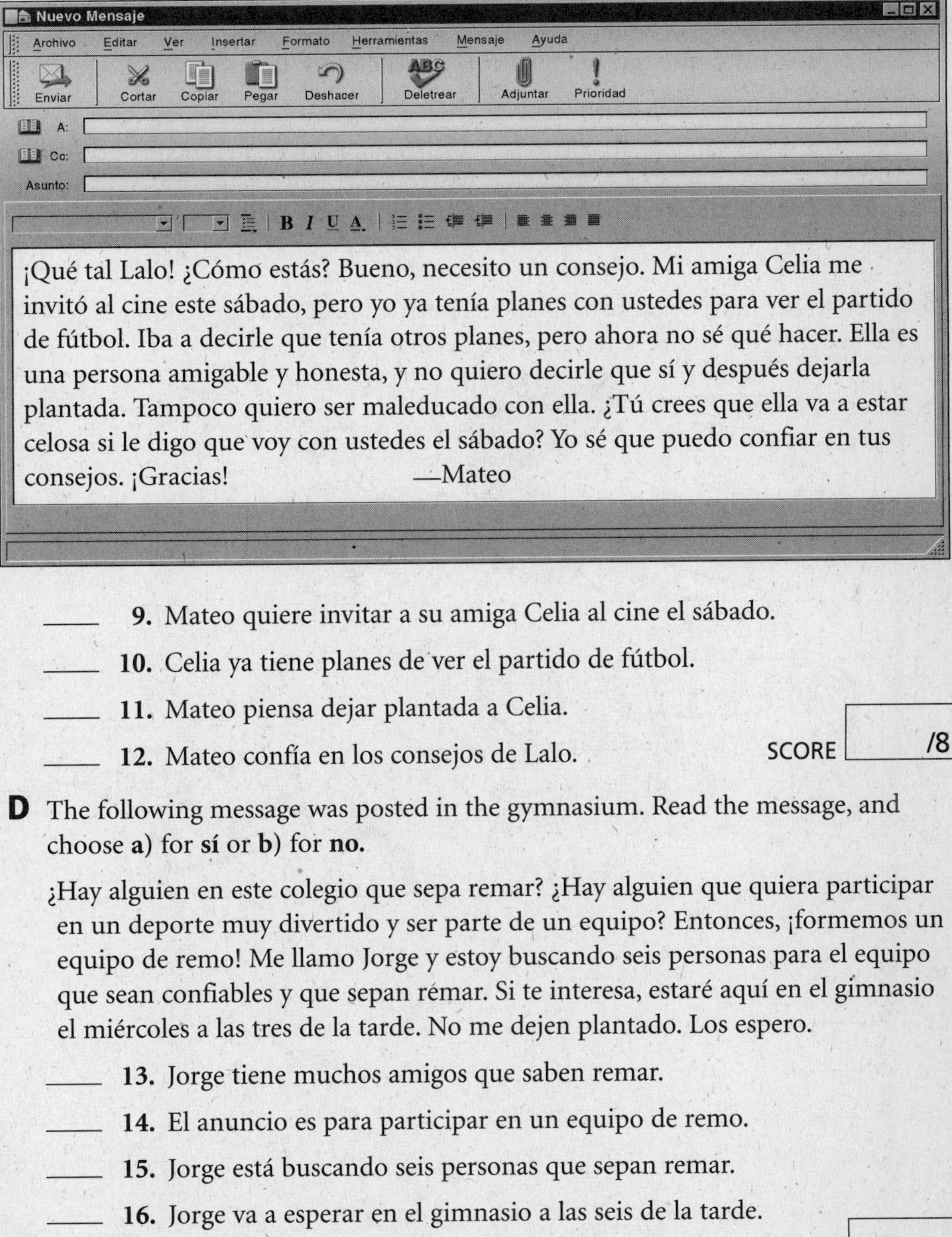

¡Qué tal Lalo! ¿Cómo estás? Bueno, necesito un consejo. Mi amiga Celia me invitó al cine este sábado, pero yo ya tenía planes con ustedes para ver el partido de fútbol. Iba a decirle que tenía otros planes, pero ahora no sé qué hacer. Ella es una persona amigable y honesta, y no quiero decirle que sí y después dejarla plantada. Tampoco quiero ser maleducado con ella. ¿Tú crees que ella va a estar celosa si le digo que voy con ustedes el sábado? Yo sé que puedo confiar en tus consejos. ¡Gracias! —Mateo

____ **9.** Mateo quiere invitar a su amiga Celia al cine el sábado.

____ **10.** Celia ya tiene planes de ver el partido de fútbol.

____ **11.** Mateo piensa dejar plantada a Celia.

____ **12.** Mateo confía en los consejos de Lalo.

SCORE ____ /8

D The following message was posted in the gymnasium. Read the message, and choose **a)** for **sí** or **b)** for **no.**

¿Hay alguien en este colegio que sepa remar? ¿Hay alguien que quiera participar en un deporte muy divertido y ser parte de un equipo? Entonces, ¡formemos un equipo de remo! Me llamo Jorge y estoy buscando seis personas para el equipo que sean confiables y que sepan remar. Si te interesa, estaré aquí en el gimnasio el miércoles a las tres de la tarde. No me dejen plantado. Los espero.

____ **13.** Jorge tiene muchos amigos que saben remar.

____ **14.** El anuncio es para participar en un equipo de remo.

____ **15.** Jorge está buscando seis personas que sepan remar.

____ **16.** Jorge va a esperar en el gimnasio a las seis de la tarde.

SCORE ____ /8

Cultura

E Complete the following sentences about **la cultura española.**

____ **17.** En España, si quieres hacer senderismo en las montañas, puedes ir ___.
a. al norte de Santander
b. a la meseta central

____ **18.** El jai-alai, o la pelota vasca, significa "___" en el idioma vasco.
a. fiesta alegre
b. pared

____ **19.** Durante los festivales de los pueblos, los vascos usaban ___ como canchas.
a. las paredes de las iglesias
b. los frontones de hoy en día

____ **20.** Si quieres ver los famosos molinos de viento de Castilla-La Mancha, debes hacer una excursión por ___.
a. los parques y reservas naturales
b. la Ruta de Don Quijote

SCORE /8

Vocabulario

F Read the descriptions below and write a vocabulary word to match each one.

__________ **21.** Tienes que ir a las montañas para hacer este deporte.

__________ **22.** Una persona a quien le gusta mucho hacer un deporte.

__________ **23.** Otro nombre para este deporte es la pelota vasca.

__________ **24.** Este deporte se hace en equipo y en un bote.

__________ **25.** Este deporte es una de las artes marciales.

SCORE /5

Nombre ______________________ Clase ______________ Fecha ______________

EXAMEN

Vocabulario

G Read the conversation between Ana and Sara. Fill in the blanks with the appropriate words from **Vocabulario.**

Ana ¿Qué te pasa, Sara? Te veo muy triste. ¿Estás (**26**) ______________ ?

Sara Sí. María no me invitó a su fiesta. No puedo creer que ella sea tan (**27**) ______________ conmigo.

Ana Pues dicen que María tiene (**28**) ______________ de ser una amiga difícil.

Sara En cambio tú, Ana, te llevas muy bien con todo el mundo. Eres muy (**29**) ______________ .

Ana Bueno, Sara, sabes bien que tú puedes (**30**) ______________ conmigo. Cuando necesites ayuda, sólo tienes que hablarme.

SCORE ____ /5

H Read the sentences below. Write an appropriate response for each sentence.

31. Soy un gran aficionado al atletismo. ¿Qué deporte te gusta a ti?

____

32. Las artes marciales me dejan frío.

____

33. Eres muy bueno(a) para el boliche, ¿verdad?

____

34. ¿Te gustaría ver la competencia de atletismo? Yo te invito.

____

35. No vayamos a remar. No aguanto el agua.

____

SCORE ____ /10

Nombre ____________________ Clase ____________ Fecha ____________

CAPÍTULO 2

EXAMEN

Gramática

I Complete each sentence with the correct form of the imperfect.

36. Cuando era niño, mi familia y yo (ir) ____________ a la playa con frecuencia.

37. Mis amigos (jugar) ____________ al fútbol americano todos los sábados.

38. Muchas veces yo (hacer) ____________ la tarea al comer el desayuno.

39. Me parece que tú siempre (tener) ____________ más amigas que yo.

40. En esos tiempos Raquel (ser) ____________ fanática de *Viaje a las Estrellas.*

SCORE ____ /5

J Read the questions below and answer each one with a **nosotros** command and an object pronoun. Answer questions followed by **sí** positively and **no** negatively.

41. ¿Hacemos una fiesta para el cumpleaños de Juana? (sí)

____

42. ¿Invitamos a los hermanos de Juana? (sí)

____

43. ¿Vemos una película durante la fiesta? (no)

____

44. ¿Practicamos el tiro con arco? (no)

____

45. ¿Guardamos el secreto hasta el día de la fiesta? (sí)

____

SCORE ____ /10

K Complete the sentences with the correct form of the subjunctive or the indicative.

46. Creo que tú y yo (ir) ____________ a llegar tarde para la competencia.

47. Me molesta que nosotros (llegar) ____________ tarde siempre.

48. ¿Conoces a alguien que (ser) ____________ puntual?

49. Al entrenador le sorprende que el equipo no (practicar) ____________ antes del juego.

50. Él piensa que un equipo (deber) ____________ estar bien preparado.

SCORE ____ /5 ⇨

Escribamos

L Write a brief conversation between two friends. One friend invites the other to do something. The other friend says he/she does not want to do this activity or is not able to at the time, and gives another idea. The first friend says it's all the same to him/her and agrees to the last suggestion. Remember to use **nosotros** commands.

____

____

____

____

____

____

____

SCORE /10

M Write a paragraph in which you describe the ideal friend. Include the qualities that this friend should have, what kind of person he or she should or should not be, and so on.

____

____

____

____

____

____

SCORE /10

TOTAL SCORE /100

Nombre ______________________ Clase ______________ Fecha ______________

CAPÍTULO 2

Score Sheet: Examen

Escuchemos

A

1. a b
2. a b
3. a b
4. a b

SCORE /8

B

5. a b c d
6. a b c d
7. a b c d
8. a b c d

SCORE /8

Leamos

C

9. a b
10. a b
11. a b
12. a b

SCORE /8

D

13. a b
14. a b
15. a b
16. a b

SCORE /8

Cultura

E

17. a b
18. a b
19. a b
20. a b

SCORE /8

Vocabulario

F

21. ______________________
22. ______________________
23. ______________________
24. ______________________
25. ______________________

SCORE /5

G

26. ______________________
27. ______________________
28. ______________________
29. ______________________
30. ______________________

SCORE /5

H

31. ____
32. ____
33. ____
34. ____
35. ____

SCORE /10

Nombre ______________________ Clase ______________ Fecha ______________

CAPÍTULO 2

SCORE SHEET: EXAMEN

Gramática

I

36. ______________
37. ______________
38. ______________
39. ______________
40. ______________

SCORE /5

J

41. ______________
42. ______________
43. ______________
44. ______________
45. ______________

SCORE /10

K

46. ______________
47. ______________
48. ______________
49. ______________
50. ______________

SCORE /5

Escribamos

L

SCORE /10

M

SCORE /10

TOTAL SCORE /100

CAPÍTULO 2

Answer Key: Examen

Escuchemos

A

1. (a) b
2. a (b)
3. a (b)
4. (a) b

SCORE /8

B

5. a (b) c d
6. a b c (d)
7. (a) b c d
8. a b (c) d

SCORE /8

Leamos

C

9. a (b)
10. a (b)
11. a (b)
12. (a) b

SCORE /8

D

13. a (b)
14. (a) b
15. (a) b
16. a (b)

SCORE /8

Cultura

E

17. (a) b
18. (a) b
19. (a) b
20. a (b)

SCORE /8

Vocabulario

F

21. la escalada deportiva
22. un(a) fanático(a) / aficionado(a)
23. el jai-alai
24. el remo
25. el kárate

SCORE /5

G Answers may vary.

26. dolida
27. seca
28. fama
29. amigable / solidaria
30. contar

SCORE /5

H Answers will vary.

31. Pues, la verdad es que me gusta mucho el remo.
32. ¿Ah, sí? Pues, yo creo que son geniales.
33. Sí, me la paso.../No, pero estoy loco(a) por...
34. No, gracias. Iba a jugar al dominó con mis amigos.
35. Como quieras. Me da lo mismo.

SCORE /10

Gramática

I

36. íbamos
37. jugaban
38. hacía
39. tenías
40. era

SCORE /5

J

41. Sí, hagámosla.
42. Sí, invitémoslos.
43. No, no la veamos.
44. No, no lo practiquemos.
45. Sí, guardémoslo.

SCORE /10

K

46. vamos
47. lleguemos
48. sea
49. practique
50. debe

SCORE /5

Escribamos

L

Answers will vary. Answers should include: ¿Te gustaría...? Yo te invito., No vayamos a... No aguanto..., No, gracias. Iba a..., Como quieras. Me da lo mismo.

SCORE /10

M

Answers will vary. Answers should include: tener mucho en común, contar con, confiar en, respetar los sentimientos, guardar los secretos, confiable, generoso(a), honesto(a), leal, abierto(a), amigable, solidario(a), atento(a), maleducado(a), seco(a), celoso(a), terco(a), chismoso(a), creído(a).

SCORE /10

TOTAL SCORE /100

Escuchemos

A. Listen to Arturo describe the ideal friend. Read the statements below, and choose **a**) for **cierto** or **b**) for **falso.**

El amigo ideal para mí es una persona abierta y amigable. Un buen amigo debe ser atento y ayudarte a resolver tus problemas. Debe ser una persona confiable, honesta y con quien puedas contar siempre. También ayuda tener mucho en común con un buen amigo. Por otro lado, un buen amigo no debe tener celos de otros amigos que tienes y no debe ser creído ni terco. Una persona chismosa no es un buen amigo porque no sabe guardar los secretos.

B. Listen to the short conversations about sports and activities. Match the letter of the image to the conversation that you hear.

5. ¿Te gustaría ir al lago a remar? Voy con Pilar, Andrés y Guillermo.
No gracias. Iba a jugar al fútbol con Francisco y Óscar.

6. Eres muy bueno para el ciclismo, ¿verdad?
Sí, me la paso practicando ciclismo. Creo que es genial.

7. Soy un fanático de los juegos de computadora.
¿Ah, sí? Pues, yo creo que son muy aburridos.

8. ¿Qué deporte te gusta a ti?
A mí me gusta el tiro con arco. Es un deporte muy divertido.

Nombre ______________________ Clase ______________ Fecha ______________

¡A pasarlo bien!

EXAMEN ORAL

Interview

A Respond to the following questions in Spanish.

1. ¿Cómo debe ser un buen amigo para ti?
2. ¿Qué te gusta y te molesta de un amigo?
3. ¿A qué deporte o juego eres gran aficionado(a)? Explica.
4. ¿Qué deporte o pasatiempo te resulta más aburrido? ¿Por qué?
5. ¿Te gusta ver tu deporte favorito por televisión o te gusta ir al estadio? ¿Por qué?

Role-Play

B Act out the following situation with a partner. You can also act it out by yourself.

Imagine that you are the sports director of your school and you have to decide which team or club each student should try out for. Greet a student, ask what his or her interests are, and suggest a club tryout for one day this week. When the student mentions that he or she has another obligation that day, ask for another interest and suggest another club.

SPEAKING RUBRIC

COMPREHENSION (ability to understand verbal cues and respond appropriately)	(POOR)	1	2	3	4	(EXCELLENT)
COMPREHENSIBILITY (ability to communicate ideas and be understood)	(POOR)	1	2	3	4	(EXCELLENT)
ACCURACY (ability to use structures and vocabulary correctly)	(POOR)	1	2	3	4	(EXCELLENT)
FLUENCY (ability to communicate clearly and smoothly)	(POOR)	1	2	3	4	(EXCELLENT)
EFFORT (inclusion of details beyond the minimum requirements)	(POOR)	1	2	3	4	(EXCELLENT)

Nombre ______________________ Clase ______________ Fecha ______________

Todo tiene solución

Escuchemos

A Listen to the following conversation between Ignacio and Margarita. Read the statements below, and choose **a**) for **cierto** or **b**) for **falso.**

____ **1.** Ignacio tiene una imagen positiva de la directora del colegio.

____ **2.** A Margarita le choca la actitud de Ignacio. Piensa que él tiene muchos prejuicios.

____ **3.** Margarita sugiere que Ignacio deje de hablar con la directora.

____ **4.** Al final, Ignacio admite su error.

SCORE ____ /8

B Listen to Ramón's comments about school and answer the questions.

____ **5.** ¿Qué clases tiene Ramón en su horario para este semestre?
a. cálculo, geografía, ciencias sociales, física, literatura
b. música, arte, geografía, español, cálculo
c. ciencias sociales, literatura, música, francés, matemáticas

____ **6.** ¿Qué le pasó en el curso de geografía?
a. Aprobó el examen.
b. Suspendió el examen.
c. Volvió a hacer el examen.

____ **7.** ¿Qué problema tiene con la clase de cálculo?
a. Le choca la actitud del profesor hacia los estudiantes.
b. Tiene que tomar muchos apuntes.
c. Han tenido muchas pruebas.

____ **8.** ¿Por qué tiene que tomar muchos apuntes en la clase de literatura?
a. Tiene un examen mañana.
b. Quiere estudiar literatura en la universidad.
c. Suspendió la última prueba.

SCORE ____ /8

EXAMEN

Leamos

C Read this article from the school newspaper. Then, read the statements that follow and choose **a)** for **cierto** or **b)** for **falso.**

> **¿Cómo combatimos la discriminación?**
>
> Hay mucho prejuicio contra las personas de diferentes culturas en nuestra comunidad. A mi parecer, la gente las juzga mal porque no las conoce. Creo que lo que tenemos que hacer es combatir la ignorancia. Es una buena manera de eliminar los estereotipos. Si yo fuera el director del colegio, empezaría un programa de intercambio. Así los estudiantes tendrían la oportunidad de conocer a gente de diferentes culturas.

____ **9.** El autor del artículo no cree que la gente tenga impresiones equivocadas de las personas de otras culturas.

____ **10.** El autor cree que la ignorancia es una causa de la discriminación.

____ **11.** La directora del colegio tiene una buena idea para combatir la ignorancia.

____ **12.** Al autor le gustaría empezar un programa de intercambio.

SCORE ____ /8

D Read Tina and Ángela's instant messages and answer the questions.

Tina He dejado de hablar con José. Voy a romper con él.

Ángela Oye, no hagas nada tan rápido. Date tiempo para pensarlo. ¿Qué hizo?

Tina Todo el mundo dice que salió con Ana.

Ángela Pues, sugiero que no hagas caso a los rumores. Primero que todo, deberías hablar con él.

Tina Sí, es un buen consejo. Es que me hirió mucho escuchar este rumor. Pero ahora no sé cómo pedirle perdón. Le daré un abrazo.

Ángela Seguramente se reconciliarán.

13. ¿Por qué quiere Tina romper con José? ______________________

14. ¿Qué le sugiere Ángela? ______________________

15. ¿Cómo piensa Tina pedirle perdón a José? ______________________

16. ¿Qué cree Ángela que va a pasar? ______________________

SCORE ____ /8 ⇨

Nombre ______________________ Clase ______________ Fecha ____________

CAPÍTULO 3

EXAMEN

Cultura

E Choose the response that best completes each of the following statements about **el mundo latinoamericano.**

____ **17.** En Puerto Rico, hoy en día, todos los estudiantes aprenden ___ en el colegio.
a. sólo inglés
b. inglés y español
c. sólo español

____ **18.** Más del 20 por ciento de los puertorriqueños va a ___.
a. colegios privados
b. colegios públicos
c. colegios internacionales

____ **19.** En Cuba, el sistema educativo es gratis desde los seis años hasta ___.
a. los once años
b. la universidad
c. la educación primaria

____ **20.** Las telenovelas latinoamericanas son ___.
a. sólo para adultos
b. una manera de convivir con la familia y los amigos
c. presentadas a las cinco y a las siete de la tarde

SCORE ____ /8

Vocabulario

F Choose a term from the box that best matches each definition.

a. el estereotipo
b. insultar
c. la reconciliación
d. la comunicación
e. suspender

____ **21.** Una persona pide perdón y la otra persona la disculpa.

____ **22.** Decir algo que ofende a otra persona.

____ **23.** El opuesto de aprobar.

____ **24.** Las personas se hablan y expresan sus ideas y sentimientos.

____ **25.** Cuando un grupo es conocido por algo y la gente cree que todos los del grupo son iguales.

SCORE ____ /5

EXAMEN

Vocabulario

G Read the following problems and choose the most logical advice.

_____ **26.** A veces mis amigos y yo discutimos sobre cosas que realmente no son importantes, y después es difícil hacer las paces.
a. En tu lugar, buscaría otros amigos.
b. En esa situación, trataría de hablar con ellos y ser muy abierto.

_____ **27.** Soy muy celoso de los amigos de mi novia. Por eso discutimos mucho.
a. Creo que deberías tratar de comunicarte mejor con ella.
b. Yo que tú, romperiá con ella porque no debe salir con otros amigos.

_____ **28.** Me peleé con mi novia y la ofendí. Pensé que ella me fue infiel, pero yo estaba equivocado. Me siento fatal.
a. En esa situación, admitiría mi error y le compraría un regalo.
b. Antes que nada, tu novia debe admitir su error.

_____ **29.** Mi hermana me insultó y estoy muy resentida. Me hirió mucho lo que me dijo, pero todavía la quiero mucho.
a. En tu lugar, le explicaría mis sentimientos y la perdonaría.
b. ¿Has pensado en comprarle un regalo?

_____ **30.** Mi novio besó a otra chica y luego me mintió. No sé qué hacer.
a. Sería una mala idea romper con él porque serías desleal.
b. Sería una buena idea romper con él. No es nada confiable.

SCORE ____ /5

H Write a response to each of the following statements using expressions from **¡Exprésate!**

31. El profesor de cálculo dice que vamos a tener un examen todos los días.

____

32. A mi parecer, no hay discriminación en nuestro país.

____

33. Mi novia siempre me insulta y nunca admite ni un error.

____

34. Me hirió mucho lo que me dijiste esta mañana.

____

35. Peleé con mi mejor amigo y no sé qué hacer.

____

SCORE ____ /10 ⇨

Nombre ______________________ Clase ____________ Fecha ____________

CAPÍTULO **3**

EXAMEN

Gramática

I Complete each sentence with the **infinitive,** the **indicative,** or the **subjunctive** of the verb in parentheses.

36. Mis amigos piensan (ir) ____________ a la playa después de clases.

37. Yo prefiero que nosotros (ver) ____________ una película.

38. Luis insiste en que tú no (invitar) ____________ a Yoli.

39. Creo que mis amigos (tener) ____________ una impresión equivocada de ella. Dicen que es muy seca.

40. No es cierto que ella (ser) ____________ seca. La verdad es que es muy tímida.

SCORE /5

J Tell what each of the following people will do when the school year is over. Use the future tense.

41. los estudiantes / disfrutar de las vacaciones

____

42. mis hermanos y yo / visitar a mis abuelos

____

43. mis papás / ir de viaje

____

44. los profesores / descansar

____

45. tú / tomar clases de piano

____

SCORE /5

K Complete each sentence using the **conditional.**

46. Si yo fuera el (la) director(a) del colegio, ______________________________

47. Si tú fueras un actor famoso, ______________________________

48. Si viviéramos en Costa Rica, ______________________________

49. Si todos pudieran hablar español, ______________________________

50. Si yo pudiera volver a hacer algo, ______________________________

SCORE /10

EXAMEN

Escribamos

L Write a paragraph describing a mistaken impression that someone has had of you. Tell how the person made you feel and how you resolved the problem. What will you do in the future to communicate better with this person?

SCORE /10

M Imagine that you had an argument with a friend and you realize you hurt his or her feelings. Write an e-mail to the friend saying that you didn't mean to hurt him or her and you're sorry. Ask your friend to take time to think things over and forgive you.

SCORE /10

TOTAL SCORE /100

Nombre ______________________ Clase ______________ Fecha ______________

CAPÍTULO 3

Score Sheet: Examen

Escuchemos

A

1. a b
2. a b
3. a b
4. a b

SCORE /8

B

5. a b c
6. a b c
7. a b c
8. a b c

SCORE /8

D

13. ______________________
14. ______________________
15. ______________________
16. ______________________

SCORE /8

Leamos

C

9. a b
10. a b
11. a b
12. a b

SCORE /8

Cultura

E

17. a b c
18. a b c
19. a b c
20. a b c

SCORE /8

Vocabulario

F

21. a b c d e
22. a b c d e
23. a b c d e
24. a b c d e
25. a b c d e

SCORE /5

G

26. a b
27. a b
28. a b
29. a b
30. a b

SCORE /5

H

31. ______________________
32. ______________________
33. ______________________
34. ______________________
35. ______________________

SCORE /10

Nombre ______________________ Clase ______________ Fecha ____________

CAPÍTULO 3

SCORE SHEET: EXAMEN

Gramática

I

36. ______________
37. ______________
38. ______________
39. ______________
40. ______________

SCORE /5

J

41. ______________
42. ______________
43. ______________
44. ______________
45. ______________

SCORE /5

K

46. ______________
47. ______________
48. ______________
49. ______________
50. ______________

SCORE /10

Escribamos

L

SCORE /10

M

SCORE /10

TOTAL SCORE /100

Answer Key: Examen

Escuchemos

A

1. a (b)
2. (a) b
3. a (b)
4. (a) b

SCORE /8

B

5. (a) b c
6. a (b) c
7. a b (c)
8. a (b) c

SCORE /8

Leamos

C

9. a (b)
10. (a) b
11. a (b)
12. (a) b

SCORE /8

D

13. Cree que él salió con otra chica.
14. Le sugiere que no haga caso a los rumores.
15. Le dará un abrazo.
16. Cree que se van a reconciliar.

SCORE /8

Cultura

E

17. a (b) c
18. (a) b c
19. a (b) c
20. a (b) c

SCORE /8

Vocabulario

F

21. a b (c) d e
22. a (b) c d e
23. a b c d (e)
24. a b c (d) e
25. (a) b c d e

SCORE /5

G

26. a (b)
27. (a) b
28. (a) b
29. (a) b
30. a (b)

SCORE /5

H Answers will vary. Possible answers:

31. ¡Esto es el colmo!
32. ¡Qué va! Eso no es cierto.
33. No me parece que sea justo. Sería una buena idea romper con ella.
34. No quise hacerte daño.
35. ¿Has pensado en pedirle perdón?

SCORE /10

Gramática

I

36. ir
37. veamos
38. invites
39. tienen
40. sea

SCORE /5

J

41. Los estudiantes disfrutarán de las vacaciones.
42. Nosotros visitaremos a mis abuelos.
43. Mis papás irán de viaje.
44. Los profesores descansarán.
45. Tú tomarás clases de piano.

SCORE /5

K Answers will vary. Possible answers:

46. ...daría más vacaciones.
47. ...me invitarías a tus fiestas.
48. ...iríamos mucho a la playa.
49. ...habría menos discriminación.
50. ...tomaría el examen de geografía otra vez.

SCORE /10

Escribamos

L

Answers will vary. Answers may include: impresión equivocada, estereotipos, la imagen, la ignorancia, combatir, juzgar, Me choca la actitud de... hacia..., Voy a..., No volveremos a...

SCORE /10

M

Answers will vary. Answers may include: Te juro que no lo volveré a hacer, Perdóname, No sé en qué estaba pensando, Créeme que fue sin querer, No lo hice a propósito, No quise hacerte daño, No quise ofenderte. Date tiempo para pensarlo, Perdóname.

SCORE /10

TOTAL SCORE /100

Escuchemos

A Listen to the following conversation between Ignacio and Margarita. Read the statements below, and choose **a)** for **cierto** or **b)** for **falso.**

Ignacio ¡No me gusta la directora para nada! A mi parecer, es antipática, creída e injusta.

Margarita ¡Qué va! Eso no es cierto. Tienes una imagen equivocada de ella.

Ignacio Además, ella insiste en que yo haga más trabajo que los otros estudiantes porque soy futbolista. A mi parecer, no hay igualdad entre los estudiantes en este colegio.

Margarita ¡Esto es el colmo! No es verdad. ¿Cómo puedes tener esos prejuicios? No quiero hablar contigo. Me voy.

Ignacio ¡Espera, Margarita! Perdóname. No quise ofenderte. Es que me molesta que la directora tenga una impresión equivocada de mí. Cree que no fui a las clases por gusto, pero en realidad estaba enfermo.

Margarita Ignacio, esto es simplemente una falta de comunicación. Yo que tú, hablaría con ella.

Ignacio Tienes razón. Discúlpame, Margarita.

B Listen to Ramón's comments about school and answer the questions.

5. Tengo un horario difícil este semestre. El consejero insiste en que tome cinco cursos: cálculo, geografía, ciencias sociales, física y literatura.
6. Suspendí el examen de geografía. ¡Esto es el colmo! Si yo pudiera volver a hacer el examen, estudiaría más.
7. Hemos tenido cinco pruebas en la clase de cálculo. ¡No aguanto más!
8. Tengo que tomar muchos apuntes en la clase de literatura porque quiero estudiar literatura española en la universidad.

Todo tiene solución

Interview

A Respond to the following questions in Spanish.

1. ¿Qué piensas de los estereotipos? Explica. ¿Qué harías para eliminar los prejuicios?
2. ¿Has tenido alguna vez una impresión equivocada de otra persona? ¿Qué pasó? ¿Qué harás en el futuro para evitar una situación similar?
3. ¿Crees que es justa la discriminación de unas personas por otras? Explica.
4. ¿Has ofendido a algún amigo injustamente? Explica. ¿Qué has hecho para reparar tu error?
5. ¿Qué piensas sobre la discriminación del hombre hacia la mujer? ¿Por qué?

Role-Play

B Act out the following situation with a partner. One of you is an exchange student meeting a student from the U.S. Both of you have some rather stereotypical ideas about the other, and both get offended, but end up resolving the problem by realizing that you have a lot in common. Use some the following phrases in your dialogue: **No quise ofenderte.**, **Perdóname.**, **No sé en qué estaba pensando.**, and **Te juro que no lo volveré a hacer.**

SPEAKING RUBRIC

COMPREHENSION (ability to understand verbal cues and respond appropriately)	(POOR)	1	2	3	4	(EXCELLENT)
COMPREHENSIBILITY (ability to communicate ideas and be understood)	(POOR)	1	2	3	4	(EXCELLENT)
ACCURACY (ability to use structures and vocabulary correctly)	(POOR)	1	2	3	4	(EXCELLENT)
FLUENCY (ability to communicate clearly and smoothly)	(POOR)	1	2	3	4	(EXCELLENT)
EFFORT (inclusion of details beyond the minimum requirements)	(POOR)	1	2	3	4	(EXCELLENT)

Nombre ______________________ Clase ______________ Fecha ______________

CAPÍTULO 4 EXAMEN

Entre familia

Escuchemos

A Listen to the following conversations, and choose the phrase that best summarizes each one.

____ **1. a.** dar una nueva noticia y reaccionar
b. hablar de la comida y dar una explicación

____ **2. a.** hablar de la familia y expresar emoción
b. reaccionar a malas noticias y dar información

____ **3. a.** contestar una pregunta y hacer una pregunta
b. reaccionar a malas noticias y dar una explicación

____ **4. a.** dar una opinión de la comida y dar una explicación
b. hablar de la familia y dar buenas noticias

SCORE ____ /8

B Listen to the conversations. Match the letter of each image to the number of the conversation that you hear.

a.

b.

c.

d.

5. ____ **7.** ____

6. ____ **8.** ____

SCORE ____ /8

EXAMEN

Leamos

C Read Alberto's essay about his family. Choose the correct word(s) to complete the sentences.

Mis padres se divorciaron cuando era pequeño. Yo vivo con mi mamá, su esposo Felipe, y mi medio hermano, Lorenzo. Mi papá está comprometido con su novia Patricia que tiene un hijo. Durante las vacaciones de verano, mi abuela me prepara bizcochos, y mi abuelo y yo pescamos en el lago. También tengo muchos parientes que sólo veo en nuestras reuniones familiares.

____ **9.** El papá y la mamá de Alberto están ____.
a. casados **b.** comprometidos **c.** divorciados

____ **10.** Alberto tiene ____.
a. una hermanastra **b.** un medio hermano **c.** una novia

____ **11.** Durante las vacaciones de verano, la abuela de Alberto ____.
a. prepara bizcochos **b.** pesca en el lago **c.** vive con su mamá

____ **12.** Alberto ve a muchos parientes ____.
a. durante los veranos **b.** cuando era pequeño **c.** en las reuniones familiares

SCORE ____ /8

D Read the conversation. Then, read the statements that follow and choose **a**) for **cierto** or **b**) for **falso.**

Mamá Francisco, ¿todavía no has limpiado tu cuarto?

Francisco Yo lo limpié ayer. Nunca entras al cuarto cuando está limpio.

Mamá Pues, ¿por qué no lo limpias ahora?

Francisco Es que estoy estudiando para un examen de cálculo.

Mamá ¿Estudiando? ¿Con los ojos cerrados? Francisco, no puedo creer que me estés mintiendo. Si no limpias el cuarto, te quedas en casa.

Francisco Pero, quería ir al nuevo restaurante con mis amigos.

Mamá Puedes ir si limpias tu cuarto y me traes un pedazo de toronja. ¿Oíste?

____ **13.** El cuarto de Francisco está limpio.

____ **14.** Francisco le está mintiendo a su mamá.

____ **15.** Francisco no quería salir con sus amigos.

____ **16.** La mamá de Francisco quiere un pedazo de fruta.

SCORE ____ /8

EXAMEN

Cultura

E Choose the words that best complete the statements about **el Caribe.**

_____ **17.** La ___ es muy importante en el Caribe porque los lazos familiares son fuertes.
a. comida **b.** familia extendida **c.** española

_____ **18.** Para los novios de muchos países latinoamericanos, ___ es más importante que la ceremonia civil.
a. la fiesta **b.** el documento **c.** la ceremonia religiosa

_____ **19.** El sofrito cubano es una salsa para sazonar ___.
a. los frijoles **b.** el arroz **c.** el plátano frito

_____ **20.** ___ es un pescado frito o al horno, y es un plato típico de Puerto Rico.
a. La ropa vieja **b.** El chillo **c.** El ceviche

SCORE ____ /8

Vocabulario

F Read the statements and choose **a**) for **cierto** or **b**) for **falso.**

_____ **21.** Los padres de mi esposo(a) son mis suegros.

_____ **22.** Cuando alguien se compromete quiere decir que se va a divorciar.

_____ **23.** Dar a luz es otra manera de decir tener un bebé.

_____ **24.** Cuando dices "esto no sabe a nada", quiere decir que te gusta la comida.

_____ **25.** La sandía es una fruta.

SCORE ____ /5

EXAMEN

G Read the following statements. In the blank, write **a**) if the person is surprised, or **b**) if the person is not surprised.

____ **26.** ¡Qué sorpresa que mi prima se haya separado de su esposo!

____ **27.** Se me hace la boca agua.

____ **28.** ¿Qué sabes de Clara?

____ **29.** Me has dejado boquiabierta.

____ **30.** Es que se me acabó el azúcar.

SCORE ____ /5

H Choose the phrases from the box that best complete the conversations.

fíjate que	**se me olvidó**	**Algo le falta, pero no sé qué**	**está seco**
andas haciendo	**se le fue la mano**	**la ensalada de frutas**	**qué pena**
se haya muerto	**un yogur con crema**		

Marcos ¿Has probado el pavo de mi tía? (**31**) ____________________

Pilar No me gustó. Creo que (**32**) ____________________ con la sal.

Silvia Roberto, hace tiempo que no te veo. ¿Qué (**33**) ____________________?

Roberto (**34**) ____________________ me comprometí con mi novia el mes pasado.

Luz María Ay, Bárbara. Tengo malas noticias. Don Enrique se murió ayer a la edad de 88 años.

Bárbara ¡(**35**) ____________________ que Don Enrique (**36**) ____________________!

Mamá Pedro, el arroz (**37**) ____________________. No puedo comerlo.

Papá Es que (**38**) ____________________ ponerle agua.

Sara Cuando llegue el mesero, voy a pedir (**39**) ____________________. Es que estoy a dieta.

Luis Yo voy a pedir (**40**) ____________________ porque no estoy a dieta.

SCORE ____ /10

Nombre ______________________ Clase ______________ Fecha ______________

CAPÍTULO

EXAMEN

Gramática

I Read the following sentences. In the blank, write **a**) if the action is still happening, or **b**) if it occurred in the past.

____ **41.** Mis padres se han divorciado.

____ **42.** Mi primo Esteban sigue estudiando en la universidad.

____ **43.** Estábamos viendo televisión cuando se fue la luz.

____ **44.** En cuanto pudo, María mandó las invitaciones.

SCORE ____ /4

J For each sentence, write **se + indirect object pronoun + the verb** in parentheses to state what happened unintentionally.

45. Al verte, a Tomás ______________________ (caer) los libros de sus manos.

46. A los niños ______________________ (quemar) el arroz que iban a comer.

47. A Uds. ______________________ (quedar) las llaves en el carro.

48. A Nora ______________________ (romper) su nueva computadora.

SCORE ____ /8

K Combine the phrases to make sentences using the correct verb tense based on the context.

49. (yo) ya / haber / preparar / el puerco asado para la cena

____

50. es triste que David / haber / enfermarse / el día antes del concierto

____

51. nosotros / estar / comer / cuando / entrar / Luisa con su esposo

____

52. los hermanos / seguir / jugar / a pesar de la lluvia

____

SCORE ____ /8

EXAMEN

Escribamos

L At a reunion, family members are catching up on the latest news and gossip. Write a conversation in which someone asks for information, and someone else gives information. Be sure to include at least three questions and answers, and the reaction of those who receive the information.

____

____

____

____

____

____

____

____

SCORE /10

M Last night, you cooked shellfish with vegetables for dinner for your family, and it was a disaster. Write your friend a letter explaining what happened. Include what you cooked for each course, how it tasted, your family's reaction, and any excuses you may have given.

____

____

____

____

____

____

____

____

SCORE /10 TOTAL SCORE /100

Nombre ______________________ Clase ______________ Fecha ____________

CAPÍTULO 4

Score Sheet: Examen

Escuchemos

A

1. a b
2. a b
3. a b
4. a b

SCORE /8

B

5. a b c d
6. a b c d
7. a b c d
8. a b c d

SCORE /8

Leamos

C

9. a b c
10. a b c
11. a b c
12. a b c

SCORE /8

D

13. a b
14. a b
15. a b
16. a b

SCORE /8

Cultura

E

17. a b c
18. a b c
19. a b c
20. a b c

SCORE /8

Vocabulario

F

21. a b
22. a b
23. a b
24. a b
25. a b

SCORE /5

G

26. a b
27. a b
28. a b
29. a b
30. a b

SCORE /5

H

31. ______________________
32. ______________________
33. ______________________
34. ______________________
35. ______________________
36. ______________________
37. ______________________
38. ______________________
39. ______________________
40. ______________________

SCORE /10

Nombre ______________ Clase ______________ Fecha ______________

CAPÍTULO **4**

SCORE SHEET: EXAMEN

Gramática

I

41. a b
42. a b
43. a b
44. a b

SCORE /4

J

45. ______________
46. ______________
47. ______________
48. ______________

SCORE /8

K

49. ______________
50. ______________
51. ______________
52. ______________

SCORE /8

Escribamos

L

____

SCORE /10

M

____

SCORE /10

TOTAL SCORE /100

CAPÍTULO 4

Answer Key: Examen

Escuchemos

A

1. a ⓑ
2. ⓐ b
3. ⓐ b
4. ⓐ b

SCORE /8

B

5. a b c ⓓ
6. a b ⓒ d
7. a ⓑ c d
8. ⓐ b c d

SCORE /8

Leamos

C

9. a b ⓒ
10. a ⓑ c
11. ⓐ b c
12. a b ⓒ

SCORE /8

D

13. a ⓑ
14. ⓐ b
15. a ⓑ
16. ⓐ b

SCORE /8

Cultura

E

17. a ⓑ c
18. a b ⓒ
19. ⓐ b c
20. a ⓑ c

SCORE /8

Vocabulario

F

21. ⓐ b
22. a ⓑ
23. ⓐ b
24. a ⓑ
25. ⓐ b

SCORE /5

G

26. ⓐ b
27. a ⓑ
28. a ⓑ
29. ⓐ b
30. a ⓑ

SCORE /5

H

31. Algo le falta, pero no sé qué
32. se le fue la mano
33. andas haciendo
34. Fíjate que
35. Qué pena
36. se haya muerto
37. está seco
38. se me olvidó
39. la ensalada de frutas
40. un yogur con crema

SCORE /10

Gramática

I

41. a (b)
42. (a) b
43. a (b)
44. a (b)

SCORE /4

J

45. se le cayeron
46. se les quemó
47. se les quedaron
48. se le rompió

SCORE /8

K

49. Ya he preparado el puerco asado para la cena.
50. Es triste que David se haya enfermado el día antes del concierto.
51. Nosotros estábamos comiendo cuando entró Luisa con su esposo.
52. Los hermanos siguen jugando afuera a pesar de la lluvia.

SCORE /8

Escribamos

L

Answers will vary. Answers should include: family members (suegro(a), sobrino(a), medio hermano(a), asking for the latest news (¿Qué anda haciendo...?), giving news (Fíjate que...), reacting to news (¡No me digas!, No me lo puedo creer), present perfect subjunctive, preterite, and past progressive.

SCORE /10

M

Answers will vary. Answers should include: preterite, past progressive, food names (camarones, langosta, apio, calabacines, chícharos, ensalada de pepino y coliflor, limón, ensalada de fruta con pasas, etc.), expressions to comment on food (Sabe delicioso.), expressions to give an excuse (Es que se me fue la mano con...), family members.

SCORE /10

TOTAL SCORE /100

Escuchemos

A Listen to the following conversations, and choose the phrase that best summarizes each one.

1. —Está listo el postre. Vengan a la mesa y vamos a probar el dulce de coco que preparó Augusto.

—¡Qué asco! El dulce de coco está salado.

—Parece que se le acabó el azúcar a Augusto y le echó sal.

2. —¿Quién más va a llegar a la reunión?

—Faltan tus suegros nada más. No iban a venir, pero por fin consiguieron un vuelo.

—¡Qué alegría que mis suegros nos vengan a visitar!

3. —¿Yo? Bueno, ya sabes. Yo sigo trabajando donde siempre.

—¿Y qué anda haciendo Ramón? ¿Sigue trabajando en el negocio familiar?

—Sí, ya conoces a Ramón. Él es muy trabajador.

4. —¿Qué tal está el bizcocho?

—La verdad es que no sabe muy dulce. ¿Qué pasó?

—Me imagino. Es que se me acabó el azúcar.

B Listen to the conversations. Match the letter of each image to the number of the conversation that you hear.

5. **Elena** ¿Has probado la comida? Está para chuparse los dedos.

Nelson No me gustó. El pescado estaba picante.

6. **Pablo** ¿Qué me cuentas de Luis e Iris?

Yolanda Fíjate que se comprometieron.

7. **Pedro** ¡Mi hermana dio a luz! Ahora tengo una sobrina con quien jugar.

Ana No puedo creer que tú sepas algo de los niños.

8. **Mesero** ¿Qué desean de comer?

Eugenio Yo quiero el caldo de pollo de entrada. Y para mi suegra, la ensalada de aguacate, por favor.

Nombre ______________________ Clase ______________ Fecha ____________

Entre familia

EXAMEN ORAL

Interview

A Respond to the following questions in Spanish.

1. ¿Con qué frecuencia ves a tus parientes? ¿De qué hablan?
2. ¿Te ha alegrado o enojado una noticia de un pariente tuyo alguna vez? Explica.
3. ¿Cómo son tus abuelos? ¿Tienes alguna noticia de ellos?
4. ¿Cuántos tíos y tías tienes? ¿Qué andan haciendo ahora?
5. ¿Qué comiste en tu última reunión familiar? ¿Qué tal estaba la comida?

Role-Play

B Get into groups of five and take turns acting out the following situation:

Each group should represent a family, as traditional or non-traditional as they would like. The groups of five should then pretend that they are at an extended family reunion. Each member of **family A** should introduce another member of his/her family to **family B,** and vice versa. Include names, ages, how that person is related to the others, and give one recent piece of news about him/her.

SPEAKING RUBRIC

COMPREHENSION (ability to understand verbal cues and respond appropriately)	(POOR)	1	2	3	4	(EXCELLENT)
COMPREHENSIBILITY (ability to communicate ideas and be understood)	(POOR)	1	2	3	4	(EXCELLENT)
ACCURACY (ability to use structures and vocabulary correctly)	(POOR)	1	2	3	4	(EXCELLENT)
FLUENCY (ability to communicate clearly and smoothly)	(POOR)	1	2	3	4	(EXCELLENT)
EFFORT (inclusion of details beyond the minimum requirements)	(POOR)	1	2	3	4	(EXCELLENT)

CAPÍTULO 5

El arte y la música

EXAMEN

Escuchemos

A Listen to the following review of a comedy. Read the statements below, and choose **a)** for **cierto** or **b)** for **falso.**

_____ **1.** El autor recomienda que el público vaya a la obra.

_____ **2.** Dice que la música de la obra es estridente.

_____ **3.** Fue a verla porque le dijeron que era entretenida.

_____ **4.** El autor dice que la obra es original y creativa.

SCORE /8

B Listen to the comments made about various artistic performances. Match the letter of the image to the statement that you hear.

a.

b.

c.

d.

5. _____ **7.** _____

6. _____ **8.** _____

SCORE /8

EXAMEN

Leamos

C Read the press release for the opening of a new school of fine arts. Then, read the statements that follow and choose **a)** for **cierto** or **b)** for **falso.**

El famoso arquitecto, el señor Rivas Mercado, acaba de inaugurar un nuevo colegio de bellas artes en el centro de la ciudad. Los edificios del colegio fueron diseñados por el mismo señor Rivas Mercado. Se construyeron varios salones para clases de pintura, escultura, baile y artes dramáticas. El arquitecto dijo que había planeado su colegio hace mucho tiempo, y declaró: "Yo quiero que los estudiantes de arte tengan un lugar donde puedan desarrollar su talento. Ahora mis estudiantes tienen un colegio moderno donde pueden crear sus obras de arte para el mundo entero".

____ **9.** El señor Rivas Mercado es un arquitecto famoso.

____ **10.** El señor Rivas Mercado diseñó los edificios del colegio.

____ **11.** Se construyeron salones para fotografía y teatro.

____ **12.** Los estudiantes pueden desarrollar su talento en el colegio.

SCORE ____ /8

D Read the conversation between Claudia and Alberto. Then, read the statements that follow and choose **a)** if Alberto would agree or **b)** if Claudia would agree.

Claudia Oye Alberto, ¿viste la presentación de baile mexicano?

Alberto No, no la vi. Además, no me gusta mucho el baile.

Claudia ¿Por qué? Es un arte hermoso y la presentación fue buenísima. El baile es mejor que la pintura o la escultura, por ejemplo.

Alberto Entonces, te sugiero que vayas a una exposición de escultura. En realidad, admiro mucho el estilo clásico. De hecho, hay una en el museo esta tarde, ¿me acompañas?

Claudia Gracias, pero no creo que sea tan divertido como el baile.

____ **13.** Admiro mucho las esculturas clásicas.

____ **14.** No creo que la escultura sea tan divertida como el baile.

____ **15.** Tienes que ir a una exposición de escultura.

____ **16.** No me gusta el baile.

SCORE ____ /8

Cultura

E Complete the following statements about **el mundo latinoamericano.**

____ **17.** Las iglesias de adobe del norte de México son ___.
a. de influencia española
b. derivadas de la arquitectura peruana del siglo XVII
c. estructuras infrecuentes y no muy típicas

____ **18.** La música norteña refleja la influencia ___.
a. española en el uso de la guitarra
b. alemana en el uso del acordeón
c. italiana en el uso del piano

____ **19.** Las obras de Frida Kahlo tienen un estilo basado en ___.
a. lo popular, lo religioso y los símbolos mexicanos
b. el folclor del Suroeste de EE.UU.
c. el arte neoclásico

____ **20.** Frida Kahlo usó ropa tradicional mexicana porque ___.
a. era una tradición en su familia
b. le gustaban los vestidos largos de colores brillantes
c. su marido, el pintor Diego Rivera, se lo sugirió

SCORE ____ /8

Vocabulario

F Choose the word that does not fit logically with each group.

____ **21.**	**a.** la fotografía	**b.** la comedia	**c.** el drama
____ **22.**	**a.** la reseña	**b.** el ritmo	**c.** la orquesta
____ **23.**	**a.** la estatua	**b.** el cuadro	**c.** la escultura
____ **24.**	**a.** la acuarela	**b.** el dibujo	**c.** la exposición
____ **25.**	**a.** antiguo	**b.** contemporáneo	**c.** moderno

SCORE /5

G Choose the phrase from the box that best describes how you would respond to the following questions.

____ **26.** ¿Qué opinas de la música clásica?

____ **27.** ¿Qué te parece la torre que está en el parque?

____ **28.** ¿Me acompañas al ensayo de la banda?

____ **29.** ¿Cuál te gusta más, la música estridente o la melodiosa?

____ **30.** ¿Por qué no vamos a la función de baile folclórico este fin de semana?

a. ¿Por qué no lo dejamos para el próximo fin de semana?
b. A decir verdad, me llama mucho la atención. Es impresionante.
c. Lo siento, pero ya tengo otro compromiso.
d. La encuentro muy aburrida, pero sí sirve para estudiar.
e. En realidad, me gustan mucho las melodías.

SCORE /5

H Respond to each item using an expression from **¡Exprésate!** to introduce or change the topic of conversation.

31. ¿Qué me dices del concierto de la sinfónica?

____

32. Hubo un robo esta mañana en el negocio de la esquina.

____

SCORE /10

Gramática

I Complete the following sentences using the passive voice with **ser** or **se.**

33. ______________________ (hacer) mucho para ayudar al desarrollo del teatro en esta ciudad.

34. Un centro cultural nuevo ______________________ (inaugurar) por el alcalde el fin de semana pasado.

35. Durante estos dos días ______________________ (presentar) muchas obras originales, clásicas y contemporáneas.

SCORE /6

J Complete the paragraph with the correct form of the verbs from the box.

visitar	**hacer**	**ver**	**llevar**	**servir**	**enseñar**

Mis amigos que llegaron de visita de México me han pedido que les (**36**) ____________ la ciudad. Yo los quiero (**37**) ____________ a muchos lugares, en especial, al Museo de Arte Moderno. Quiero que nosotros (**38**) ____________ varias salas y que (**39**) ____________ algunas de las obras surrealistas. Después, voy a sugerir que todos (**40**) ____________ un tour de la ciudad vieja y que cenemos allá, en un restaurante donde yo sé que deben (**41**) ____________ comida deliciosa. Les va a encantar.

SCORE /6

K Complete the following sentences using the past perfect.

42. Nosotros pasamos por Miguel, pero él ya ______________________ .

43. Cuando llegamos al teatro, el concierto ya ______________________ .

44. Cerraron las puertas y nosotros todavía no ______________________ a Miguel.

45. Pensamos que algo le ______________________ y decidimos irnos a casa.

SCORE /8

Escribamos

L Write a brief review of a play, a concert, or any other artistic event, real or imaginary. Describe the event and compare it to at least one other you've seen (in reality or in your imagination). Include which work was the most or least impressive and explain why. Make a recommendation to see it or offer an alternative suggestion.

SCORE /10

M Ricardo wants to go to a cultural event with his friend Marta, but both have very busy schedules. Write a conversation between Ricardo and Marta where they try to agree on an event to attend. Both Ricardo and Marta have to turn down at least one invitation before they come to an agreement.

Ricardo _______________

Marta _______________

Ricardo _______________

Marta _______________

Ricardo _______________

Marta _______________

SCORE /10 TOTAL SCORE /100

Nombre ______________________ Clase ____________ Fecha ____________

CAPÍTULO 5

Score Sheet: Examen

Escuchemos

A

1. a b
2. a b
3. a b
4. a b

SCORE /8

B

5. a b c d
6. a b c d
7. a b c d
8. a b c d

SCORE /8

Leamos

C

9. a b
10. a b
11. a b
12. a b

SCORE /8

D

13. a b
14. a b
15. a b
16. a b

SCORE /8

Cultura

E

17. a b c
18. a b c
19. a b c
20. a b c

SCORE /8

Vocabulario

F

21. a b c
22. a b c
23. a b c
24. a b c
25. a b c

SCORE /5

G

26. a b c d e
27. a b c d e
28. a b c d e
29. a b c d e
30. a b c d e

SCORE /5

H

31. ______________________________

32. ______________________________

SCORE /10

Nombre ______________________ Clase ______________ Fecha ______________

CAPÍTULO 5

SCORE SHEET: EXAMEN

Gramática

I

33. ______________
34. ______________
35. ______________

SCORE /6

J

36. ______________
37. ______________
38. ______________
39. ______________
40. ______________
41. ______________

SCORE /6

K

42. ______________________
43. ______________________
44. ______________________
45. ______________________

SCORE /8

Escribamos

L

____

____

____

____

____

____

SCORE /10

M

____

____

____

____

____

____

SCORE /10

TOTAL SCORE /100

Answer Key: Examen

Escuchemos

A

1. a (b)
2. (a) b
3. (a) b
4. a (b)

SCORE /8

B

5. a b c (d)
6. a (b) c d
7. a b (c) d
8. (a) b c d

SCORE /8

Leamos

C

9. (a) b
10. (a) b
11. a (b)
12. (a) b

SCORE /8

D

13. (a) b
14. a (b)
15. (a) b
16. (a) b

SCORE /8

Cultura

E

17. (a) b c
18. a (b) c
19. (a) b c
20. a b (c)

SCORE /8

Vocabulario

F

21. (a) b c
22. (a) b c
23. a (b) c
24. a b (c)
25. (a) b c

SCORE /5

G

26. a b c (d) e
27. a (b) c d e
28. a b (c) d e
29. a b c d (e)
30. (a) b c d e

SCORE /5

H Answers will vary. Possible answers:

31. **Pues, muy melodioso. A propósito, ¿qué has oído tú de la ópera?**
32. **Hablando de robos, ¿te enteraste de lo que le pasó a Marta?**

SCORE /10

Gramática

I

33. Se hace
34. fue inaugurado
35. se presentaron

SCORE /6

J

36. enseñe
37. llevar
38. visitemos
39. veamos
40. hagamos
41. servir

SCORE /6

K Answers will vary. Possible answers:

42. se había ido
43. había comenzado
44. habíamos encontrado
45. había pasado

SCORE /8

Escribamos

L

Answers will vary. Answers should include: Giving opinions: A decir verdad, me parece..., Lo/La encuentro muy..., En realidad, admiro...; Comparatives of equality and superlatives: fue tan ... como ..., fue la más impresionante de...; Making suggestions and recommendations: Es mejor que veas..., Es formidable., Sería buena idea ir..., Te aconsejo que vayas a...

SCORE /10

M

Answers will vary. Answers should include: To invite someone to do something: ¿Quieres ir a ver...?, ¿Te interesa ir a...?, ¿Me acompañas a....?, ¿Por qué no vamos a...?; To turn down an invitation: Gracias por invitarme, pero ya lo/la he visto., Lo siento, pero ya tengo otros planes/otro compromiso., Gracias, pero tengo mucho que hacer., La próxima vez iré; Hoy no, gracias., ¿Por qué no lo dejamos para la próxima semana?

SCORE /10

TOTAL SCORE /100

Escuchemos

A Listen to the following review of a comedy. Read the statements below, and choose **a**) for **cierto** or **b**) for **falso.**

Si te gustan las obras de mal gusto, te recomiendo que vayas a ver "Invasores de otro mundo". La obra es un ejemplo incomprensible del teatro contemporáneo, y además su música es estridente. Mis amigos me habían dicho que era una comedia muy entretenida y original. Por eso fui a verla; sin embargo, me di cuenta durante la primera escena de que era pésima. A decir verdad, es la obra menos original y creativa que he visto. Si quieres disfrutar una obra de calidad, te sugiero que no veas ésta y vayas a ver un drama o una tragedia.

B Listen to the comments made about various artistic performances. Match the letter of the image to the statement that you hear.

5. Sugiero que veas la tragedia porque es una obra original y entretenida.

6. Oye Fernando, espero que no te hayas perdido el concierto. ¡Estuvo buenísimo! El grupo interpretó la letra de una nueva canción.

7. ¿Me acompañas al museo? Hay una exposición de arte antiguo formidable.

8. Anoche fuimos a ver el ballet. Es impresionante cómo las bailarinas se mueven al ritmo de la música.

Nombre ____________________ Clase ____________ Fecha ____________

CAPÍTULO 5

El arte y la música

EXAMEN ORAL

Interview

A Respond to the following questions in Spanish.

1. ¿Qué tipo de arte te gusta más? ¿Por qué?
2. ¿Hay un tipo de arte que sabes hacer bien?
3. ¿Qué opinas de la pintura de Picasso? ¿Cómo comparas sus obras con las de Georgia O'Keefe?
4. ¿Te gustan los murales de Diego Rivera? ¿Por qué?
5. ¿Qué música te gusta? ¿Quién es tu cantante favorito?

Role-Play

B Act out the following situation with the entire class. You can also act it out by yourself.

Form different activity groups with your classmates (chorus, band, painting, and sculpture). You should introduce yourself, explain which type of art you would most like to do as part of a group, and explain why. You should also mention your prior experience in that type of art.

SPEAKING RUBRIC

COMPREHENSION (ability to understand verbal cues and respond appropriately)	(POOR)	1	2	3	4	(EXCELLENT)
COMPREHENSIBILITY (ability to communicate ideas and be understood)	(POOR)	1	2	3	4	(EXCELLENT)
ACCURACY (ability to use structures and vocabulary correctly)	(POOR)	1	2	3	4	(EXCELLENT)
FLUENCY (ability to communicate clearly and smoothly)	(POOR)	1	2	3	4	(EXCELLENT)
EFFORT (inclusion of details beyond the minimum requirements)	(POOR)	1	2	3	4	(EXCELLENT)

Examen parcial

Escuchemos

A Listen to the following conversations. Then, match the letter of the image to the conversation that you hear.

a.

b.

c.

d.

1. ____ 3. ____

2. ____ 4. ____

SCORE /8

B Listen to Joaquín and Clara talk about what they did during the summer break. Then, read the statements below and choose **a**) for **cierto** or **b**) for **falso.**

____ **5.** Joaquín acaba de regresar de vacaciones.

____ **6.** Joaquín no hizo nada durante el verano.

____ **7.** Clara hizo windsurfing y montó a caballo durante sus vacaciones.

____ **8.** A Joaquín le encanta la esgrima.

____ **9.** Clara es buena para el patinaje en línea.

____ **10.** Clara le enseñará a Joaquín a jugar al jai-alai.

SCORE  /12

Nombre ______________________ Clase ______________ Fecha ____________

EXAMEN PARCIAL

Leamos

C Read the following advertisement for a new recreational center. Then, read the statements below and choose **a**) for **cierto** or **b**) for **falso.**

¿Estás cansado de hacer ejercicio solo? Entonces, el centro recreativo Elizondo tiene la solución para ti. El centro recreativo Elizondo ofrece clases de jai-alai, esgrima, natación, kárate, ejercicios aeróbicos y muchas más. Tenemos algo para todos los aficionados al deporte y en toda clase de horarios: mañanas, tardes y noches hasta las diez. Así, hasta la persona más ocupada tendrá la oportunidad de hacer ejercicio. Y para aquéllos que siguen una dieta balanceada, tenemos una cafetería con platos especiales que están para chuparse los dedos. Entonces, ¿qué esperas? Aquí puedes mantenerte en forma y hacer amigos al mismo tiempo. Si quieres más información, puedes visitar nuestro centro en persona. ¡Te aconsejo que vengas a tomar una de nuestras clases hoy mismo!

____ **11.** El centro recreativo Elizondo es una galería de pinturas clásicas.

____ **12.** El centro recreativo Elizondo es para personas que quieren mantenerse en forma.

____ **13.** En el centro recreativo se pueden tomar clases de esgrima y jai-alai.

____ **14.** Una persona no puede tomar clases en el centro por la tarde.

____ **15.** El centro tiene comida especial para la gente que sigue una dieta.

SCORE ____ /5

D Read the following statements, and choose the most appropriate answer based on the reading.

____ **16.** El centro recreativo Elizondo ofrece clases de ___.
a. kárate **b.** natación **c.** todos los anteriores

____ **17.** El centro recreativo Elizondo tiene algo para todos los ___.
a. perezosos **b.** aficionados al deporte **c.** artistas

____ **18.** Si eres una persona muy ocupada, el centro está abierto ___.
a. hasta las diez **b.** a medianoche **c.** siempre

____ **19.** La cafetería tiene platos especiales para las personas interesadas en ___.
a. los deportes **b.** una dieta balanceada **c.** los ejercicios

____ **20.** En el centro recreativo, puedes mantenerte en forma y ___.
a. hacer rompecabezas **b.** hacer amigos **c.** jugar al golf

SCORE ____ /5 ⇨

EXAMEN PARCIAL

E Read the conversation between Inés and Rubén. Then, read the statements that follow and write the letter of the phrase that best completes each statement.

Inés ¿Qué tal, Rubén? ¿Qué clases estás tomando este semestre?

Rubén ¡Ay, Inés! Si supieras, no querrías estar en mi lugar. Tengo un horario pesado. Tengo literatura, cálculo y geografía por la mañana, y tengo física y ciencias sociales por la tarde.

Inés ¡Qué va! Ese horario no está tan pesado como dices. Yo estoy tomando los mismos cursos.

Rubén ¿Ah, sí? Pues, la verdad es que he estado buscando con quién estudiar. Mi profesor insiste en que estudie con un compañero de clase. ¿Qué dices? ¿Me acompañas a la biblioteca para estudiar un rato?

Inés ¿Por qué no lo dejamos para esta tarde? Iba a ayudar a Gloria ahora con su tarea de álgebra. Te veré en la biblioteca a las cinco, ¿está bien?

Rubén De acuerdo, nos vemos a las cinco.

____ **21.** Rubén piensa que tiene ___.
a. un horario pesado **b.** tarea de álgebra **c.** una clase de literatura

____ **22.** Inés no está de acuerdo con Rubén porque ella tiene ___.
a. más tarea que Rubén **b.** una fiesta **c.** las mismas clases

____ **23.** Rubén tiene la clase de ___ por la tarde.
a. literatura **b.** álgebra **c.** ciencias sociales

____ **24.** El profesor de Rubén insiste en que ___.
a. tome otra clase **b.** estudie con alguien **c.** estudie solo

____ **25.** Inés recomienda que vayan a ___ a las cinco.
a. la clase de literatura **b.** la biblioteca **c.** la casa de Gloria

SCORE ____ /5

EXAMEN PARCIAL

Cultura

F Choose a term from the box that best matches its description below.

a. la norteña	**b.** el ceviche	**c.** el Baile de la Soldadesca
d. el mazapán	**e.** el congrí	

_____ **26.** Es un evento en el cual la gente se viste con ropa típica toledana y hay danzas folclóricas llamadas **animeros.**

_____ **27.** Según una leyenda, esta comida se hizo en un convento cuando la ciudad de Toledo estaba sitiada.

_____ **28.** Es un plato típico de Cuba que es una combinación de arroz y frijoles.

_____ **29.** Esta comida se hace con pescado crudo y una combinación de jugo de limón y otros ingredientes.

_____ **30.** Un género de música popular en México que tiene sus orígenes en las polkas de Europa.

SCORE ____ /10

Vocabulario

G Complete the following paragraph with the words from the box.

jugar al boliche	**discutimos**	**insulté**	**creído**	**la escultura**

Hace poco, mi novia rompió conmigo porque le dije que era una persona superficial. Es que a ella no le gustan las artes como (**31**) ________________ y la pintura, que a mí me gustan muchísimo. Siempre (**32**) ________________ los fines de semana porque nunca estamos de acuerdo en qué queremos hacer. Por ejemplo, yo quiero ver una obra de teatro, y ella quiere salir con sus amigas y (**33**) ________________. El fin de semana pasado la (**34**) ________________ con algo que le dije. Ella me dijo que soy muy (**35**) ________________ y no me ha hablado desde aquel día. Me gustaría admitir mi error y pedirle perdón.

SCORE ____ /5

EXAMEN PARCIAL

H Read Pedro's letter to Aracelis. Then read Aracelis' response and fill in the blanks with the correct form of the words from the box.

hacer las paces	**ofender**	**pedir perdón**	**cometer un error**	**la comunicación**
una buena idea	**grosero**	**resentida**	**dejar de hablarse**	**malentendido**

Querida Aracelis:

¡No sé qué hacer! Creo que ayer (**36**) ______________ a mi amiga Marta y ella (**37**) ______________. Quiero (**38**) ______________ con ella porque (**39**) ______________. Quiero decirle que fui muy (**40**) ______________ con ella y que no volverá a pasar. ¿Qué dices?

Querido Pedro:

Tienes razón, sería (**41**) ______________ admitir tu error. Tienes que hablar con ella. (**42**) ______________ es muy importante. Puede que ella esté (**43**) ______________ contigo ahora, pero si le (**44**) ______________, a ella se le olvidará el (**45**) ______________ que tuvieron. Si la quieres como amiga, seguirás este consejo.

SCORE ____ /5

I Disagree with these statements using expressions from **¡Exprésate!**

46. Yo creo que las mujeres no son muy buenas para el kárate.

____

47. A mi parecer, no hay igualdad entre los chicos y las chicas en los deportes.

____

48. Jugar al dominó es más peligroso que escalar.

____

49. Los hombres y las mujeres no deben competir juntos en las Olimpiadas.

____

50. Los hombres sólo saben jugar bien al fútbol.

____

SCORE ____ /5

EXAMEN PARCIAL

J One of your relatives is asking you about your future plans. He is also asking about family members and giving you news about others. Respond to each statement by giving or reacting to the latest news.

51. Dime, ¿qué piensas estudiar al terminar la escuela?

____

52. ¿Qué anda haciendo tu primo Enrique?

____

53. ¿Qué me cuentas de tu hermano?

____

54. Te juro que tu tía Alejandra dio a luz hace una semana.

____

55. Tu tío Ignacio se separó de su esposa hace poco tiempo.

____

SCORE ____ /5

Gramática

K Complete the following sentences with the correct word or phrase in parentheses.

56. Juan, ¿qué ____________ (les / te) parece esta estatua?

57. Pienso que es más grande que ____________ (ése / aquélla) que vimos ayer.

58. Mira este puente. Es ____________ (el más grande de / más grande que) la ciudad.

59. Y ____________ (aquélla / aquella) torre allá en el parque también es muy grande.

60. La arquitectura aquí es impresionante. ____________ (Ningún / Ninguna) ciudad es tan bonita como ésta.

SCORE ____ /5

Nombre ______________________ Clase ______________ Fecha ____________

EXAMEN PARCIAL

L Ángel has had a misunderstanding with his girlfriend and is telling his best friend Antonio what happened. Complete each sentence with the correct form of the verb in parentheses.

61. Yo que tú, ____________ (haré / haría) las paces con tu novia.

62. Créeme que quise hablar con ella ayer, pero no ____________ (podía / pude). También yo estoy herido.

63. Está muy resentida y no creo que ____________ (quiere / quiera) escucharme.

64. Creyó los chismes de sus amigas y dijo que yo le ____________ (había / haya) mentido.

65. Siento tanto que nosotros ____________ (hemos / hayamos) tenido este malentendido. Yo le estaba diciendo la verdad.

SCORE | /5

M Beatriz is describing her ideal friend. Read each sentence, and write the correct form of the **indicative** or the **subjunctive** of the verb in parentheses.

66. Busco un amigo que ____________ (ser) leal.

67. Pero no conozco a nadie que ____________ (tener) mucho en común conmigo.

68. ¿Conoces a alguien que ____________ (saber) guardar un secreto y que sea leal?

69. Creo que yo ____________ (conocer) a muchas personas en las que puedo confiar.

70. Es verdad que un buen amigo ____________ (ser) algo difícil de encontrar.

SCORE | /5

EXAMEN PARCIAL

N Combine the phrases to write sentences using the verb forms you have learned.

71. yo / ir a estudiar anoche / pero / dormirme

____

72. yo / estar en el colegio / cuando / ver a Héctor

____

73. cuando nosotros / llegar a clase / él buscar su tarea

____

74. Héctor y yo / hablar más de ahora en adelante

____

75. hacer cinco minutos / Héctor / encontrar su tarea

____

SCORE /5

Escribamos

O Write a paragraph describing what you and your family were like ten years ago. Where did you go on vacation and what did you do to amuse yourselves?

____

____

____

____

____

____

SCORE /10

P A friend wrote you about a problem he/she has with a friend and asks you for advice. Write your friend a short note with advice on how to solve the problem.

____

____

____

____

____

____

SCORE /5 TOTAL SCORE /100

Nombre ______________________ Clase ______________ Fecha ______________

Score Sheet: Examen parcial

Escuchemos

A

1. a b c d
2. a b c d
3. a b c d
4. a b c d

SCORE /8

B

5. a b
6. a b
7. a b
8. a b
9. a b
10. a b

SCORE /12

Leamos

C

11. a b
12. a b
13. a b
14. a b
15. a b

SCORE /5

D

16. a b c
17. a b c
18. a b c
19. a b c
20. a b c

SCORE /5

E

21. a b c
22. a b c
23. a b c
24. a b c
25. a b c

SCORE /5

Cultura

F

26. a b c d e
27. a b c d e
28. a b c d e
29. a b c d e
30. a b c d e

SCORE /10

Vocabulario

G

31. ______________
32. ______________
33. ______________
34. ______________
35. ______________

SCORE /5

H

36. ______________
37. ______________
38. ______________
39. ______________
40. ______________
41. ______________
42. ______________
43. ______________
44. ______________
45. ______________

SCORE /5

Nombre ______________________ Clase ______________ Fecha ______________

SCORE SHEET: EXAMEN PARCIAL

Vocabulario

I

46. ______________________

47. ______________________

48. ______________________

49. ______________________

50. ______________________

SCORE ___ /5

J

51. ______________________

52. ______________________

53. ______________________

54. ______________________

55. ______________________

SCORE ___ /5

Gramática

K

56. ______________
57. ______________
58. ______________
59. ______________
60. ______________

SCORE ___ /5

L

61. ______________
62. ______________
63. ______________
64. ______________
65. ______________

SCORE ___ /5

M

66. ______________
67. ______________
68. ______________
69. ______________
70. ______________

SCORE ___ /5

N

71. ______________________________________
72. ______________________________________
73. ______________________________________
74. ______________________________________
75. ______________________________________

SCORE ___ /5

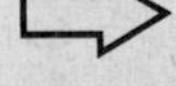

Nombre ______________________ Clase ______________ Fecha ____________

SCORE SHEET: EXAMEN PARCIAL

Escribamos

O

SCORE /10

P

SCORE /5

TOTAL SCORE /100

Answer Key: Examen parcial

Escuchemos

A

1. a b (c) d
2. a (b) c d
3. a b c (d)
4. (a) b c d

SCORE /8

B

5. a (b)
6. a (b)
7. (a) b
8. (a) b
9. (a) b
10. a (b)

SCORE /12

Leamos

C

11. a (b)
12. (a) b
13. (a) b
14. a (b)
15. (a) b

SCORE /5

D

16. a b (c)
17. a (b) c
18. (a) b c
19. a (b) c
20. a (b) c

SCORE /5

E

21. (a) b c
22. a b (c)
23. a b (c)
24. a (b) c
25. a (b) c

SCORE /5

Cultura

F

26. a b (c) d e
27. a b c (d) e
28. a b c d (e)
29. a (b) c d e
30. (a) b c d e

SCORE /10

Vocabulario

G

31. la escultura
32. discutimos
33. jugar al boliche
34. insulté
35. creído

SCORE /5

H

36. ofendí
37. dejó de hablarme
38. hacer las paces
39. cometí un error
40. grosero
41. una buena idea
42. La comunicación
43. resentida
44. pides perdón
45. malentendido

SCORE /5

Vocabulario

I Answers will vary.

46. ¡Qué va! Eso no es cierto. Hay muchas mujeres que hacen kárate.
47. ¡Al contrario! No estoy de acuerdo.
48. Eso no es cierto. Jugar al dominó es más seguro.
49. No me parece justo que los hombres y las mujeres no compitan juntos.
50. Yo que tú, no diría eso en público.

SCORE /5

J Answers will vary.

51. Pienso estudiar ingeniería.
52. Fíjate que ha cambiado de colegio.
53. Según tengo entendido, se comprometió con su novia.
54. ¡No me digas! / No me lo puedo creer.
55. Qué pena que se hayan separado.

SCORE /5

Gramática

K

56. te
57. aquélla
58. el más grande de
59. aquella
60. Ninguna

SCORE /5

L

61. haría
62. pude
63. quiera
64. había
65. hayamos

SCORE /5

M

66. sea
67. tenga
68. sepa
69. conozco
70. es

SCORE /5

N Answers will vary.

71. Yo iba a estudiar anoche, pero me dormí.
72. Yo estaba en el colegio cuando vi a Héctor.
73. Cuando nosotros llegamos a clase, él estaba buscando su tarea.
74. Héctor y yo hablaremos más de ahora en adelante.
75. Hace cinco minutos Héctor encontró su tarea.

SCORE /5

Escribamos

O

Answers will vary. Answers should include: imperfect (Nos gustaba..., Íbamos a..., Viajábamos a..., Lo pasábamos de película/de maravilla, Lo/La encontrábamos muy interesante), Talking about what you liked and used to do (De niño(a), me gustaba..., Cuando tenía 10 años me encantaba..., Siempre disfrutábamos de..., De pequeño, me lo pasaba bomba..., Lo encontrábamos genial...), ir a + infinitive in the imperfect (íbamos a esquiar todos los veranos, solíamos hacer...), Comparisons, demonstrative adjectives and pronouns (Disfrutábamos más que nadie..., Teníamos más planes que..., Esos veranos eran los mejores...),To express happiness (Estábamos entusiasmados porque...) and vocabulary (mi cuñada, mi hermanastro, la reunión familiar, dar una caminata, pasear, las montañas, montar a caballo...)

SCORE /10

P

Answers will vary. Answers should include: vocabulary: atento(a), confiar en, grosero(a), maleducado(a), resolver problemas, contar con, mentir, querer, leal, terco(a), chismoso(a), hacer las paces, tener celos de, respetar sentimientos, guardar un secreto, inseguro(a), confiable, leal / poco leal, romper con, ¿Has pensado en…?, (No) te conviene…, Te aconsejo que…, Sería una buena idea…, Te recomiendo que…, No te olvides de…, Sugiero que…, Date tiempo para pensarlo.

SCORE /5 TOTAL SCORE /100

Escuchemos

A Listen to the following conversations. Then, match the letter of the image to the conversation that you hear.

1. —Lo siento mucho, Daniela. No quise ofenderte. ¿Me perdonas?
   —Ya no aguanto más. Me has ofendido muchas veces. No te perdonaré.
2. —Elena, mira la catedral. Es muy bonita.
   —Sí, la arquitectura es impresionante. Esta catedral es más antigua que aquélla que vimos en Santo Domingo. ¿Me puedes sacar una foto enfrente de la catedral?
3. —No puedo creer que Rodolfo me haya dejado plantada otra vez. ¡Esto es el colmo! Un buen amigo no hace cosas así.
   —No creo que lo haya hecho a propósito. Tú sabes que Rodolfo no tiene fama de llegar a tiempo a las citas.
4. —¿Qué hiciste ayer?
   —Salí con mis amigos y ¡jugamos al fútbol todo el día! Lo pasé de película.

B Listen to Joaquín and Clara talk about what they did during the summer break. Then, read the statements below and choose **a**) for **cierto** or **b**) for **falso.**

Joaquín Hola, Clara, ¿cómo estás?

Clara Bien, Joaquín, gracias. Acabo de regresar de vacaciones.

Joaquín ¿Qué tal lo pasaste?

Clara Lo pasé de película. Fui a la costa con mi familia y me divertí mucho en la playa. Coleccioné caracoles, di caminatas por la playa, hice windsurfing, monté a caballo por primera vez, en fin, hice muchas cosas que no he podido hacer aquí.

Joaquín ¡Qué bien! Si pudiera hacer windsurfing, me iría ahora mismo a la playa.

Clara Y tú, Joaquín, ¿qué hiciste este verano?

Joaquín Pues, yo pensaba hacer muchas cosas, pero no pude hacer todo. Fui a las montañas a escalar con mis amigos. También la pasé montando mi bicicleta y tomando clases de esgrima. Oye, Clara, tú eres muy buena para el patinaje en línea, ¿verdad?

Clara Sí, me la paso patinando. ¡Es genial! Hablando del patinaje en línea, ¿te interesa intentarlo? Yo te enseñaré.

Joaquín De acuerdo. Gracias, Clara.

Nombre _______________ Clase _______________ Fecha _______________

CAPÍTULO 6

¡Ponte al día!

EXAMEN

Escuchemos

A Listen to the statements. In the blank, write **a**) if the speaker expresses **certainty,** or **b**) if the speaker expresses **doubt.**

1. ____

2. ____

3. ____

4. ____

SCORE /8

B Listen to the following statements. Match the letter of the image to the statement that you hear.

a.

b.

c.

d.

5. ____

6. ____

7. ____

8. ____

SCORE /8

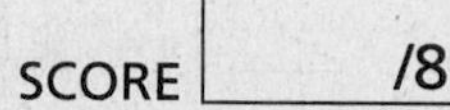

EXAMEN

Leamos

C Read the President's interview. Then, read the statements and choose **a)** for **cierto** or **b)** for **falso.**

Reportero Señor Presidente, ¿le parece que hay una crisis ambiental?

Presidente Es evidente que hay una crisis ambiental y que podemos hacer algo para mejorar la situación. Por ejemplo, todos podemos reciclar.

Reportero ¿Es cierto que la economía está decayendo?

Presidente No, no es cierto. Ayer los expertos afirmaron que está mejorando.

Reportero Finalmente, ¿qué opina de las noticias con enfoque mundial?

Presidente Son importantísimas. Por eso, estoy bien informado.

____ **9.** El presidente duda que el reciclaje mejore la crisis ambiental.

____ **10.** El presidente cree que la economía está decayendo.

____ **11.** Los expertos declararon que la economía está mejorando.

____ **12.** El presidente está bien informado sobre las noticias con enfoque mundial.

SCORE ____ /8

D Read the conversation. Then, read the statements and choose **a)** for **cierto** or **b)** for **falso.**

Gilberto Pásame los anuncios clasificados. Quiero buscar un trabajo.

Raquel Es dudoso que encuentres trabajo. Anoche, hubo un reportaje sobre la economía, y anunciaron que el desempleo está aumentando.

Mamá Ese reportero siempre pasa por alto muchos detalles importantes.

Gilberto Bueno, yo leí otra perspectiva sobre este tema.

Raquel Todo el mundo sabe que no lees el periódico. ¿Dónde leíste eso?

Gilberto Leo las noticias en línea. Sin duda alguna, los informes por Internet son detallados y tratan los temas a fondo.

____ **13.** Gilberto busca un trabajo en los anuncios clasificados.

____ **14.** Anoche, Raquel vio un reportaje sobre la economía.

____ **15.** Mamá está convencida de que el reportero es fiable.

____ **16.** A Gilberto le parece que las noticias en línea son informativas.

SCORE ____ /8

Nombre ______________________ Clase ______________ Fecha ____________

CAPÍTULO 6

EXAMEN

Cultura

E Choose the letter of the word that best completes each of the following sentences.

a. Univisión	**b.** México	**c.** The Latin America Data Base	**d.** Estados Unidos

____ **17.** Los primeros programas en español transmitidos por EE.UU. provenían de ___.

____ **18.** Los boletines de noticias en línea en Latinoamérica se conocen como ___.

____ **19.** ___ emite *A millón,* versión en español de *Who Wants to Be a Millionaire?*

____ **20.** Algunos canales adaptan programas en inglés de ___ y crean versiones españolas.

SCORE ____ /8

Vocabulario

F Choose the phrase that best completes each statement.

____ **21.** ___ hay una gran crisis ambiental.
a. Es evidente que **b.** Dudo que

____ **22.** No creo que Pablo ___ de la sección de moda.
a. está seguro **b.** sepa algo

____ **23.** En los editoriales puedo leer ___.
a. la sección de cocina **b.** comentarios controvertidos

____ **24.** Mis padres escuchan las noticias ___.
a. por la emisora **b.** en línea

____ **25.** El periodista reseña las nuevas películas en ___.
a. los titulares **b.** la sección de ocio

____ **26.** Los noticieros deben informar de modo ___.
a. parcial **b.** imparcial

____ **27.** El reportero es poco fiable porque ___ los detalles.
a. pasa por alto **b.** está al tanto de

____ **28.** Papá nunca tiene tiempo; por eso sólo lee ___.
a. los titulares **b.** los artículos

____ **29.** ___ los concursos de belleza sean tan populares.
a. Estás segura que **b.** Parece mentira que

____ **30.** Se anunció la muerte de la actriz en ___.
a. los obituarios **b.** la primera plana

SCORE ____ /5

EXAMEN

G Complete the following sentences with the words from the box.

alguno que otro	telenovelas	la locutora
está al tanto	nos suscribimos	

31. Lisa siempre ______________________ de las noticias con enfoque local, nacional y mundial.
32. Nora dice que ______________________ del Canal 6 no está bien informada.
33. Mucha gente ve ______________________ y opina sobre ellas.
34. Hace poco nosotros ______________________ al periódico. Siempre leemos artículos sobre arte y las tiras cómicas.
35. Anunciaron que la crisis sorprendió a todo el mundo, pero solamente alcancé a escuchar ______________________ detalle.

SCORE /5

H David and Nicolás have been assigned to follow the national news. Follow the instructions to create a conversation they had about the assignment.

36. Nicolás asks if David found out the results of the elections.

____

37. David says he doesn't understand a thing about politics.

____

38. Nicolás says he understands a little about politics, but nothing about financial news.

____

39. David says he doubts Nicolás is so poorly informed about the economy, as he passed the social science test.

____

40. Nicolás asks how David found out about the result of the test.

____

SCORE /10

EXAMEN

Gramática

I Complete each sentence with the correct word in parentheses.

41. No puedo lavar los platos porque se rompió __________ (los / el) lavaplatos.

42. Hay __________ (ningunas / algunas) recetas en la sección de cocina.

43. No podemos creer que __________ (nada / nadie) lea las noticias en línea.

44. __________ (El / La) periodista Camila Caraballo es de Perú.

SCORE /5

J Combine the phrases to form sentences using different forms of **haber.**

45. anoche / haber / varios documentales sobre la moda europea

____

46. haber / varios estudiantes sentados cuando entré al salón de clases

____

47. hoy en día / haber / mucha censura en la prensa

____

48. los científicos dudan que / haber / extraterrestres en la Luna

____

SCORE /5

K Write a sentence telling whether you believe each headline or not using an expression of certainty or doubt followed by the **subjunctive** or the **indicative.**

49. "Una mujer vio a Elvis Presley en un restaurante"

____

50. "Presidente ganó las elecciones por un solo voto"

____

51. "Concurso de belleza ofrece premio de un millón de dólares"

____

52. "La censura es buena para la prensa"

____

SCORE /10

EXAMEN

Escribamos

L Write a paragraph about some surprising news you learned recently on television or while surfing the Internet, for example a claim that an asteroid might strike the Earth. Tell where you got your information, and say whether you believe or doubt the story. Use expressions of certainty or doubt followed by the subjunctive or indicative where appropriate.

SCORE ____ /10

M Write a conversation between two people about a controversial topic, for example environmental policy or biotechnology. One of the participants is well-informed about the issue, the other one less so. They talk about what they understand and don't understand about the issue, and they discuss what newspaper or magazine they read to find out about the topic.

SCORE ____ /10

TOTAL SCORE ____ /100

Nombre ______________________ Clase ______________ Fecha ______________

CAPÍTULO 6

Score Sheet: Examen

Escuchemos

A

1. a b
2. a b
3. a b
4. a b

SCORE /8

B

5. a b c d
6. a b c d
7. a b c d
8. a b c d

SCORE /8

Leamos

C

9. a b
10. a b
11. a b
12. a b

SCORE /8

D

13. a b
14. a b
15. a b
16. a b

SCORE /8

Cultura

E

17. a b c d
18. a b c d
19. a b c d
20. a b c d

SCORE /8

Vocabulario

F

21. a b
22. a b
23. a b
24. a b
25. a b
26. a b
27. a b
28. a b
29. a b
30. a b

SCORE /5

G

31. ______________________
32. ______________________
33. ______________________
34. ______________________
35. ______________________

SCORE /5

H

36. ______________________
37. ______________________
38. ______________________
39. ______________________
40. ______________________

SCORE /10

Nombre ______________________ Clase ______________ Fecha ______________

CAPÍTULO 6

SCORE SHEET: EXAMEN

Gramática

I

41. ______________
42. ______________
43. ______________
44. ______________

SCORE /5

J

45. ______________________________
____
46. ______________________________
____
47. ______________________________
____
48. ______________________________
____

SCORE /5

K

49. ______________________________
50. ______________________________
51. ______________________________
52. ______________________________

SCORE /10

Escribamos

L

____
____
____
____

SCORE /10

M

____
____
____
____

SCORE /10

TOTAL SCORE /100

CAPÍTULO

Answer Key: Examen

Escuchemos

A

1. (a) b
2. (a) b
3. a (b)
4. a (b)

SCORE /8

B

5. a b (c) d
6. a b c (d)
7. a (b) c d
8. (a) b c d

SCORE /8

Leamos

C

9. a (b)
10. a (b)
11. (a) b
12. (a) b

SCORE /8

D

13. (a) b
14. (a) b
15. a (b)
16. (a) b

SCORE /8

Cultura

E

17. a (b) c d
18. a b (c) d
19. (a) b c d
20. a b c (d)

SCORE /8

Vocabulario

F

21. (a) b
22. a (b)
23. a (b)
24. (a) b
25. a (b)
26. a (b)
27. (a) b
28. (a) b
29. a (b)
30. (a) b

SCORE /5

G

31. **está al tanto**
32. **la locutora**
33. **telenovelas**
34. **nos suscribimos**
35. **alguno que otro**

SCORE /5

H **Answers will vary.**

36. **¿Supiste los resultados de las elecciones?**
37. **No entiendo ni jota de política.**
38. **Entiendo algo de política, pero nada de las noticias financieras.**
39. **Dudo que estés tan mal informado sobre la economía, pues aprobaste el examen de ciencias sociales.**
40. **¿Cómo te enteraste del resultado del examen?**

SCORE /10

Gramática

I

41. el
42. algunas
43. nadie
44. La

SCORE /5

J

45. Anoche hubo varios documentales sobre la moda europea.
46. Había varios estudiantes sentados cuando entré al salón de clases.
47. Hoy en día hay mucha censura en la prensa.
48. Los científicos dudan que haya extraterrestres en la Luna.

SCORE /5

K Answers will vary.

49. No pienso que una mujer haya visto a Elvis Presley en un restaurante.
50. Estoy convencido(a) de que el presidente ganó las elecciones por un solo voto.
51. Es increíble que un concurso de belleza ofrezca un premio de un millón de dólares.
52. No creo que la censura sea buena para la prensa.

SCORE /10

Escribamos

L

Answers will vary. Answers should include: Vocabulary: electronic media (la radio, la televisión, Internet), estar al tanto de…, tratar un tema a fondo; Expressions of doubt, disbelief, or certainty: Dudo que…, Estoy convencido(a) de que…, No estoy seguro(a) de que…; Grammar: Indicative and subjunctive after expressions of certainty or doubt.

SCORE /10

M

Answers will vary. Answers should include: print media (el periódico, la sección de…, la prensa); Asking about information and explaining where you found it: Lo leí en…, Estaba en la primera plana., Talking about what you know and don't know: Entiendo algo de…, ¿Qué sé yo de…?; Grammar: Indefinite expressions.

SCORE /10

TOTAL SCORE /100

Escuchemos

A Listen to the statements. In the blank, write **a**) if the speaker expresses **certainty,** or **b**) if the speaker expresses **doubt.**

1. Estamos convencidos de que debemos cuidar el medio ambiente.

2. Todo el mundo sabe que los documentales son educativos.

3. No puedo creer que haya extraterrestres en el planeta Marte.

4. Es dudoso que Andrés esté al tanto de las noticias.

B Listen to the following statements. Match the letter of the image to the statement that you hear.

5. Me parece que el reportero del Canal 8 es poco fiable. Anunció esta mañana que iba a estar soleado, pero hace muchísimo frío.

6. Me gusta estar al tanto de las noticias sobre la economía mundial y la política.

7. ¡Qué lástima! Me enteré en los obituarios de que doña Lola se murió hace poco tiempo.

8. No puedo creer que estés informado de las noticias porque te la pasas viendo telenovelas todo el día.

¡Ponte al día!

Interview

A Respond to the following questions in Spanish.

1. ¿Qué medio de comunicación te gusta más para enterarte de las noticias?
2. ¿Crees que los noticieros de la televisión son fiables?
3. ¿Disfrutas leyendo las noticias en línea? ¿Por qué?
4. ¿Cuál de los medios de comunicación te inspira más confianza? ¿Por qué?
5. ¿Qué programas de televisión te gustan más: los concursos, las telenovelas, las entrevistas? Explica.

Role-Play

B Take turns acting out the following situation.

Imagine that you are a reporter giving the news for a popular television station. Introduce yourself to the class and present your top stories. Inform the class about at least three different news stories. The news stories you present can be imaginary.

SPEAKING RUBRIC

COMPREHENSION (ability to understand verbal cues and respond appropriately)	(POOR)	1	2	3	4	(EXCELLENT)
COMPREHENSIBILITY (ability to communicate ideas and be understood)	(POOR)	1	2	3	4	(EXCELLENT)
ACCURACY (ability to use structures and vocabulary correctly)	(POOR)	1	2	3	4	(EXCELLENT)
FLUENCY (ability to communicate clearly and smoothly)	(POOR)	1	2	3	4	(EXCELLENT)
EFFORT (inclusion of details beyond the minimum requirements)	(POOR)	1	2	3	4	(EXCELLENT)

Mis aspiraciones

Escuchemos

A Listen to the statements. In the blank, write **a)** for **pasado, b)** for **futuro,** or **c)** for **habitual.**

1. _____

2. _____

3. _____

4. _____

SCORE /8

B Listen to the conversations, and match the letter of the image to the conversation that you hear.

a.

b.

c.

d.

5. _____ **7.** _____

6. _____ **8.** _____

SCORE /8

EXAMEN

Leamos

C Read the essay and the statements below, and choose **a**) for **cierto** or **b**) for **falso.**

Me crié en un pueblo pequeño de Alabama. La vida era muy tranquila. El año pasado, todo cambió. Mi papá perdió su trabajo, por eso nos mudamos a Atlanta, una ciudad grandísima. Me costó trabajo asimilar el estilo de vida de la ciudad. Además, tuve que enfrentar muchos obstáculos porque no conocía a nadie en Atlanta. Los estudiantes de mi nuevo colegio me discriminaban porque venía del campo. Poco a poco me acostumbré a la vida rápida de la ciudad. Es verdad que extraño poder montar a caballo, pero sé que algún día lo volveré a hacer. Cuando sea mayor, me gustaría vivir en el campo de nuevo.

____ **9.** El narrador se crió en una ciudad grandísima.

____ **10.** Para el narrador fue fácil adaptarse a la ciudad.

____ **11.** El narrador cree que el estilo de vida de la ciudad es rápido.

____ **12.** El narrador sueña con vivir en el campo otra vez.

SCORE ____ /8

D Read the conversation and choose the best answer for the questions that follow.

Mercedes Pascual, lo que debes hacer es prestar atención en clase. A menos de que te enfoques en los estudios, no vas a graduarte.

Pascual Todo el mundo dice que debo empeñarme por sacar buenas notas, pero yo no tengo planes de ir a la universidad.

Mercedes Entonces, ¿qué aspiraciones tienes para el futuro?

Pascual Sueño con ser un agente del FBI.

Mercedes Para ser agente se necesita un diploma. Debes ir a la universidad.

Pascual No sabía que era necesario. Después de que nos graduemos, iré a la universidad. Ahora, ¿me ayudas con la tarea?

____ **13.** ¿Qué quiere Pascual que haga Mercedes?
a. que le ayude con la tarea **b.** que vaya a la universidad

____ **14.** ¿Que pasará a menos de que Pascual se enfoque en sus estudios?
a. Llegará a ser agente. **b.** No se va a graduar.

____ **15.** ¿Por qué debe ir Pascual a la universidad?
a. Él necesita más tarea. **b.** Él necesita un diploma.

____ **16.** ¿Qué hará Pascual en cuanto se gradúe?
a. Irá a la universidad. **b.** Estudiará para el examen del FBI.

SCORE ____ /8

Geocultura

E Choose the word or phrase that best completes each statement about **los Andes.**

____ **17.** Al español de los Andes que ha incorporado indigenismos lo llaman ____.
- **a.** español de la cordillera
- **b.** español andino
- **c.** español indigenista

____ **18.** Otavalo es un pueblo andino de Ecuador famoso por ____.
- **a.** tener un mercado de artesanías
- **b.** no hablar quechua
- **c.** no mantener sus costumbres

____ **19.** Los Uros son ____.
- **a.** un grupo de 40 islas del Lago Titicaca
- **b.** los habitantes indígenas de las islas del Lago Titicaca
- **c.** un grupo de 40 islas y sus habitantes indígenas

____ **20.** Los incas se destacaron por sus logros en ____.
- **a.** arquitectura e ingeniería
- **b.** agricultura, arquitectura e ingeniería
- **c.** agricultura y arquitectura

SCORE ____ /8

Vocabulario

F Choose the word or phrase that best completes each statement.

____ **21.** Tuvimos que hacer un gran ____ para mantener nuestras raíces.
a. objetivo **b.** esfuerzo **c.** origen

____ **22.** Debemos ____ a nuestros antepasados por la tradición.
a. estar agradecidos **b.** aprovechar **c.** expresarnos

____ **23.** Cuando sea mayor, me gustaría ____ médico.
a. acostumbrarme **b.** establecerme **c.** llegar a ser

____ **24.** ____ en la vida se debe a saber aprovechar buenas oportunidades.
a. El grupo étnico **b.** El éxito **c.** El compromiso

____ **25.** Para mí es ____ ser cubano.
a. un orgullo **b.** un sacrificio **c.** una costumbre

SCORE ____ /5

G Choose the word or phrase that does not belong.

____ **26.** **a.** seguir adelante **b.** deberse a **c.** empeñarse en

____ **27.** **a.** encajar en **b.** asimilar **c.** modo de ser

____ **28.** **a.** mantener **b.** contribuir **c.** aporte

____ **29.** **a.** triunfar **b.** soñar con **c.** tener éxito

____ **30.** **a.** esforzarse **b.** luchar **c.** discriminar

SCORE ____ /5

H Complete the interview with the words or phrases from the box.

aspiraciones	**alcanzar**	**tengo la intención de**	**me enfoco**	**ascendencia**
antes de que	**me crié**	**costó trabajo**	**en cuanto**	**enfrentaron**

Penélope ¿Cuál es tu herencia cultural?

Ken Yun Soy de (**31**) ________________ china, pero (**32**) ________________ en Estados Unidos.

Penélope ¿Tus padres (**33**) ________________ algunos obstáculos cuando llegaron a este país?

Ken Yun Sí, les (**34**) ________________ aprender inglés porque algunos sonidos en inglés no se encuentran en el idioma chino.

Penélope ¿Qué (**35**) ________________ tienes para el futuro?

Ken Yun (**36**) ________________ cumpla los dieciocho años, iré a la universidad para estudiar psicología.

Penélope ¿Cómo podrás (**37**) ________________ tus metas?

Ken Yun Siempre trabajo duro y (**38**) ________________ en mis estudios; por lo tanto sé que lograré realizar mis sueños.

Penélope ¿Qué quieres hacer (**39**) ________________ empiecen las clases?

Ken Yun (**40**) ________________ viajar a China para visitar a mis abuelos.

SCORE ____ /10

Nombre ______________________ Clase ______________ Fecha ____________

EXAMEN

Gramática

I Complete the following sentences with **lo** or **lo que.**

41. ________ malo de mudarse a otro país es que se necesita asimilar un nuevo estilo de vida.

42. ________ tienes que hacer es esforzarte para que puedas alcanzar tus metas.

43. ¿Podemos hablar de ________ me contaste ayer?

44. ________ bueno de cumplir dieciocho años es que puedo graduarme del colegio.

45. ________ me gusta del trabajo es que gano dinero.

SCORE /5

J Complete the sentences with the preterite or imperfect.

46. El año pasado, yo ____________ (estar) en Costa Rica por dos semanas.

47. Alejandro ____________ (tener) que lavar los platos, pero no lo hizo.

48. Ester sabía que ____________ (poder) lograr sus sueños algún día.

49. Anabel ____________ (tener) malas noticias de su familia ayer.

50. De niña, mis primas ____________ (ser) mis compañeras preferidas.

SCORE /10

K Complete the sentences using the indicative or the subjunctive and your own ideas.

51. Mis padres me compraron un carro cuando...

____

52. Voy a visitar el museo de arte colonial antes que...

____

53. Quiero visitar un país hispanohablante a menos que...

____

54. Reservaré tres lugares en caso de que ustedes...

____

55. Leo el periódico por las mañanas en cuanto...

____

SCORE /5

EXAMEN

Escribamos

L Write an essay about your cultural heritage. Explain where your ancestors are from, what challenges they have had to face, and any customs or traditions you have learned from your parents or grandparents.

SCORE /10

M Write an essay about your accomplishments so far and your future goals. Explain what you want to achieve, what you will have to do, and whose support you will need.

SCORE /10

TOTAL SCORE /100

Nombre ______________________ Clase ______________ Fecha ______________

CAPÍTULO 7

Score Sheet: Examen

Escuchemos

A

1. a b c
2. a b c
3. a b c
4. a b c

SCORE /8

B

5. a b c d
6. a b c d
7. a b c d
8. a b c d

SCORE /8

Leamos

C

9. a b
10. a b
11. a b
12. a b

SCORE /8

D

13. a b
14. a b
15. a b
16. a b

SCORE /8

Cultura

E

17. a b c
18. a b c
19. a b c
20. a b c

SCORE /8

Vocabulario

F

21. a b c
22. a b c
23. a b c
24. a b c
25. a b c

SCORE /5

G

26. a b c
27. a b c
28. a b c
29. a b c
30. a b c

SCORE /5

H

31. ______________________
32. ______________________
33. ______________________
34. ______________________
35. ______________________
36. ______________________
37. ______________________
38. ______________________
39. ______________________
40. ______________________

SCORE /10

SCORE SHEET: EXAMEN

Gramática

I

41. ______________
42. ______________
43. ______________
44. ______________
45. ______________

SCORE /5

J

46. ______________
47. ______________
48. ______________
49. ______________
50. ______________

SCORE /10

K

51. ______________
52. ______________
53. ______________
54. ______________
55. ______________

SCORE /5

Escribamos

L

____

____

____

____

____

SCORE /10

M

____

____

____

____

____

SCORE /10

TOTAL SCORE /100

CAPÍTULO 7

Answer Key: Examen

Escuchemos

A

1. a (b) c
2. a b (c)
3. (a) b c
4. a (b) c

SCORE /8

B

5. a (b) c d
6. a b c (d)
7. (a) b c d
8. a b (c) d

SCORE /8

Leamos

C

9. a (b)
10. a (b)
11. (a) b
12. (a) b

SCORE /8

D

13. (a) b
14. a (b)
15. a (b)
16. (a) b

SCORE /8

Cultura

E

17. a (b) c
18. (a) b c
19. a b (c)
20. a (b) c

SCORE /8

Vocabulario

F

21. a (b) c
22. (a) b c
23. a b (c)
24. a (b) c
25. (a) b c

SCORE /5

G

26. a (b) c
27. a b (c)
28. (a) b c
29. a (b) c
30. a b (c)

SCORE /5

H

31. ascendencia
32. me crié
33. enfrentaron
34. costó trabajo
35. aspiraciones
36. En cuanto
37. alcanzar
38. me enfoco
39. antes de que
40. Tengo la intención de

SCORE /10

Gramática

I

41. Lo
42. Lo que
43. lo que
44. Lo
45. Lo que

SCORE /5

J

46. estuve
47. tenía
48. podía
49. tuvo
50. fueron

SCORE /10

K Answers will vary. Possible answers:

51. conseguí trabajo a medio tiempo en un restaurante.
52. termine la exhibición de arte indígena.
53. cueste demasiado dinero.
54. puedan ir conmigo.
55. termino el desayuno.

SCORE /5

Escribamos

L

Answers will vary. Answers should include: vocabulario (mis antepasados..., soy de ascendencia...); grammatical reflexives (se mudaron, me crié), preterite (tuvieron que...), imperfect (sabían que podían...), indicative with habitual or past actions (cuando llegaron, no hablaban inglés...), expressions with lo + adjective, and lo que

SCORE /10

M

Answers will vary. Answers should include: vocabulario (metas, aspiraciones, apoyo), grammatical reflexives (graduarme, esforzarme), subjunctive with future actions (Estudiaré hasta que me gradúe.), subjunctive with adverbial conjunctions (A menos de que me esfuerce por mis objetivos, no lograré mis metas.)

SCORE /10

TOTAL SCORE /100

Escuchemos

A. Listen to the statements. In the blank, write **a)** for **pasado, b)** for **futuro,** or **c)** for **habitual.**

1. Tendrás que estudiar mucho para que puedas lograr tu sueño de ser profesora. Si no apruebas los exámenes del estado, no te darán el puesto en ningún colegio.

2. Tan pronto como llego de clases, hago la tarea. Me gusta tener las noches libres para ver televisión.

3. Cuando nos mudamos a esta ciudad, nos costó trabajo acostumbrarnos al clima.

4. A menos de que haya una tormenta, irás al colegio. No te aceptaré ninguna excusa ya que mañana tienes el examen de biología.

B. Listen to the conversations, and match the letter of the image to the conversation that you hear.

5. Josefina ¿Cuál es el sueño de tu vida?
Allan Sueño con ser un jugador de béisbol. Creo que lo lograré si sigo practicando.

6. Eva ¿Qué quieres hacer antes de que empiecen las clases?
Sonia Quisiera ir a la playa. ¿Me acompañas?

7. Alfredo ¿Cómo te fue cuando llegaste por primera vez a esta ciudad?
Carolina Al principio no encajaba en ningún grupo, pero ahora tengo muchos amigos.

8. Sebastián Dime, ¿cómo lograste graduarte de la universidad?
Daisy Mi éxito en la universidad se debe al esfuerzo y al trabajo duro.

Nombre ______________________ Clase ______________ Fecha ____________

Mis aspiraciones

EXAMEN ORAL

Interview

A Respond to the following questions in Spanish.

1. ¿A qué grupo étnico pertenecen tus padres y cuál es su país de origen? Explica dónde se encuentra.
2. ¿Qué desafíos enfrentaron tus antepasados cuando llegaron a Estados Unidos?
3. ¿Te ha sido difícil adaptarte a un nuevo país? ¿Por qué?
4. ¿Cuáles son tus aspiraciones para el futuro? Explica.
5. ¿Qué cualidades crees que son necesarias para triunfar en la vida?

Role-Play

B Act out the following situation with a partner.

Imagine that you are a young child who immigrated from a foreign country to the United States. Tell your partner your name, country of origin, how you felt when you first arrived, how your life has changed since then, and what your ambitions for the future are. Then switch roles.

SPEAKING RUBRIC

COMPREHENSION (ability to understand verbal cues and respond appropriately)	(POOR)	1	2	3	4	(EXCELLENT)
COMPREHENSIBILITY (ability to communicate ideas and be understood)	(POOR)	1	2	3	4	(EXCELLENT)
ACCURACY (ability to use structures and vocabulary correctly)	(POOR)	1	2	3	4	(EXCELLENT)
FLUENCY (ability to communicate clearly and smoothly)	(POOR)	1	2	3	4	(EXCELLENT)
EFFORT (inclusion of details beyond the minimum requirements)	(POOR)	1	2	3	4	(EXCELLENT)

CAPÍTULO **8** EXAMEN

¿A qué te dedicas?

Escuchemos

A Listen to the speakers. Then, complete the following statements based on their answers.

_____ **1.** Si algún día ganara la lotería, ____ .

a. donaría su tiempo y dinero **b.** no trabajaría jamás

_____ **2.** Susana ____ porque no sabe utilizar su agenda electrónica.

a. no tiene talento **b.** está frustrada

_____ **3.** Daniel le adjuntó ____ a la carta de solicitud.

a. un sobre grande **b.** su currículum vitae

_____ **4.** La vida con un robot sería estupenda porque ____ .

a. el robot le facilitaría todo el trabajo **b.** el robot sería competente

SCORE ____ /8

B Listen to the statements and match the letter of the image to the statement that you hear.

a.

b.

c.

d.

5. _____ **7.** _____

6. _____ **8.** _____

SCORE ____ /8

Leamos

C Read the news article. Then, read the statements that follow and choose **a)** for **cierto** or **b)** for **falso.**

La tecnología: Una amenaza al mundo

Enfrentamos una amenaza constante del lugar menos pensado. Declaro que la tecnología nos está destruyendo. Sólo se necesita ver los accidentes causados por el uso de los teléfonos celulares. Por otro lado, una epidemia de obesidad está afectando a gente de todas las edades. Esto se debe a la inactividad causada por el uso de los videojuegos, las computadoras y la televisión. Estoy seguro de que si no existiera esta tecnología, los niños preferirían montar en bicicleta en vez de ver televisión. Al mismo tiempo, los padres en todas partes están perdiendo la batalla contra los medios de comunicación que transmiten material que no es apropiado para niños. En fin, debemos examinar el uso de los adelantos tecnológicos en nuestra vida diaria. Está claro que si se eliminara la tecnología dañina *(harmful)*, viviríamos en un mundo más seguro.

____ **9.** El autor afirma que la tecnología nos amenaza en la vida diaria.

____ **10.** Los teléfonos celulares no causan ningún daño.

____ **11.** Una desventaja de los adelantos tecnológicos es la facilidad con que los niños pueden obtener material que no es apropiado para su edad.

____ **12.** El autor declara que aunque elimináramos la tecnología dañina, el mundo no sería más seguro.

SCORE ____ /8

D Read Julia's essay about her dream job and the statements that follow. In the blanks, write **a)** for **lo haría** or **b)** for **no lo haría.**

Siempre he sido aficionada a los deportes. De pequeña mi papá y yo veíamos partidos por televisión y jugábamos en el parque. Aunque tengo habilidades para toda clase de deportes, no sueño con ser atleta. El sueño de mi vida es encontrar empleo como reportera. Así, iría gratis a todos los partidos, entrevistaría a mis atletas favoritos y viajaría por todo el país. Además, ganaría mucho dinero y tendría tiempo libre. Si mi canal favorito me ofreciera el puesto de reportera deportiva, lo aceptaría en un santiamén.

____ **13.** A Julia le gustaría ser jugadora para su equipo de béisbol favorito.

____ **14.** Si tuviera la oportunidad, Julia sería reportera de deportes.

____ **15.** Con su empleo ideal, Julia entrevistaría a sus actores favoritos.

____ **16.** Si le ofrecieran el puesto de reportera, Julia lo aceptaría.

SCORE ____ /8

EXAMEN

Cultura

E Choose the word or phrase that best completes each statement.

____ **17.** El precio de acceso a Internet en Perú ___.

a. ha subido desde hace dos años
b. ha bajado en los últimos años

____ **18.** El gobierno peruano está tratando de ___.

a. invertir en la red de carreteras del Estado
b. mejorar el sistema de telecomunicaciones

____ **19.** En Latinoamérica, al graduarte de la universidad ___.

a. el título que recibes se llama "licenciatura"
b. debes hacer un examen que se llama "licenciada"

____ **20.** Tradicionalmente en Latinoamérica y España, ___.

a. las horas de trabajo han sido de las ocho de la mañana a las cinco de la tarde
b. la gente volvía a casa a comer y dormir la "siesta" entre las dos y las cuatro

SCORE ____ /8

Vocabulario

F Fill in the blank with the word or phrase that best completes each statement.

____ **21.** Juan trabaja ___ . Dona su tiempo para ayudar a los niños discapacitados.

a. a tiempo completo **b.** de voluntario **c.** a medio tiempo

____ **22.** Una ventaja de ___ es que puedes organizar tus ideas en un tren o un avión y no necesitas papel.

a. la agenda electrónica **b.** el empleo **c.** un robot competente

____ **23.** ___ de la medicina, como la máquina de ultrasonido, mejoran la vida de mucha gente.

a. Los beneficios **b.** Las desventajas **c.** Los adelantos

____ **24.** Tengo que ___ mi currículum vitae antes de la entrevista.

a. adjuntar **b.** actualizar **c.** solicitar

____ **25.** Hay varios ___ para ser profesor(a). Uno es el título universitario.

a. salarios **b.** horarios **c.** requisitos

SCORE ____ /5 ⇨

EXAMEN

G Choose the word or phrase that does NOT belong.

		a.	b.	c.
____	**26.**	**a.** la fotocopiadora	**b.** el contestador automático	**c.** el puesto de trabajo
____	**27.**	**a.** el empleado	**b.** el gerente	**c.** el jefe
____	**28.**	**a.** no poder	**b.** ser capaz de	**c.** costar trabajo
____	**29.**	**a.** empeorar	**b.** facilitar	**c.** ventaja
____	**30.**	**a.** el seguro médico	**b.** los beneficios	**c.** la entrevista

SCORE /5

H Answer the following questions with words from **Vocabulario** and your opinion.

31. ¿Crees que los adelantos tecnológicos facilitan o empeoran la vida diaria? Explica.

____

____

32. ¿Hay algo que tratarías de cambiar del mundo? ¿Por qué o por qué no?

____

____

33. ¿Qué te gustaría estudiar? ¿Por qué?

____

____

34. ¿Hay algo que no logras entender de la vida moderna? Explica.

____

____

35. ¿Qué tienes que hacer para que tus sueños estén a tu alcance?

____

____

SCORE /10

EXAMEN

Gramática

I Decide if each statement is a) **pasado,** b) **presente,** or c) **hipotético.**

_____ **36.** Si me dieran el puesto, trabajaría duro para poder ganar dinero.

_____ **37.** Me gustan los niños, por eso trabajo en una guardería infantil.

_____ **38.** Mi hermano me aconsejó que terminara los estudios.

_____ **39.** A Esteban le gustaría que creáramos una empresa.

_____ **40.** Mi madre dirige el departamento de recursos humanos en la empresa.

SCORE _____ /5

J Complete the statements with the correct word or phrase from the box.

se dice que	**les resulta**	**tuviera**	**preferían que**	**se puso**

41. A mis padres ______________ bastante difícil utilizar la computadora.

42. ______________ en el futuro, los robots competentes facilitarán la vida diaria.

43. Luis ______________ triste cuando oyó la mala noticia.

44. Si Ana ______________ el dinero, ella viajaría a Otavalo.

45. Sus padres ______________ fuera abogado, pero Santos se hizo pintor.

SCORE _____ /5

K Combine the phrases to make sentences, using the **conditional** or the **past subjunctive** of the verbs provided.

46. si el director lo / aceptar / Alberto / irse / a estudiar a Harvard

____

47. a mis padres / resultar / fácil utilizar las nuevas tecnologías

____

48. Leticia / llegar a ser / buena pintora si / interesarle / el arte

____

49. Juan / decidirse a comprar / un teléfono celular si / tener dinero

____

50. a nosotros / molestar / tener / malos compañeros de trabajo

____

SCORE _____ /10 ⇨

EXAMEN

Escribamos

L Write a formal letter responding to a want ad. Explain what position you are interested in and your qualifications (you can make them up). The letter can be addressed to the teacher.

SCORE ____ /10

M Write an essay about your ideal work environment. Describe what your work hours, benefits, boss, and co-workers would be like, and what contributions you would make to a good work environment.

SCORE ____ /10

TOTAL SCORE ____ /100

Nombre ______________________ Clase ______________ Fecha ____________

CAPÍTULO 8

Score Sheet: Examen

Escuchemos

A

1. a b
2. a b
3. a b
4. a b

SCORE /8

B

5. a b c d
6. a b c d
7. a b c d
8. a b c d

SCORE /8

Leamos

C

9. a b
10. a b
11. a b
12. a b

SCORE /8

D

13. a b
14. a b
15. a b
16. a b

SCORE /8

Cultura

E

17. a b
18. a b
19. a b
20. a b

SCORE /8

Vocabulario

F

21. a b c
22. a b c
23. a b c
24. a b c
25. a b c

SCORE /5

G

26. a b c
27. a b c
28. a b c
29. a b c
30. a b c

SCORE /5

H

31. ____
32. ____
33. ____
34. ____
35. ____

SCORE /10

Nombre ______________ Clase ______________ Fecha ______________

CAPÍTULO **8**

SCORE SHEET: EXAMEN

Gramática

I

36. a b c
37. a b c
38. a b c
39. a b c
40. a b c

SCORE /5

J

41. ______________
42. ______________
43. ______________
44. ______________
45. ______________

SCORE /5

K

46. ______________
47. ______________
48. ______________
49. ______________
50. ______________

SCORE /10

Escribamos

L

SCORE /10

M

SCORE /10

TOTAL SCORE /100

CAPÍTULO **8**

Answer Key: Examen

Escuchemos

A

1. (a) b
2. a (b)
3. a (b)
4. (a) b

SCORE /8

B

5. a (b) c d
6. a b c (d)
7. a b (c) d
8. (a) b c d

SCORE /8

Leamos

C

9. (a) b
10. a (b)
11. (a) b
12. a (b)

SCORE /8

D

13. a (b)
14. (a) b
15. a (b)
16. (a) b

SCORE /8

Cultura

E

17. a (b)
18. a (b)
19. (a) b
20. a (b)

SCORE /8

Vocabulario

F

21. a (b) c
22. (a) b c
23. a b (c)
24. a (b) c
25. a b (c)

SCORE /5

G

26. a b (c)
27. (a) b c
28. a (b) c
29. (a) b c
30. a b (c)

SCORE /5

H Answers will vary. Possible answers:

31. Creo que los adelantos tecnológicos empeoran la vida diaria porque la gente se hace perezosa.
32. Si pudiera, trataría de bajar el costo de la medicina porque hay muchas familias que necesitan servicios médicos y no los pueden pagar.
33. Me gustaría estudiar psicología para niños porque me gusta trabajar con ellos.
34. No logro entender por qué no hay robots para prepararte una pizza o una hamburguesa cuando tienes hambre.
35. Para que mi sueño esté a mi alcance, tengo que buscar trabajo de voluntario que me permita participar en una exploración del océano.

SCORE /10 

Gramática

I

36. a b (c)
37. a (b) c
38. (a) b c
39. a b (c)
40. a (b) c

SCORE /5

J

41. les resulta
42. Se dice que
43. se puso
44. tuviera
45. preferían que

SCORE /5

K

46. Si el director lo aceptara, Alberto se iría a estudiar a Harvard.
47. A mis padres les resultaría fácil utilizar las nuevas tecnologías.
48. Leticia llegaría a ser una buena pintora si le interesara el arte.
49. Juan se decidiría a comprar un teléfono celular si tuviera dinero.
50. A nosotros nos molestaría tener malos compañeros de trabajo.

SCORE /10

Escribamos

L

Answers will vary. Answers should include: vocabulary (estimado, por medio de la presente...), conditional (trabajaría duro...), subjunctive with hypothetical statements (Si tuviera la oportunidad...), indirect object pronouns (le adjunto...)

SCORE /10

M

Answers will vary. Answers should include: vocabulary (beneficios, empleados...), conditional (haría todo lo posible por...), past subjunctive (preferiría que mi jefe...), past subjunctive with hypothetical statements (si pudiera..., facilitaría/mejoraría...), indirect object pronouns (les daría..., les conseguiría...)

SCORE /10

TOTAL SCORE /100

Escuchemos

A Listen to the speakers. Then, complete the following statements based on their answers.

1. —¿Qué harías si algún día ganaras la lotería?
—Si fuera rico, haría trabajo voluntario en África y donaría mucho dinero a varias causas.

2. —¿Por qué Susana está tan frustrada?
—A Susana le cuesta trabajo utilizar su agenda electrónica. Ella no tiene talento para la tecnología y se frustra rápidamente.

3. —¿Por qué necesitaba un sobre tan grande para la carta?
—Es que Daniel le adjuntó una copia de su currículum vitae a la carta de solicitud.

4. —¿Cómo sería tu vida diaria con un robot?
—¡Sería estupendo tener un robot! Un robot competente me facilitaría el trabajo, limpiaría la casa y cocinaría.

B Listen to the statements and match the letter of the image to the statement that you hear.

5. El trabajo de un hombre de negocios es bastante difícil. Hay mucho que hacer y las horas de trabajo son muy largas.

6. Si Ana tuviera dinero, iría a España. Siempre ha soñado con viajar a Madrid, ver el Palacio Real y conocer el museo del Prado.

7. Como auxiliar administrativa tengo que hacer varias cosas a la vez. Me gustaría tener un robot para que me facilitara el trabajo.

8. Me resulta fácil usar este programa. Siempre he tenido talento para las computadoras.

Nombre ______________________ Clase ____________ Fecha ____________

¿A qué te dedicas?

EXAMEN ORAL

Interview

A Respond to the following questions in Spanish.

1. ¿Crees que tienes talento especial para algún trabajo o actividad? Explica.
2. ¿A qué te gustaría dedicarte cuando empieces a trabajar? ¿Por qué?
3. ¿Crees que podrías dirigir una empresa? Explica.
4. ¿Te gustaría hacer trabajo voluntario en algún país pobre? ¿Por qué?
5. ¿Qué opinas de los robots? ¿Mejoran la vida moderna?

Role-Play

B Work with a partner and act out the following situation.

You are a job applicant at an interview. Introduce yourself and explain why you are there and what your skills and abilities are. Be creative; the job can be as outlandish as you like. There is something you just can't understand about the job, but you eventually get the idea. Say good-bye, and then switch roles.

SPEAKING RUBRIC

COMPREHENSION (ability to understand verbal cues and respond appropriately)	(POOR)	1	2	3	4	(EXCELLENT)
COMPREHENSIBILITY (ability to communicate ideas and be understood)	(POOR)	1	2	3	4	(EXCELLENT)
ACCURACY (ability to use structures and vocabulary correctly)	(POOR)	1	2	3	4	(EXCELLENT)
FLUENCY (ability to communicate clearly and smoothly)	(POOR)	1	2	3	4	(EXCELLENT)
EFFORT (inclusion of details beyond the minimum requirements)	(POOR)	1	2	3	4	(EXCELLENT)

Nombre ______________________ Clase ____________ Fecha ____________

CAPÍTULO 9

Huellas del pasado

EXAMEN

Escuchemos

A Listen to the following story. Read the statements below, and choose **a)** for **cierto** or **b)** for **falso.**

_____ **1.** La princesa se sentía muy sola.

_____ **2.** El hechicero le dio un líquido mágico que liberaría al príncipe encantado.

_____ **3.** La princesa podía regar cualquiera de las flores con el líquido mágico.

_____ **4.** La princesa no pudo encontrar al príncipe, y el jardín desapareció.

SCORE /8

B Listen to the following statements. Then, match the letter of the image to the statement that you hear.

a.

b.

c.

d.

5. _____ **7.** _____

6. _____ **8.** _____

SCORE /8

EXAMEN

Leamos

C Read the legend about the Russian alphabet. Then, read the statements that follow and choose **a**) for **cierto** or **b**) for **falso.**

Se cuenta que el día que se crearon los idiomas, un hechicero envió a un niño de cada país con una cesta a buscar las letras que habrían de componer el alfabeto de los diferentes idiomas. Los niños tenían que atravesar un bosque y, al regresar, ya con su cesta llena, el niño de Rusia se puso a jugar y se le cayó su cesta. Según nos dicen, cuando recogió las letras, éstas se le mezclaron con semillas y hojas secas de los árboles. Es por eso que desde entonces, el idioma ruso tiene un alfabeto tan diferente al alfabeto romano.

_____ **9.** Un hechicero envió a los niños a buscar las letras.

_____ **10.** Por el camino, los niños tenían que atravesar un lago.

_____ **11.** Los niños llevaban cestas para traer las letras.

_____ **12.** El niño de Rusia mezcló las letras con las cestas.

SCORE /8

D Read part of Patricio's essay about his country's struggle for independence. Then read the statements that follow, and choose **a**) for **cierto** or **b**) for **falso.**

En 1868, mi país comenzó la lucha de independencia contra el imperio que lo había controlado durante varias décadas. Después de muchas batallas sangrientas, nuestros soldados derrotaron al enemigo, y el país por fin ganó su libertad. El pueblo se regocijó con la victoria y desde entonces, los ciudadanos han honrado a sus héroes con un desfile cada año. También hay un gran monumento en el centro de la ciudad para conmemorar a todas las víctimas de la guerra, y después del desfile hay un momento de silencio. Todos están de acuerdo en que valieron la pena los sacrificios que hicieron estas personas, y es una buena manera de honrar su memoria.

_____ **13.** El imperio comenzó una lucha de independencia contra otro imperio.

_____ **14.** Los soldados vencieron a las tropas del imperio después de muchas batallas.

_____ **15.** El pueblo se regocijó porque el monumento fue muy hermoso.

_____ **16.** El monumento sólo honra a los soldados que murieron en la guerra.

SCORE /8

EXAMEN

Cultura

E Answer the following questions about **El Cono Sur.**

_____ **17.** ¿Cuáles son los colores de la bandera chilena?
a. blanco, azul y rojo **b.** amarillo, azul y rojo **c.** blanco, verde y rojo

_____ **18.** ¿Qué grupos indígenas existían en Argentina antes de la llegada de los europeos?
a. diaguita y guaraní **b.** inca y maya **c.** azteca y maya

_____ **19.** ¿Qué quiere decir la palabra **iguazú** en guaraní?
a. altas montañas **b.** verdes bosques **c.** grandes aguas

_____ **20.** ¿El gobierno de qué presidente fue derrotado por Augusto Pinochet en 1973?
a. Alberto Fujimori **b.** Salvador Allende **c.** Fidel Castro

SCORE /8

Vocabulario

F Read the definitions and choose a word from the box that best fits each one.

_____ **21.** Los ciudadanos se regocijaron cuando al final los dos países ___ la paz.
a. lamentaron **b.** acordaron **c.** traicionaron

_____ **22.** ___ quiere decir lo mismo que **en cuanto.**
a. Tan pronto como **b.** A partir de **c.** Hace tiempo que

_____ **23.** Lorenzo aceptará su ___ porque ya se ha arrepentido de haber sido tan malvado.
a. castigo **b.** traición **c.** poder

_____ **24.** Débora no podía creer lo que pasó; le pareció que todo había sido ___.
a. un hecho **b.** un sueño **c.** un campo desconocido

_____ **25.** Después de la revolución, el pueblo se decidió a honrar a ___.
a. los encantados **b.** los traidores **c.** las tropas

SCORE /5

Vocabulario

G Complete Paco and Ana's conversation with the words from the box.

soldados	bandera	esperanzas	víctimas	justicia
honra	declararon la guerra	sabios	victoria	héroes

Paco ¿Crees que las trece colonias tenían (**26**) ______________ de ganar su lucha por la independencia en 1776?

Ana Claro, por eso las colonias (**27**) ______________ contra Inglaterra. Y en 1787, después de la (**28**) ______________, los (**29**) ______________ del país formaron un congreso para crear la Constitución.

Paco ¿Hubo muchas (**30**) ______________ de las batallas?

Ana Sí, muchos se sacrificaron para lograr la (**31**) ______________ política.

Paco Pienso que los (**32**) ______________ fueron muy valientes.

Ana ¿Cómo se (**33**) ______________ la victoria hoy en día?

Paco Cada 4 de julio se conmemora a los (**34**) ______________ con desfiles y se celebra también la (**35**) ______________ tricolor que simboliza nuestro país.

SCORE /5

H Use an expression from **¡Exprésate!** to answer each question.

36. ¿Qué esperas de las manifestaciones en las calles?

____

37. ¿Qué hicieron las mujeres soldado después de que fueron liberadas?

____

38. ¿Qué hace el presidente al ver a las tropas de su país sufrir tanto?

____

39. ¿Qué le pasó al malvado del cuento?

____

40. ¿Qué se supo al final del cuento?

____

SCORE /10 

CAPÍTULO **9**

EXAMEN

Gramática

I Complete each sentence with **por** or **para.**

41. La tarea de matemáticas es ____________ mañana.

42. Los autos deportivos pueden ir a muchos kilómetros ____________ hora.

43. El templo fue diseñado ____________ un arquitecto famoso.

44. Tenemos que entrenar mucho ____________ correr en el maratón.

SCORE /4

J Complete the following sentences with the **preterite, imperfect,** or **past progressive** of the verbs in parentheses.

45. Mi hermano ____________ (estudiar) en el colegio cuando vio a su novia por primera vez.

46. Todas las mañanas, Andrea ____________ (correr) treinta minutos antes de ir a trabajar.

47. Hace muchos años, en el pueblo no ____________ (haber) cine ni teatro.

48. Cuando a Pablo le dijeron que había sido aceptado en la universidad, ____________ (empezar) a saltar de alegría.

SCORE /8

K Based on the cues provided, complete the following sentences using either the **present** or **past subjunctive.**

49. Me sorprende que ____

____

50. Nuestros profesores quieren que ______________________________________

____

51. Anoche nuestros padres nos pidieron que ________________________________

____

52. Ayer me sorprendió que ____

____

SCORE /8

EXAMEN

Escribamos

L Write a fairy tale or a myth that you know or invent your own. You can include a mysterious person, a princess, a prince, and other characters.

SCORE /10

M Imagine that you are the new president. You are going to be interviewed about what you expect for the future of your country. Write the questions you think you will be asked and answer them.

SCORE /10

TOTAL SCORE /100

Nombre ______________________ Clase ______________ Fecha ______________

CAPÍTULO 9

Score Sheet: Examen

Escuchemos

A

1. a b
2. a b
3. a b
4. a b

SCORE /8

B

5. a b c d
6. a b c d
7. a b c d
8. a b c d

SCORE /8

Leamos

C

9. a b
10. a b
11. a b
12. a b

SCORE /8

D

13. a b
14. a b
15. a b
16. a b

SCORE /8

Cultura

E

17. a b c
18. a b c
19. a b c
20. a b c

SCORE /8

Vocabulario

F

21. a b c d e
22. a b c d e
23. a b c d e
24. a b c d e
25. a b c d e

SCORE /5

G

26. ______________
27. ______________
28. ______________
29. ______________
30. ______________
31. ______________
32. ______________
33. ______________
34. ______________
35. ______________

SCORE /5

H

36. ______________________________
37. ______________________________
38. ______________________________
39. ______________________________
40. ______________________________

SCORE /10

Nombre ______________________ Clase ______________ Fecha ______________

CAPÍTULO 9

SCORE SHEET: EXAMEN

Gramática

I

41. ______________
42. ______________
43. ______________
44. ______________

SCORE /4

J

45. ______________
46. ______________
47. ______________
48. ______________

SCORE /8

K

49. ______________
50. ______________
51. ______________
52. ______________

SCORE /8

Escribamos

L

SCORE /10

M

SCORE /10

TOTAL SCORE /100

CAPÍTULO 9

Answer Key: Examen

Escuchemos

A

1. (a) b
2. (a) b
3. a (b)
4. a (b)

SCORE /8

B

5. a b (c) d
6. (a) b c d
7. a b c (d)
8. a (b) c d

SCORE /8

Leamos

C

9. (a) b
10. a (b)
11. (a) b
12. a (b)

SCORE /8

D

13. a (b)
14. (a) b
15. a (b)
16. a (b)

SCORE /8

Cultura

E

17. (a) b c
18. (a) b c
19. a b (c)
20. a (b) c

SCORE /8

Vocabulario

F

21. a (b) c d e
22. (a) b c d e
23. (a) b c d e
24. a (b) c d e
25. a b (c) d e

SCORE /5

G

26. esperanzas
27. declararon la guerra
28. victoria
29. sabios
30. víctimas
31. justicia
32. soldados
33. honra
34. héroes
35. bandera

SCORE /5

H Answers will vary. Possible answers:

36. Es de esperar que las manifestaciones no resulten en violencia.
37. Las mujeres soldado les agradecieron a sus libertadores.
38. El presidente se arrepiente de que las tropas hayan tenido que sufrir.
39. Según nos dicen, el malvado fue castigado por el rey.
40. Al final, nos dimos cuenta de que el sabio tenía razón.

SCORE /10

Gramática

I

41. para
42. por
43. por
44. para

SCORE /4

J

45. estudiaba / estaba estudiando
46. corría
47. había
48. empezó

SCORE /8

K Answers will vary. Possible answers:

49. Me sorprende que haya tanta gente pobre en nuestro país.
50. Nuestros profesores quieren que estudiemos más.
51. Anoche nuestros padres nos pidieron que llegáramos temprano de la fiesta.
52. Ayer me sorprendió que mi abuelo recordara todos los detalles del cuento.

SCORE /8

Escribamos

L

Answers will vary. Answers should include: vocabulary (cuento de hadas, leyenda, mito, príncipe, princesa, enamorarse, un sabio, poderes mágicos, fantasma, misterioso, desconocido), preterite and imperfect (Érase una vez..., Se cuenta que..., A causa de esto..., A partir de entonces, ..., Tan pronto como..., Al final, nos dimos cuenta de...), por and para (Pasó por el bosque..., Durmió por cien años..., Vino para el palacio...), sequence of tenses (El rey dijo que...)

SCORE /10

M

Answers will vary. Answers should include: vocabulary (justicia, libertad, tener esperanzas de, acordar la paz, arrepentirse de, es lamentable que..., declarar la guerra), use of subjunctive (Sugiero que..., Te recomiendo que..., Ojalá que..., Con tal de que..., En cuanto...), por and para (Para mí..., Estoy aquí para..., Haremos muchas cosas por la gente)

SCORE /10

TOTAL SCORE /100

Escuchemos

A Listen to the following story. Read the statements below, and choose **a**) for **cierto** or **b**) for **falso.**

Hace mucho tiempo en un país muy lejano, vivía una hermosa princesa. La joven se sentía muy sola y todas las mañanas salía a caminar por los jardines de su palacio. Un día, se encontró con un anciano misterioso. El anciano, que era un hechicero, le dijo que una de las flores de su jardín era un príncipe encantado. Entonces le dio un líquido mágico que ella debía usar para liberar al príncipe. Le advirtió que primero tenía que encontrar al príncipe, porque si regaba la flor equivocada con el líquido mágico, todo el jardín iba a desaparecer. La princesa buscó y buscó por el jardín. Finalmente, vio una flor muy triste; parecía que estaba llorando. La princesa regó la flor con cuidado y de repente, la flor se convirtió en un hermoso príncipe. El príncipe le dio las gracias por haberlo rescatado, y a partir de entonces, vivieron siempre felices.

B Listen to the following statements. Then, match the letter of the image to the statement that you hear.

5. Los aztecas tenían mitos para explicar fenómenos naturales como la creación de los volcanes Popocatépetl e Iztaccíhuatl.

6. Las civilizaciones antiguas construían templos para sus dioses.

7. No hay guerra que no tenga víctimas. Pero a veces, las guerras son necesarias.

8. El príncipe y la princesa se casaron y vivieron siempre felices.

Huellas del pasado

EXAMEN ORAL

Interview

A Respond to the following questions in Spanish.

1. ¿Qué trataban de explicar los pueblos antiguos con sus mitos?
2. Por lo general, ¿quiénes son y cómo son los personajes (*characters*) de los mitos? ¿de las leyendas?
3. ¿Tenías un cuento de hadas favorito cuando eras niño(a)? ¿Por qué? ¿Cómo querías que terminaran los cuentos que te contaban?
4. Compara el tratamiento de la realidad en las leyendas, los mitos y los cuentos de hadas.

Role-Play

B Act out one of the following situations with a partner. You can also act either one out by yourself.

1. Imagine that you and a classmate are soldiers. Take turns asking each other about the meaning and the consequences of different types of wars.
2. Take turns telling each other what you were like as a child. What did you use to do? Did you have a lifelong dream? Explain. Did you want the world to change or stay the same? Why?

SPEAKING RUBRIC

COMPREHENSION (ability to understand verbal cues and respond appropriately)	(POOR)	1	2	3	4	(EXCELLENT)
COMPREHENSIBILITY (ability to communicate ideas and be understood)	(POOR)	1	2	3	4	(EXCELLENT)
ACCURACY (ability to use structures and vocabulary correctly)	(POOR)	1	2	3	4	(EXCELLENT)
FLUENCY (ability to communicate clearly and smoothly)	(POOR)	1	2	3	4	(EXCELLENT)
EFFORT (inclusion of details beyond the minimum requirements)	(POOR)	1	2	3	4	(EXCELLENT)

El mundo en que vivimos

Escuchemos

A Listen to the following conversation between Raquel and Andrés. Read the statements below and choose **a)** for **cierto** or **b)** for **falso.**

____ **1.** Andrés va al colegio en autobús y no se preocupa por el medio ambiente.

____ **2.** Raquel piensa que Andrés quiere bajar de peso.

____ **3.** Raquel no ve una manera de mejorar la calidad del aire.

____ **4.** Andrés sabe que existen otras fuentes de energía.

SCORE ____ /8

B Listen to the following statements. Then, match the letter of the image to the statement that you hear.

a.

b.

c.

d.

5. ____ **7.** ____

6. ____ **8.** ____

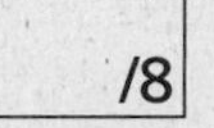
SCORE ____ /8

EXAMEN

Leamos

C Read the following interview of an exchange student from Germany. Then, read the statements that follow and choose **a**) for **cierto** or **b**) for **falso.**

Hans, ¿de dónde eres? ¿Qué hacías en tu tiempo libre? ¿Por qué decidiste venir a Estados Unidos?

Soy de Berlín. En mi tiempo libre, me reunía con un grupo de amigos a quienes les preocupaba el medio ambiente. Teníamos un club de reciclaje. Vine a Estados Unidos a aprender inglés y a aprender más sobre lo que se puede hacer para conservar el medio ambiente.

¿Qué piensas del uso de los recursos no renovables en Estados Unidos?

Creo que es un país muy rico que desperdicia mucho sus recursos.

¿Qué planes tienes para el tiempo que estés aquí?

Voy a explicarles a mis amigos el programa de reciclaje de mi país.

_____ **9.** Hans es de Berlín.

_____ **10.** Hans y sus amigos jugaban al fútbol en su tiempo libre.

_____ **11.** Él piensa que en Estados Unidos se desperdician los recursos.

_____ **12.** Hans les va a enseñar alemán a sus nuevos amigos.

SCORE /8

D Read Gloria's essay about her volunteer work planting trees. Then, read the statements that follow and choose **a**) for **cierto** or **b**) for **falso.**

Estoy estudiando ecología en la universidad. Aprendí que los bosques están desapareciendo muy rápido. Por eso, debemos sembrar muchos árboles para proteger los bosques porque son los pulmones del planeta. Los árboles producen oxígeno y también detienen el proceso de la erosión. Durante mis vacaciones de primavera trabajé como voluntaria en un proyecto de reforestación de árboles frutales. Como parte del programa, cada participante debía adoptar un árbol: llevarlo a su casa, sembrarlo y cuidarlo como si fuera un hijo. Cuando me gradúe de la universidad, me gustaría enseñar a la gente la importancia de los bosques para que empiecen a conservarlos.

_____ **13.** Gloria estudia ecología en la universidad.

_____ **14.** Gloria piensa que no es importante sembrar árboles.

_____ **15.** Los bosques son los pulmones del planeta porque producen oxígeno.

_____ **16.** Durante sus vacaciones, Gloria trabajó en un proyecto de reforestación.

SCORE /8

EXAMEN

Cultura

E Read the following questions about the **Cono Sur** and choose the most appropriate answer.

____ **17.** ¿Dónde está ubicada la ciudad de Buenos Aires?
a. en el río Paraná
b. en el río Uruguay
c. en el Río de la Plata

____ **18.** ¿Cuál de las siguientes oraciones sobre Chile es cierta?
a. Es el único país que cultiva papas orgánicas.
b. Es el primer país del mundo que usó la energía solar.
c. Es el primer país latinoamericano que se hizo socio comercial de Estados Unidos.

____ **19.** ¿Dónde ocurrió el terremoto más grande del siglo XX?
a. en Argentina
b. en Chile
c. en Paraguay

____ **20.** ¿Dónde se encuentra la mayor parte de los recursos naturales de Argentina?
a. en las Pampas
b. en Buenos Aires
c. en el Río de la Plata

SCORE ____ /8

Vocabulario

F Choose a word from the box that best matches its description below.

a. desperdiciar
b. la contaminación
c. implementar
d. los pesticidas
e. innovador

____ **21.** Poner algo en efecto, como una ley.

____ **22.** Gastar de manera incorrecta o excesiva.

____ **23.** Daño causado al medio ambiente por efecto de la actividad humana.

____ **24.** Una idea o cosa que no existía antes es algo…

____ **25.** Sustancia química para eliminar parásitos de los cultivos.

SCORE ____ /5

Nombre ______________________ Clase ______________ Fecha ______________

CAPÍTULO **10**

EXAMEN

Vocabulario

G Complete the following conversation with the words from the box.

cooperación	**solidaridad**	**espantosas**	**indiferencia**	**destrucción**
erupción	**conmovedor**	**desastre**	**trágico**	**bomba**

Marieta Hernán, ¿viste la (**26**) ____________ del volcán en las noticias?

Hernán Sí, eran unas imágenes (**27**) ____________ ; daban mucho miedo. Causó mucha (**28**) ____________ en los pueblos cercanos.

Marieta Ese (**29**) ____________ natural es uno de los peores que existen.

Hernán Es cierto. Es un acontecimiento más que triste, realmente (**30**) ____________ . Dijeron que muchas personas están sin hogar.

Marieta En uno de los pueblos parecía que había estallado una (**31**) ____________ . Todo estaba cubierto de cenizas. Las ciudades vecinas mostraron su (**32**) ____________ al ayudar a las víctimas.

Hernán Sí, todos estaban ansiosos por ofrecer su (**33**) ____________ .

Marieta Cuando un acontecimiento es tan (**34**) ____________ , la gente no puede reaccionar con (**35**) ____________ o falta de interés.

SCORE ____ /5

H Write a question that fits each of the following answers.

36. Son los productos que se cultivan sin usar sustancias contaminantes.

____

37. Volver a usar productos o materiales en lugar de tirarlos a la basura.

____

38. Una fuente de energía alternativa es la energía solar.

____

39. Son elementos naturales del planeta disponibles para nuestro uso, como los bosques, por ejemplo.

____

40. Creando leyes a favor del uso de carros eléctricos e híbridos.

____

SCORE ____ /10 

EXAMEN

Gramática

I Complete each sentence with the correct form of **haber.**

41. Mi padre __________ terminado todo para la noche.

42. Pienso que yo todavía no __________ estudiado lo suficiente.

43. Cuando llegué al colegio, no __________ nadie en los pasillos.

44. Me dijeron que __________ un accidente terrible en la autopista.

SCORE ____ /4

J Make complete sentences with the phrases below, using different forms of the present progressive (with **estar, seguir, andar**...). Use the subjunctive if necessary.

45. yo / desperdiciar papel / antes de que / empezar / programa de reciclaje en el colegio

____

46. los profesores / dudar / los estudiantes / reciclar / después de que / salir del colegio

____

47. es la tercera vez que / todos nosotros / leer / sobre la contaminación

____

48. hacer / cuatro años / los estudiantes / sembrar / árboles en su colegio

____

SCORE ____ /8

K Write a sentence with **ir a** + the infinitive or the future tense of the verb given and use the **subjunctive** in the subordinate clause.

49. Elena y Gustavo (reciclar) las botellas mañana en cuanto...

____

50. Lorena (ir a) comprarse un carro eléctrico en un año cuando...

____

51. Marta (sembrar) un árbol en el parque este sábado a menos que...

____

52. Yo (ir a) comer frutas y verduras orgánicas tan pronto como...

____

SCORE ____ /8 

EXAMEN

Escribamos

L Write a paragraph describing a new environmental or ecology club at your school. Talk about the programs the club members have in mind and how the community will benefit from them.

SCORE /10

M Write a dialogue between you and a friend about a natural disaster you both experienced, such as a severe storm or a big fire. Talk about what you were doing and how you felt about it. Discuss whether you can predict a similar event happening again in the future.

SCORE /10

TOTAL SCORE /100

Nombre ______________________ Clase ____________ Fecha __________

CAPÍTULO 10

Score Sheet: Examen

Escuchemos

A

1. a b
2. a b
3. a b
4. a b

SCORE /8

B

5. a b c d
6. a b c d
7. a b c d
8. a b c d

SCORE /8

Leamos

C

9. a b
10. a b
11. a b
12. a b

SCORE /8

D

13. a b
14. a b
15. a b
16. a b

SCORE /8

Cultura

E

17. a b c
18. a b c
19. a b c
20. a b c

SCORE /8

Vocabulario

F

21. a b c d e
22. a b c d e
23. a b c d e
24. a b c d e
25. a b c d e

SCORE /5

G

26. ______________________
27. ______________________
28. ______________________
29. ______________________
30. ______________________
31. ______________________
32. ______________________
33. ______________________
34. ______________________
35. ______________________

SCORE /5

H

36. ____
____
37. ____
____
38. ____
____
39. ____
____
40. ____
____

SCORE /10

Nombre ______________________ Clase ______________ Fecha ____________

CAPÍTULO **10**

SCORE SHEET: EXAMEN

Gramática

I

41. ______________________
42. ______________________
43. ______________________
44. ______________________

SCORE /4

J

45. ______________________
46. ______________________
47. ______________________
48. ______________________

SCORE /8

K

49. ______________________
50. ______________________
51. ______________________
52. ______________________

SCORE /8

Escribamos

L

SCORE /10

M

SCORE /10

TOTAL SCORE /100

CAPÍTULO 10

Answer Key: Examen

Escuchemos

A

1. a (b)
2. (a) b
3. a (b)
4. (a) b

SCORE /8

B

5. a (b) c d
6. a b (c) d
7. (a) b c d
8. a b c (d)

SCORE /8

Leamos

C

9. (a) b
10. a (b)
11. (a) b
12. a (b)

SCORE /8

D

13. (a) b
14. a (b)
15. (a) b
16. (a) b

SCORE /8

Cultura

E

17. a b (c)
18. a b (c)
19. a (b) c
20. (a) b c

SCORE /8

Vocabulario

F

21. a b (c) d e
22. (a) b c d e
23. a (b) c d e
24. a b c d (e)
25. a b c (d) e

SCORE /5

G

26. erupción
27. espantosas
28. destrucción
29. desastre
30. trágico
31. bomba
32. solidaridad
33. cooperación
34. conmovedor
35. indiferencia

SCORE /5

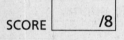

H Answers will vary. Possible answers:

36. ¿Qué son los productos de cultivo biológico?
37. ¿Qué es reciclar?
38. Nombra una fuente de energía alternativa.
39. ¿Qué son los recursos naturales?
40. ¿Cómo podemos conservar mejor la calidad del aire y del agua?

SCORE /10

Gramática

I

41. habrá
42. he
43. había
44. hubo

SCORE /4

J

45. Yo estaba desperdiciando papel antes de que empezara el programa de reciclaje en el colegio.
46. Los profesores dudan que los estudiantes anden reciclando después de que salgan del colegio.
47. Es la tercera vez que todos nosotros estamos leyendo sobre la contaminación.
48. Hace cuatro años que los estudiantes están sembrando árboles en su colegio.

SCORE /8

K Answers may vary. Possible answers:

49. Elena y Gustavo reciclarán las botellas mañana en cuanto se despierten.
50. Lorena va a comprarse un carro eléctrico en un año cuando tenga el dinero.
51. Marta sembrará un árbol en el parque este sábado a menos que llueva.
52. Voy a comer frutas y verduras orgánicas tan pronto como pueda.

SCORE /8

Escribamos

L

Answers will vary. Answers should include: reciclar, un aire más puro, conservar, fuentes de energía alternativas...

SCORE /10

M

Answers will vary. Answers should include: vocabulario (¿Te acuerdas de...?, espantoso, refugiados, A lo mejor habrá...), the verb haber (Hubo un accidente aterrador...), past progressive (Estábamos viendo la televisión cuando...), future (De ahora en adelante calcularán/van a calcular...), subjunctive with doubt, denial, and feelings (Es una lástima que haya ocurrido algo así)

SCORE /10

TOTAL SCORE /100

Escuchemos

A Listen to the following conversation between Raquel and Andrés. Read the statements below and choose **a)** for **cierto** or **b)** for **falso.**

Raquel ¡Hola Andrés! Ahora vienes en bicicleta al colegio todos los días. ¿Quieres bajar de peso y estar en forma?

Andrés No, no lo hago por eso. He leído mucho sobre la contaminación del medio ambiente. Me preocupa la calidad del aire que respiramos.

Raquel ¿Y cómo piensas ayudar con tu bicicleta?

Andrés El petróleo de los carros es uno de los combustibles que daña la calidad del aire. Los científicos buscan fuentes de energía alternativas.

Raquel ¿Como tus propios músculos?

Andrés Sí, pero también existen la energía solar, la energía eléctrica y la energía nuclear. En algunos lugares como California, se utiliza incluso la energía del viento.

Raquel Me imagino que si muchas personas hicieran como tú, respiraríamos aire más limpio. A partir de mañana, voy a venir al colegio en patines.

B Listen to the following statements. Then, match the letter of the image to the statement that you hear.

5. Los adelantos tecnológicos son fantásticos. Ahora, en vez de ir al cine, puedo ver mis películas favoritas en la comodidad de mi casa.

6. Un huracán puede ser un desastre natural aterrador. Los fuertes vientos y las lluvias pueden causar mucha destrucción.

7. Muchas veces tiramos cosas a la basura que podemos utilizar de nuevo. Es importante promover programas de reciclaje.

8. El petróleo es un combustible que empeora la calidad del aire. En cambio, los carros eléctricos no contaminan el medio ambiente.

El mundo en que vivimos

Interview

A Respond to the following questions in Spanish.

1. ¿Qué sabes de los desastres naturales y cómo lo sabes?
2. ¿Qué ocurre durante un terremoto?
3. ¿Cómo puedes ayudar a conservar el medio ambiente?
4. ¿Qué podemos hacer para mejorar la calidad del aire?
5. ¿Qué pasará en el futuro si no dejamos de contaminar el medio ambiente?

Role-Play

B Act out the following situation with a partner. You can also act out this situation in larger groups.

Imagine that you and a classmate are scientists from different countries. Take turns asking each other about the environment, natural resources, and alternative energy sources. Ask each other about the laws for recycling, energy conservation, and the protection of the environment that exist in your countries.

SPEAKING RUBRIC

COMPREHENSION (ability to understand verbal cues and respond appropriately)	(POOR)	1	2	3	4	(EXCELLENT)
COMPREHENSIBILITY (ability to communicate ideas and be understood)	(POOR)	1	2	3	4	(EXCELLENT)
ACCURACY (ability to use structures and vocabulary correctly)	(POOR)	1	2	3	4	(EXCELLENT)
FLUENCY (ability to communicate clearly and smoothly)	(POOR)	1	2	3	4	(EXCELLENT)
EFFORT (inclusion of details beyond the minimum requirements)	(POOR)	1	2	3	4	(EXCELLENT)

Nombre ______________________ Clase ______________ Fecha ______________

Examen final

Escuchemos

A Listen to the statements. Then, match the letter of the image to the statement that you hear.

a.

b.

c.

d.

1. ____ **3.** ____

2. ____ **4.** ____

SCORE /8

B Listen to the speakers. Then, read the statements below and choose **a)** for **cierto** or **b)** for **falso.**

____ **5.** Tan pronto como se levantan, todos pelean por la sección deportiva del periódico.

____ **6.** El narrador piensa que su talento para las matemáticas lo ayudará a tener una carrera como contador.

____ **7.** El narrador viajaría a otros países y ayudaría donando su dinero y su tiempo.

____ **8.** El reportero trató el tema a fondo.

____ **9.** En el cuento de la editora, la princesa rescata al príncipe.

____ **10.** El soldado regresó a su casa después de ganar la guerra.

SCORE 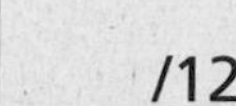 /12 

EXAMEN FINAL

Leamos

C Read Vladimir's essay on his experiences as a Russian immigrant and the statements that follow. In the blank, write the letter of the statement that Vladimir would agree with.

Me llamo Vladimir y soy de ascendencia rusa. Me crié en una aldea pequeña muy lejos de Moscú. En Rusia, éramos muy pobres. Una vez al mes, hacíamos fila para poder recibir una pequeña ración de comida del gobierno. La mantequilla y el aceite eran un lujo *(luxury)* en nuestro país. Sólo los ricos podían obtenerlos. Si nos enfermábamos, no teníamos la atención necesaria porque no había médicos disponibles, y el hospital quedaba a una hora de nuestra casa. Durante esta época de extrema pobreza, mis padres decidieron que nos mudaríamos a Estados Unidos. No le fue fácil, pero mi padre pudo obtener permiso del gobierno soviético para que nos dejara ir. Cuando llegamos a este país, tuvimos que enfrentar muchos obstáculos. No hablábamos inglés y mucha gente discriminaba a los inmigrantes de Rusia. En el colegio, me llamaban comunista y se burlaban de mi acento. Poco a poco, pude asimilar el estilo de vida. Hice amigos en el colegio y aprendí inglés. Ahora tengo muchas aspiraciones para el futuro. Tengo planes de ir a la universidad, con la intención de estudiar medicina. Me gustaría graduarme de médico para unirme a la organización *Médicos Sin Fronteras.* Quisiera ayudar a la gente en los países pobres. Sé lo que es vivir en la pobreza y quiero hacer todo lo posible para cambiar el mundo.

____ **11.** **a.** Me crié cerca de Moscú.
b. Me crié en Rusia.
c. Me crié en Estados Unidos.

____ **12.** **a.** Hacíamos fila para obtener una ración de comida.
b. Hacíamos fila para obtener mantequilla y aceite.
c. Los ricos hacían fila para obtener comida del gobierno.

____ **13.** **a.** Vivíamos cerca del hospital.
b. Los médicos llegaban tan pronto como nos enfermábamos.
c. No teníamos atención médica.

____ **14.** **a.** Mi familia se burlaba de mi acento.
b. Logré aprender inglés.
c. Nadie discriminaba a los inmigrantes rusos.

____ **15.** **a.** Me gustaría ayudar a la gente pobre.
b. Quisiera graduarme de leyes.
c. No es posible cambiar el mundo.

SCORE ____ /5

EXAMEN FINAL

D Read the conversation. Then, read the statements that follow and choose **a)** for **cierto** or **b)** for **falso.**

Alberto Anoche hubo un documental sobre la contaminación del aire. Me parece que el reportero no está bien informado porque dio su informe de modo muy parcial. ¿Lo viste?

Catalina No, cuando empezó, ya había salido de casa. ¿Qué dijo?

Alberto El reportero declaró que la tecnología causa la contaminación.

Catalina Tiene razón. Es cierto que los carros contaminan el aire.

Alberto No estoy de acuerdo en que todos los adelantos tecnológicos contaminen el aire.

Catalina ¿Hay algún adelanto tecnológico que no dañe el medio ambiente?

Alberto Claro que sí. ¿Te has olvidado de los carros eléctricos, la energía solar y el reciclaje? Todos son el resultado de la tecnología, y con ellos podemos mejorar la crisis ambiental.

Catalina Es evidente que sabes mucho sobre el tema, pero no creo que podamos hacer nada para mejorar la situación.

Alberto Al contrario, podemos hacer mucho. Se puede hacer trabajo voluntario con organizaciones ambientales, o donar dinero a una organización que trabaje en la reforestación.

Catalina Si pudiera donar dinero, lo haría, pero no tengo ni un centavo.

Alberto Te sugiero que te unas al club de ecología de nuestro colegio. Si lo hicieras, podrías participar en nuestros programas de reciclaje y plantación de árboles, y aprenderías más sobre el tema.

Catalina Me has convencido. Creo que lo haré.

_____ **16.** A Alberto le gustó el documental sobre la contaminación del aire.

_____ **17.** Catalina está de acuerdo con el reportero.

_____ **18.** Todos los adelantos tecnológicos dañan el medio ambiente.

_____ **19.** Alberto cree que se puede donar tiempo a organizaciones para mejorar la situación.

_____ **20.** Alberto convenció a Catalina de que se uniera al club de ecología del colegio.

SCORE ______ /10

Nombre ______________________ Clase ______________ Fecha ____________

EXAMEN FINAL

Cultura

E Choose a term from the box that best matches its description below.

a. los incas	**b.** los diaguitas	**c.** Buenos Aires
d. la bandera de Chile		**e.** la siesta

____ **21.** Se la conoce como "la París de América del Sur".

____ **22.** Construyeron carreteras que se usan hoy en día.

____ **23.** La gente regresa del trabajo a su casa para dormir unas horas.

____ **24.** Vivían en el noroeste de Argentina, cerca de Bolivia.

____ **25.** Tiene una estrella cuyas puntas simbolizan los poderes del estado.

SCORE ____ /10

Vocabulario

F Choose the answer that best completes each statement.

____ **26.** En la sección de ___ se anuncian las muertes.
a. la sociedad **b.** los obituarios **c.** la moda

____ **27.** Tener éxito quiere decir ___.
a. triunfar **b.** lograr tus metas **c. a** y **b**

____ **28.** La persona que administra una empresa es el (la) ___.
a. gerente **b.** empleado **c.** auxiliar médico

____ **29.** Una persona que tiene poderes mágicos es un ___.
a. hechicero **b. a** y **c** **c.** valiente

____ **30.** Si quieres conservar los recursos, no debes ___.
a. reciclarlos **b.** desperdiciarlos **c.** aumentarlos

SCORE ____ /5

EXAMEN FINAL

G Choose the word or phrase that best completes each sentence.

____ **31.** Nunca tengo tiempo por las mañanas, por eso sólo leo ___ .
a. la sección de ocio **b.** los titulares **c.** los artículos

____ **32.** ¿Tus abuelos ___ obstáculos cuando llegaron a este país?
a. enfrentaron **b.** soñaron **c.** alcanzaron

____ **33.** Durante el día no tengo mucho estrés porque ___ donde trabajo es muy relajado.
a. el requisito **b.** el beneficio **c.** el ambiente

____ **34.** El 4 de julio se conmemora a ___ de la independencia estadounidense.
a. los enemigos **b.** los dictadores **c.** los héroes

____ **35.** La erupción del volcán causó mucha ___ en los pueblos cercanos.
a. destrucción **b.** cooperación **c.** discriminación

____ **36.** Para estar bien informado, puedes ___ .
a. suscribirte al periódico **b.** ver las telenovelas **c.** reseñar una película

____ **37.** Roberto no ___ y pudo lograr su sueño de ser profesor.
a. recibió apoyo **b.** se empeñó **c.** se dio por vencido

____ **38.** Si pudiera, ___ a un programa para niños pobres para hacer un aporte a la sociedad.
a. buscaría empleo **b.** donaría tiempo **c.** sería capaz

____ **39.** ___ y las vacaciones son beneficios de un puesto de trabajo.
a. Los requisitos **b.** La carrera **c.** El seguro médico

____ **40.** Los productos de cultivo biológico se cosechan sin utilizar ___ .
a. la energía solar **b.** los pesticidas **c.** la contaminación

SCORE /10

EXAMEN FINAL

H Answer the following questions with your opinion.

41. ¿Cómo te mantienes al tanto de las noticias?

____

42. ¿Qué harás en cuanto cumplas los veintiún años?

____

43. ¿Qué puesto te gustaría tener en una compañía? ¿Por qué?

____

44. ¿Crees que las leyendas están basadas en elementos misteriosos y desconocidos?

____

45. ¿Qué podemos hacer para mejorar la crisis ambiental?

____

SCORE [/5]

Gramática

I Read each statement, and choose the most appropriate response from the box.

Cómprate un contestador automático. Te sugiero que dones tiempo o dinero a la Cruz Roja. No me extraña que estés mal informado con esos programas no educativos. Hay un club de reciclaje en su colegio al cual se pueden unir. Deben hacer una lista de metas y empeñarse por alcanzarlas.

46. Me gustaría estar bien informado, pero sólo veo las telenovelas.

____

47. No tenemos ningunas aspiraciones para el futuro.

____

48. Mis amigos no pueden dejarme mensajes cuando no estoy en casa.

____

49. Quisiera ayudar a las víctimas de las inundaciones *(floods)*.

____

50. Alberto y Nancy están preocupados por el medio ambiente.

____

SCORE [/5] ⇨

EXAMEN FINAL

J Complete the following sentences with the correct word in parentheses.

51. Quiero leer la sección de cocina para ver si hay __________ (ningunas / algunas) recetas para el arroz.

52. Alejandro y Laura __________ (fueron / iban) a Argentina dos veces el año pasado.

53. Si me __________ (dan / dieran) el puesto, trabajaría muy duro.

54. La princesa fue rescatada de la torre alta __________ (para / por) el príncipe azul.

55. Elena y Josué __________ (están / estaban) entrenando ahora para el maratón del domingo que viene.

SCORE ____ /5

K Combine the phrases to make sentences, using the correct form of the verb(s).

56. mis padres nunca / haber / creído que los políticos / decir / la verdad

____

57. a menos de que Manuel me / haber / invitado, no / ir / a la fiesta

____

58. yo que tú / jugar / para el equipo de fútbol

____

59. las víctimas / esperar que / la guerra no / repetirse / en el futuro

____

60. el reportero / anunciar / que / haber / un terremoto en Japón esta mañana

____

SCORE ____ /5

EXAMEN FINAL

L Complete the following paragraph with the correct form of the verb in parentheses. Pay attention to the verb tense in the main clause.

Amparo dijo que ella (**61**) ____________ (ir) a ver el reportaje sobre la tasa de desempleo en el noticiero. Según ella, los expertos habían dicho que la tasa de desempleo (**62**) ____________ (subir) en los próximos meses. De hecho, el alcalde ha dicho que (**63**) ____________ (hablar) del tema en una conferencia de prensa la semana que viene. Espero que él no nos (**64**) ____________ (dar) malas noticias sobre la situación porque Amparo quería que yo la (**65**) ____________ (acompañar) a una entrevista mañana.

SCORE ____ /5

Escribamos

M Answer the following questions with your opinion.

66. ¿Has visto algún programa interesante por televisión últimamente? ¿De qué trataba?

____

67. Si pudieras hacer un documental para la televisión, ¿qué tema escogerías? ¿Por qué?

____

68. ¿Cómo crees que los adelantos tecnológicos afectarán a la vida en el futuro?

____

69. ¿Qué podríamos hacer para conservar el medio ambiente?

____

70. ¿Qué ventajas crees que tiene el uso de un carro eléctrico?

____

SCORE ____ /10

N Write a paragraph about an obstacle you faced at school last year. Talk about how you overcame the obstacle.

____

____

____

____

____

SCORE ____ /5 TOTAL SCORE ____ /100

Nombre ______________________ Clase ______________ Fecha ____________

Score Sheet: Examen final

Escuchemos

A

1. a b c d
2. a b c d
3. a b c d
4. a b c d

SCORE /8

B

5. a b
6. a b
7. a b
8. a b
9. a b
10. a b

SCORE /12

Leamos

C

11. a b c
12. a b c
13. a b c
14. a b c
15. a b c

SCORE /5

D

16. a b
17. a b
18. a b
19. a b
20. a b

SCORE /10

Cultura

E

21. a b c d e
22. a b c d e
23. a b c d e
24. a b c d e
25. a b c d e

SCORE /10

Vocabulario

F

26. a b c
27. a b c
28. a b c
29. a b c
30. a b c

SCORE /5

G

31. a b c
32. a b c
33. a b c
34. a b c
35. a b c
36. a b c
37. a b c
38. a b c
39. a b c
40. a b c

SCORE /10

H

41. ____________________________________
42. ____________________________________
43. ____________________________________
44. ____________________________________
45. ____________________________________

SCORE /5

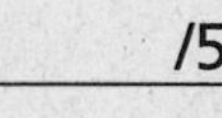

Nombre ______________________ Clase ______________ Fecha ____________

SCORE SHEET: EXAMEN FINAL

Gramática

I

46. ______________________________
____

47. ______________________________
____

48. ______________________________
____

49. ______________________________
____

50. ______________________________
____

SCORE /5

J

51. ______________
52. ______________
53. ______________
54. ______________
55. ______________

SCORE /5

K

56. ______________________________
____

57. ______________________________
____

58. ______________________________
____

59. ______________________________
____

60. ______________________________
____

SCORE /5

L

61. ______________
62. ______________
63. ______________
64. ______________
65. ______________

SCORE /5

Nombre ______________________ Clase ______________ Fecha ____________

SCORE SHEET: EXAMEN FINAL

Escribamos

M

66. ____

67. ____

68. ____

69. ____

70. ____

SCORE /10

N

____

____

____

____

____

____

____

SCORE /5

TOTAL SCORE /100

Answer Key: Examen final

Escuchemos

A

1. a b (c) d
2. a b c (d)
3. (a) b c d
4. a (b) c d

SCORE /8

B

5. a (b)
6. (a) b
7. (a) b
8. a (b)
9. a (b)
10. (a) b

SCORE /12

Leamos

C

11. a (b) c
12. (a) b c
13. a b (c)
14. a (b) c
15. (a) b c

SCORE /5

D

16. a (b)
17. (a) b
18. a (b)
19. (a) b
20. (a) b

SCORE /10

Cultura

E

21. a b (c) d e
22. (a) b c d e
23. a b c d (e)
24. a (b) c d e
25. a b c (d) e

SCORE /10

Vocabulario

F

26. a (b) c
27. a b (c)
28. (a) b c
29. (a) b c
30. a (b) c

SCORE /5

G

31. a (b) c
32. (a) b c
33. a b (c)
34. a b (c)
35. (a) b c
36. (a) b c
37. a b (c)
38. a (b) c
39. a b (c)
40. a (b) c

SCORE /10

H Answers will vary. Possible answers:

41. Leo el periódico para estar al tanto de las noticias.
42. En cuanto cumpla los veintiún años, voy a trabajar como periodista en un periódico importante.
43. Me gustaría ser el jefe porque así tendría un buen salario, seguro médico y beneficios.
44. Creo que las leyendas están basadas en elementos misteriosos y desconocidos, pero también en mitos históricos.
45. Podemos reciclar, caminar en vez de ir en auto y comprar productos de cultivo biológico.

SCORE /5

Gramática

I

46. No me extraña que estés mal informado con esos programas no educativos.
47. Deben hacer una lista de metas y empeñarse por alcanzarlas.
48. Cómprate un contestador automático.
49. Te sugiero que dones tiempo o dinero a la Cruz Roja.
50. Hay un club de reciclaje en su colegio al cual se pueden unir.

SCORE /5

J

51. algunas
52. fueron
53. dieran
54. por
55. están

SCORE /5

K

56. Mis padres nunca han (habían, habrían) creído que los políticos digan (dijeran) la verdad.
57. A menos de que Manuel me haya (hubiera) invitado, no iré (iría) a la fiesta.
58. Yo que tú, jugaría para el equipo de fútbol.
59. Las víctimas esperan / esperaban que la guerra no se repita / repitiera en el futuro.
60. El reportero anunció que hubo un terremoto en Japón esta mañana.

SCORE /5

L

61. iba
62. subiría
63. hablará
64. dé
65. acompañara

SCORE /5

Escribamos

M Answers will vary. Possible answers:

66. Me parece que la semana pasada hubo un documental sobre los carros híbridos.
67. Si pudiera, haría un documental sobre los terremotos y presentaría los adelantos tecnológicos que nos ayudan a saber cuándo van a pasar.
68. Los adelantos tecnológicos nos ayudarán a conservar el medio ambiente.
69. Podríamos reciclar más para conservar el medio ambiente.
70. Es evidente que un carro eléctrico no contamina el aire.

SCORE /10

N

Answers will vary. Answers should include: vocabulary (trabajé duro, por eso..., esfuerzo, enfrentar obstáculos), talking about accomplishments (con el tiempo pude asimilar..., gracias al apoyo de...), preterite and imperfect, grammatical reflexives (me empeñé, me esforcé), indicative after expressions of certainty (es cierto que..., estaba seguro de que...), haber, lo malo / bueno, lo que más...

SCORE /5 TOTAL SCORE /100

Escuchemos

A Listen to the statements. Then, match the letter of the image to the statement that you hear.

1. Aunque estoy de acuerdo en que la esclavitud fue horrible, creo que debemos estudiar ese acontecimiento histórico para ver cómo influye en el presente.
2. Debemos usar otros modos de transporte como los carros eléctricos, la transportación pública o las bicicletas para mejorar la calidad del aire.
3. No es cierto que todos los programas de televisión sean malos. Hay algunos programas como los documentales y las noticias que son educativos e informativos.
4. José enfrentó muchos obstáculos cuando llegó a Estados Unidos. Había gente que lo discriminaba porque no hablaba inglés. Se empeñó mucho en la universidad y ahora es el jefe de una empresa.

B Listen to the speakers. Then, read the statements below and choose **a**) for **cierto,** or **b**) for **falso.**

5. Tan pronto como nos levantamos los domingos por la mañana, leemos el periódico. Papá y Rolando pelean por la sección deportiva, mamá toma la sección de moda y yo me siento en el sofá con la sección de ocio.
6. En cuanto cumpla los dieciocho años, iré a la universidad para estudiar computación. Creo que mi talento para las matemáticas me ayudará a tener una carrera como contador.
7. Si fuera rico, haría trabajo voluntario en países pobres, viajaría a otros países para ayudar a las víctimas de las guerras civiles y donaría dinero para las víctimas de los desastres naturales. En fin, haría todo lo posible para cambiar el mundo.
8. Ayer hubo un documental sobre la crisis ambiental. No me gustó la forma parcial en que el reportero dio su informe. Está claro que pasó por alto muchos detalles importantes como el reciclaje, el carro híbrido y la energía solar.
9. Durante el día trabajo como editora para un periódico local. Pero cuando llego a casa, escribo cuentos para niños. Ahora mismo estoy terminando un cuento de hadas donde un príncipe que no sabe nadar, es atrapado por un hechicero malvado en una isla pequeña en el medio de un lago. No sé si la princesa hermosa debe rescatar al príncipe o no. No estoy segura de cómo debe terminar el cuento.
10. Dos meses después del comienzo de la Segunda Guerra Mundial, un chico se unió a las tropas militares estadounidenses. Cuando las tropas aliadas ganaron la guerra, el soldado regresó a su casa. Junto a su familia, conmemoró a las víctimas y a los héroes valientes.

Alternative Assessment

Table of Contents

ALTERNATIVE ASSESSMENT

To the Teacher

Alternative Assessment

Students learn differently and progress at different rates in developing their oral and written skills. The Alternative Assessment accommodates those differences and offers opportunities for all students to be evaluated in ways that enable them to succeed. This guide contains suggestions for three types of assessment that go beyond the standard quizzes and tests: portfolio suggestions, performance assessment, and picture sequences. Each section of the guide offers specific suggestions for incorporating each type of assessment into your instructional plan.

Portfolio Suggestions

Student portfolios benefit foreign language students and teachers alike because they provide documentation of a student's efforts, progress, and achievements over a given period of time. In addition, students receive both positive feedback and constructive criticism by sharing their portfolios with teachers, family, and peers.

Setting up the Portfolios

The first step in implementing portfolios is to determine the purpose for which they will be used: to assess an individual student's growth and progress, to make students active in the assessment process, to provide evidence and documentation of students' work for more effective communication with parents, or to evaluate an instructional program of curriculum. Both the content of the portfolio and the manner in which it is evaluated will depend directly on the purpose(s) the portfolio is to serve. Portfolios are especially useful tools for assessing written and oral work. Written items can be in a variety of forms, depending on the level and needs of the students. Oral items may be recorded on audio- or videocassette for incorporation into the portfolio. Whatever the format, both written and oral work can include evidence of the developmental process, such as notes from brainstorming or early drafts, as well as the finished product.

Selecting Materials for the Portfolio

Work to be included in the portfolio should be selected on the basis of the portfolio's purpose and evaluation criteria to be used. Many teachers prefer to let students choose samples of their best work to include in their portfolios. This option gives students a feeling of ownership that is likely to increase as their involvement at the decision-making level increases. Some teachers prefer that portfolios contain students' responses to prompts or activities, allowing the teacher to focus attention on specific functions, vocabulary items, and grammar points. A third option is some combination of the two approaches.You can assign specific activities from which students may choose what to include in their portfolios, or you can assign some specific activities and allow students to choose others on their own.

Using the Portfolio Checklists

The checklists on pages 367 and 368 will help you and your students keep their portfolios organized. The Student's Portfolio Checklist will help students track the items they include. The Teacher's Portfolio Checklist is a list of items you expect students to include.

Peer Editing

The Alternative Assessment includes a Peer Editing Rubric (p. 365) to encourage peer editing and to aid students in this part of the evaluation process. Using the rubric, students can exchange compositions (usually a first draft) and edit each other's work according to a clearly designed, step-by-step process. The Peer Editing Rubric can be used with any written assignment.

Evaluating the Portfolio

Students' portfolios should be evaluated at regular intervals. Establish the length of the assessment period in advance: six weeks, a quarter, a semester, and so on. The Portfolio Self-Evaluation and Portfolio Evaluation forms on pages 369 and 370 are designed to aid you and your students in assessing the portfolio at the end of each assessment period.

Performance Assessment

Performance assessment uses authentic situations as contexts for performing communicative, competency-based tasks. Suggestions in this section give students the opportunity to demonstrate both acquired language proficiency and cultural competence in interviews, conversations, or skits that can be performed for the entire class, or recorded or videotaped for evaluation at a later time. Such recordings can be included in student portfolios.

Using Picture Sequences for Assessment

The picture sequences in the *Assessment Program* can be used in a variety of ways. As the basis for a speaking test, you can have students describe what they see in the picture or use the pictures to narrate a story. As a written assessment, you can ask for the same things but have students write their responses. The picture sequences are especially good for the visual learners in the class. They are also a comfortable first step in putting your students on the road to advanced placement testing.

Oral Rubric A • Presentational Communication

Use the following criteria to evaluate oral assignments in which only one student is speaking.

	Content	Comprehensibility	Accuracy	Fluency
4	**Complete**	**Comprehensible**	**Accurate**	**Fluent**
	Speaker consistently uses the appropriate structures and vocabulary necessary to communicate.	Listener understands all of what the speaker is trying to communicate.	Speaker uses language correctly, including grammar and word order.	Speaker speaks clearly without hesitation. Pronunciation and intonation seem natural.
3	**Generally complete**	**Usually comprehensible**	**Usually accurate**	**Moderately fluent**
	Speaker usually uses the appropriate structures and vocabulary necessary to communicate.	Listener understands most of what the speaker is trying to communicate.	Speaker usually uses language correctly, including grammar and word order.	Speaker has few problems with hesitation, pronunciation, and intonation.
2	**Somewhat complete**	**Sometimes comprehensible**	**Sometimes accurate**	**Somewhat fluent**
	Speaker sometimes uses the appropriate structures and vocabulary necessary to communicate.	Listener understands less than half of what the speaker is trying to communicate.	Speaker sometimes uses language correctly.	Speaker has some problems with hesitation, pronunciation, and intonation.
1	**Incomplete**	**Seldom comprehensible**	**Seldom accurate**	**Not fluent**
	Speaker uses few of the appropriate structures and vocabulary necessary to communicate.	Listener understands little of what the speaker is trying to communicate.	Speaker seldom uses language correctly.	Speaker hesitates frequently and struggles with pronunciation and intonation.

Oral Rubric B • Interpersonal Communication

Use the following criteria to evaluate oral assignments in which two or more students are speaking.

	Content	Comprehension	Comprehensibility	Accuracy	Fluency
4	**Complete**	**Total comprehension**	**Comprehensible**	**Accurate**	**Fluent**
	Speaker consistently uses the appropriate structures and vocabulary necessary to communicate.	Speaker understands all of what is said to him or her.	Listener understands all of what the speaker is trying to communicate.	Speaker uses language correctly, including grammar and word order.	Speaker speaks clearly without hesitation. Pronunciation and intonation seem natural.
3	**Generally complete**	**General comprehension**	**Usually comprehensible**	**Usually accurate**	**Moderately fluent**
	Speaker usually uses the appropriate structures and vocabulary necessary to communicate.	Speaker understands most of what is said to him or her.	Listener understands most of what the speaker is trying to communicate.	Speaker usually uses language correctly, including grammar and word order.	Speaker has few problems with hesitation, pronunciation, and intonation.
2	**Somewhat complete**	**Moderate comprehension**	**Sometimes comprehensible**	**Sometimes accurate**	**Somewhat fluent**
	Speaker sometimes uses the appropriate structures and vocabulary necessary to communicate.	Speaker understands some of what is said to him or her.	Listener understands less than half of what the speaker is trying to communicate.	Speaker sometimes uses language correctly.	Speaker has some problems with hesitation, pronunciation, and intonation.
1	**Incomplete**	**Little comprehension**	**Seldom comprehensible**	**Seldom accurate**	**Not fluent**
	Speaker uses few of the appropriate structures and vocabulary necessary to communicate.	Speaker understands little of what is said to him or her.	Listener understands little of what the speaker is trying to communicate.	Speaker seldom uses language correctly.	Speaker hesitates frequently and struggles with pronunciation and intonation.

Nombre ______________________ Clase ______________ Fecha ____________

Oral Progress Report

OVERALL IMPRESSION

☐ Excellent ☐ Good ☐ Satisfactory ☐ Unsatisfactory

Some particularly good aspects of this item are ______________________

Some areas that could be improved are ______________________

To improve your speaking, I recommend ______________________

Additional Comments ______________________

Written Rubric A

Use the following criteria to evaluate written assignments.

	4	3	2	1
Content	**Complete**	**Generally complete**	**Somewhat complete**	**Incomplete**
	Writer uses the appropriate functions and vocabulary for the topic.	Writer usually uses the appropriate functions and vocabulary for the topic.	Writer uses few of the appropriate functions and vocabulary for the topic.	Writer uses none of the appropriate functions and vocabulary for the topic.
Comprehensibility	**Comprehensible**	**Usually comprehensible**	**Sometimes comprehensible**	**Seldom comprehensible**
	Reader can understand all of what the writer is trying to communicate.	Reader can understand most of what the writer is trying to communicate.	Reader can understand less than half of what the writer is trying to communicate.	Reader can understand little of what the writer is trying to communicate.
Accuracy	**Accurate**	**Usually accurate**	**Sometimes accurate**	**Seldom accurate**
	Writer uses grammar, spelling, word order, and punctuation correctly.	Writer usually uses grammar, spelling, word order and punctuation correctly.	Writer has some problems with language usage.	Writer makes a significant number of errors in language usage.
Organization	**Well-organized**	**Generally well-organized**	**Somewhat organized**	**Poorly organized**
	Presentation is logical and effective.	Presentation is generally logical and effective with a few minor problems.	Presentation is somewhat illogical and confusing in places.	Presentation lacks logical order and organization.
Effort	**Excellent effort**	**Good effort**	**Moderate effort**	**Minimal effort**
	Writer exceeds the requirements of the assignment and has put care and effort into the process.	Writer fulfills all of the requirements of the assignment.	Writer fulfills some of the requirements of the assignment.	Writer fulfills few of the requirements of the assignment.

Nombre ______________________ Clase ______________ Fecha ____________

Written Progress Report

OVERALL IMPRESSION

☐ Excellent ☐ Good ☐ Satisfactory ☐ Unsatisfactory

Some particularly good aspects of this item are ______________________

Some areas that could be improved are ______________________

To improve your written work, I recommend ______________________

Additional Comments ______________________

Nombre ______________________ Clase ____________ Fecha ____________

Peer Editing Rubric

Chapter _____

I. Content: Look for the following elements in your partner's composition. Put a check next to each category when you finish it.

1. ___ Vocabulary — Does the composition use enough new vocabulary from the chapter? Underline all the new vocabulary words you find from this chapter. What additional words do you suggest that your partner try to use?

2. ___ Organization — Is the composition organized and easy to follow? Can you find an introduction and a conclusion?

3. ___ Comprehensibility — Is the composition clear and easy to understand? Is there a specific part that was hard to understand? Did you understand the author's meaning? Draw a box around any sections that were particularly hard to understand.

4. ___ Target Functions and Grammar — Ask your teacher what functions and grammar you should focus on for this chapter and list them below.

Focus: ______________________________

II. Proofreader's checklist: Circle any errors you find in your partner's composition, so that your partner can correct his or her errors. See the chart for some examples.

incorrect form of the verb	Yo (coma) una hamburguesa. [como]
Adjective–noun agreement Subject–verb agreement	Mi casa es (blanco). ← blanca Las amigas son (inteligente). [inteligentes] Los perros (es) bonitos. [son]
Spelling	Eres (intelligente). ← inteligente
Article	(El) casa es bonita. [La]
Transition words (if they apply to chapter)	primero, después, y, o, por eso...
Accents/Punctuation	Buenos (dias) ← días ¡Qué bueno ( ) ← !

III. Explain your content and grammar suggestions to your partner. Answer any questions about your comments.

Peer Editor's signature: ______________________ Date: ____________

Documentation of Group Work

Item ______________________________________ Chapter __________

Group Members: ______________________________________

____

____

____

____

____

____

Description of Item: ______________________________________

____

____

____

____

____

____

Personal Contribution: ______________________________________

____

____

____

____

____

____

Please rate your personal contribution to the group's work.

☐ Excellent ☐ Good ☐ Satisfactory ☐ Unsatisfactory

Nombre ______________________ Clase ______________ Fecha ____________

Student's Portfolio Checklist

To the Student This form should be used to keep track of the materials you are including in your portfolio. It is important that you keep this list up-to-date so that your portfolio will be complete at the end of the assessment period. As you build your portfolio, try to include pieces of your work that demonstrate progress in your ability to speak and write in Spanish.

	Type of Item	Date Completed	Date Placed in Portfolio
Item #1			
Item #2			
Item #3			
Item #4			
Item #5			
Item #6			
Item #7			
Item #8			
Item #9			
Item #10			
Item #11			
Item #12			

Nombre ______________________ Clase ____________ Fecha ____________

Teacher's Portfolio Checklist

To the Teacher This form should be used to keep track of the materials you expect your students to keep in their portfolios for the semester. Encourage students to keep their lists up-to-date so that their portfolios will be complete at the end of the assessment period.

	Type of Item	Date Assigned	Date Due in Portfolio
Item #1			
Item #2			
Item #3			
Item #4			
Item #5			
Item #6			
Item #7			
Item #8			
Item #9			
Item #10			
Item #11			
Item #12			

Nombre ______________________ Clase ______________ Fecha ____________

Portfolio Self-Evaluation

To the Student Your portfolio consists of selections of your written and oral work. You should consider all the items in your portfolio as you evaluate your progress. Read the statements below and mark a box to the right of each statement to show how well you think your portfolio demonstrates your skills and abilities in Spanish.

	Strongly Agree	Agree	Disagree	Strongly Disagree
1. My portfolio contains all of the required items.				
2. My portfolio provides evidence of my progress in speaking and writing Spanish.				
3. The items in my portfolio demonstrate that I can communicate my ideas in Spanish.				
4. The items in my portfolio demonstrate accurate use of Spanish.				
5. The items in my portfolio show that I understand and can use a wide variety of vocabulary.				
6. When creating the items in my portfolio, I tried to use what I have learned in new ways.				
7. The items in my portfolio provide an accurate picture of my skills and abilities in Spanish.				

The item I like best in my portfolio is ______________________

because (please give at least three reasons) ______________________

____

____

____

____

____

____

I find my portfolio to be (check one):

☐ Excellent ☐ Good ☐ Satisfactory ☐ Unsatisfactory

Nombre ______________________ Clase ______________ Fecha ____________

Portfolio Evaluation

To the Student I have reviewed the items in your portfolio and want to share with you my reactions to your work.

Teacher's signature: ______________________________ Date: ____________

	Strongly Agree	Agree	Disagree	Strongly Disagree
1. Your portfolio contains all the required items.				
2. Your portfolio provides evidence of your progress in speaking and writing Spanish.				
3. The items in your portfolio demonstrate that you can communicate your ideas in Spanish.				
4. The items in your portfolio demonstrate accurate use of Spanish.				
5. The items in your portfolio show that you understand and can use a wide variety of Spanish vocabulary.				
6. The items in your portfolio demonstrate that you have tried to use what you have learned in new ways.				
7. The items in your portfolio provide an accurate picture of your skills and abilities in Spanish.				

The item I like best in your portfolio is ______________________________

because ______________________________

____

____

One area in which you seem to need improvement is ______________________________

____

For your next portfolio collection, I would like to suggest ______________________________

____

I find your portfolio to be (check one):

☐ Excellent ☐ Good ☐ Satisfactory ☐ Unsatisfactory

Picture Sequence Assessment

Nombre ______________________ Clase ______________ Fecha ____________

CAPÍTULO 1

¡Adiós al verano!

PICTURE SEQUENCE

Cuenta la historia que se desarrolla en los siguientes dibujos.

1

2

3

4

5

6

Nombre ________________ Clase ____________ Fecha ____________

CAPÍTULO 2

¡A pasarlo bien!

PICTURE SEQUENCE

Cuenta la historia que se desarrolla en los siguientes dibujos.

1

2

3

4

5

6

Nombre ______________________ Clase ______________ Fecha ______________

CAPÍTULO 3

Todo tiene solución

PICTURE SEQUENCE

Cuenta la historia que se desarrolla en los siguientes dibujos.

1

2

3

4

5

6

Nombre ______________________ Clase ______________ Fecha ____________

CAPÍTULO 4

Entre familia

PICTURE SEQUENCE

Cuenta la historia que se desarrolla en los siguientes dibujos.

1

2
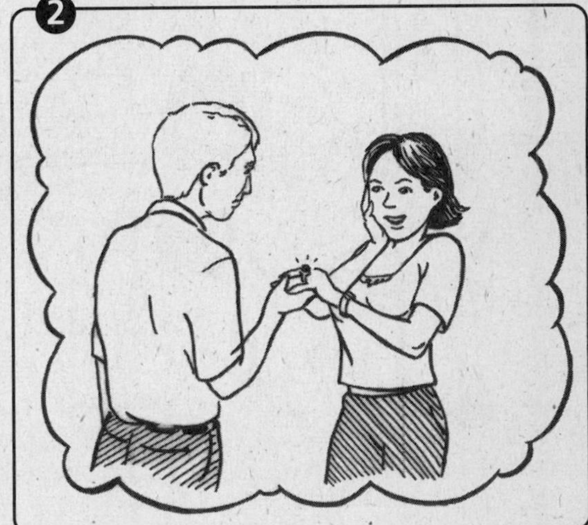

3

4
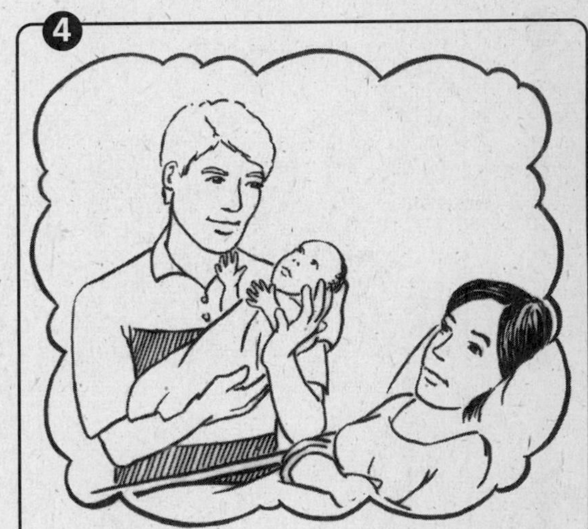

5

6

Nombre ______________________ Clase ______________ Fecha ____________

CAPÍTULO 5

El arte y la música

PICTURE SEQUENCE

Cuenta la historia que se desarrolla en los siguientes dibujos.

1

2

3

4

5

6

Nombre ______________________ Clase ______________ Fecha ______________

CAPÍTULO 6

¡Ponte al día!

PICTURE SEQUENCE

Cuenta la historia que se desarrolla en los siguientes dibujos.

Nombre ______________________ Clase ______________ Fecha ______________

CAPÍTULO 7

Mis aspiraciones

PICTURE SEQUENCE

Cuenta la historia que se desarrolla en los siguientes dibujos.

1

2

3

4

5

6

Nombre ______________________ Clase ______________ Fecha ______________

¿A qué te dedicas?

Cuenta la historia que se desarrolla en los siguientes dibujos.

Nombre ______________________ Clase ______________ Fecha ______________

CAPÍTULO 9

Huellas del pasado

PICTURE SEQUENCE

Cuenta la historia que se desarrolla en los siguientes dibujos.

1

2

3

4

5

6

Nombre ______________________ Clase ______________ Fecha ____________

CAPÍTULO 10

El mundo en que vivimos

PICTURE SEQUENCE

Cuenta la historia que se desarrolla en los siguientes dibujos.

1

2

3

4

5

6

Portfolio Suggestions

¡Adiós al verano!

Written Activity

TASK Students create a slide show that describes the activities they did last summer. (Activities can be made up.)

PURPOSE to use chapter vocabulary, to use **ser** and **estar** to describe scenes, to use the preterite and imperfect, to use the subjunctive with giving advice and recommendations, to make comparisons, to use time constructions

ACTIVITY Have students create "slides" from index cards and either sketch the "pictures" in their slide show or cut out pictures from a magazine. They should describe the scenes and tell where they were. They should also compare several activities they did, tell which ones they liked best, and include how long ago they did those activities. Finally, students should make a recommendation to a friend about an activity that he or she should do.

MATERIALS index cards, pencils, markers, scissors, glue, magazines

Oral Activity

TASK Students imagine that they are standing in a city square while leafing through a guide book or looking at a map, and need to decide which activities to do.

PURPOSE to use demonstrative adjectives, to use negative constructions, to use the subjunctive with recommendations

ACTIVITY Students should take turns proposing two similar activities or destinations at a time to each other (for example, **¿Vamos a esta catedral o aquélla?**) using the proper demonstrative adjectives. The other student should say which one they prefer or recommend, and explain why (**Prefiero que vayamos a ver este monumento porque no me gustan las catedrales.**), and then suggest another pair of activities to the first student. Students should continue until they have decided on six activities (three per student). At least one pair of activities should be rejected completely by each student (**Ninguno de los dos me interesa.**).

MATERIALS guide book, city maps, pencil, paper

¡A pasarlo bien!

Written Activity

TASK Students write a page for a magazine about how to be a good friend.

PURPOSE to use chapter vocabulary, to describe the ideal friend, to use object pronouns, to use the subjunctive with expressions of feelings

ACTIVITY Have students create a magazine article about how to be a good friend. They should come up with a catchy title and design the page in an attractive way. They may wish to write one article about how to be a good friend, or they may wish to compile several short paragraphs written by different people about their experiences. The article should be tied together by one general theme.

MATERIALS paper, markers, scissors (or they may want to design the page on a computer)

Oral Activity

TASK Students work in small groups. They imagine they are making plans for the weekend.

PURPOSE to express interest and displeasure, to invite someone to do something, to use **nosotros** commands, to use **ir a** + infinitive in the imperfect

ACTIVITY Students should take turns proposing activities to the rest of the group using expressions to invite someone to do something or **nosotros** commands. Each member of the group will be handed an item indicating the activity he or she should propose. Someone should turn down each invitation until the last student makes his or her proposal.

MATERIALS bike helmet, karate belt, oar, puzzle, dominoes, a computer game

Todo tiene solución

PORTFOLIO SUGGESTIONS

Written Activity

TASK Students write an opinion column in response to an article in the newspaper.

PURPOSE to talk about attitudes and opinions, to use subjunctive with will or wish, to use subjunctive with negation or denial, to express an opinion, to use the future tense, to talk about problems and solutions

ACTIVITY Have students look through the newspaper of their choice and find an article that deals with issues of stereotypes, discrimination, or prejudice. Ask them to write an opinion column in response to the article. Have them tell what parts of the article they agree with and what parts they disagree with. They should talk about their own attitudes and opinions about the issue, discuss what they hope will happen in the future, and give advice to their community about solutions.

MATERIALS newspaper, computer, paper

Oral Activity

TASK Students work in pairs to discuss their schedules.

PURPOSE to talk about school courses, to complain, to express an opinion, to use the conditional, to use the future tense, to use the subjunctive with will or wish, to use the subjunctive with negation or denial

ACTIVITY Students should take turns telling each other about their schedules for this semester. They talk about their classes and tell which ones they like, and they complain about the classes they do not like. If students have some of the same classes, they may wish to express an opinion or disagree. Students should discuss the reasons they don't like certain classes and ask for advice. The partner should give advice or say what he or she would do in each situation. Both students should talk about their hopes and wishes for this year.

MATERIALS school books, class schedules

Entre familia

Written Activity

TASK Students write a review of a restaurant based on meals served to a group of four people.

PURPOSE to comment on food, to explain and give excuses, to use the preterite, to use **se** + indirect object pronoun, to use the past progressive

ACTIVITY Have students imagine they are food critics, and they have just eaten at a Caribbean restaurant with three friends. Tell them to write a review of the restaurant, describing what each person ordered. They should explain which dishes were excellent, and which had problems. They should also tell what excuses the waiter gave when they complained about some of the meals. Have them cut out pictures of the food items from magazines to illustrate the review.

MATERIALS paper, scissors, glue, food magazines

Oral Activity

TASK Students imagine that they are at a family reunion with their in-laws, a Caribbean family.

PURPOSE to talk about family members, relationships, and family events; to ask about the latest news, to respond, and to react; to use the present progressive, present perfect indicative, and present perfect subjunctive

ACTIVITY Divide the class into two groups and have each group act out the following situation. One student has just married into a large Caribbean family. He or she has been given the task of passing out name tags, but he/she does not know who everyone is. The student must go around asking about the latest news in order to learn more about the family members. The other members of the group respond, telling about various family relationships.

MATERIALS name tags

CAPÍTULO 5

El arte y la música

PORTFOLIO SUGGESTIONS

Written Activity

TASK Students write an instant message conversation with a friend or pen pal in a Spanish-speaking country about artistic events such as concerts, plays, or movies.

PURPOSE to have students use art-related vocabulary; to use adjectives to describe music and art; to use expressions to change the subject; to make recommendations; to ask for opinions

ACTIVITY Students can begin their instant messaging conversation casually and change the subject to music and art. Once they have at least eight exchanges using vocabulary and expressions from the chapter, have students print out their conversation. They may then edit their conversations, making a version that only contains information about art or music, to read aloud in class.

MATERIALS computer, paper

Oral Activity

TASK Students imagine that they are a tour guide in an art gallery with paintings, sculptures, drawings, wood carvings, and so on. They will greet visitors and tell them about what is in the gallery.

PURPOSE to use art-related vocabulary; to use expressions to ask for an opinion about art; to describe works of art using chapter vocabulary; to respond to opinions

ACTIVITY Have students work in groups of four to act out the scene. Ask them to choose a person to be the gallery tour guide. The remaining students in the group will be the gallery visitors. The tour guide will take visitors through the gallery, telling them the types of art that are in the gallery, their age, style, and so on. The tour guide will then ask visitors their opinions. Visitors will respond to questions. Visitors may also ask the tour guide his or her opinion of the works of art. Have students alternate between the role of the tour guide and visitors.

MATERIALS (optional) props for gallery such as picture frames, clay or wooden sculptures, drawings

¡Ponte al día!

Written Activity

TASK Students write a letter to the editor stating their opinions about a recent article on a controversial topic.

PURPOSE to use expressions of certainty and doubt, to use expressions of affirmation and negation, to use vocabulary expressions, to use the indicative and the subjunctive, to use the present, preterite, imperfect, and present subjunctive forms of **haber**

ACTIVITY Have students choose and research a controversial news topic such as the economy, the environment, violence on TV, politics, arts education in schools, and so on. Students should find at least two articles on their topic where journalists give opposing points of view. Students may print out a copy of the articles from an online news source, or clip the articles from newspapers or magazines to use in a visual representation. The visual representation should be a simple illustration of the topic and the main points of each article. Students will then write a letter to the editor explaining which article they are responding to, their opinions on the article, and why they agree or disagree with it.

MATERIALS access to online news sources, magazines, newspapers, glue, scissors, and paper

Oral Activity

TASK Students will debate a controversial news topic.

PURPOSE to use expressions of certainty and doubt, to use expressions of affirmation and negation, to use vocabulary expressions, to use the indicative and the subjunctive, to use the present, preterite, imperfect, and present subjunctive forms of **haber**

ACTIVITY Divide the class into two teams, and assign each team a different point of view on a controversial topic. Have each team prepare for a debate by finding articles from online news sources, newspapers, and magazines that support their position. They should also prepare to counteract the other team's point of view. Each student should present at least one or two sentences in defense of their team's position and take notes on the opposing team's opinions. Choose one student to begin the debate by presenting the team's position. A student from the opposing team should then counteract by disagreeing with that point of view and presenting his team's position. Continue the debate until all students have taken part and all the evidence from both sides has been presented. Have a post-activity discussion as a class. (Did anyone change his or her mind during the research or debate process? Was a compromise or a solution reached?) Collect notes and add them to students' portfolios.

MATERIALS access to online news sources, magazines, newspapers, pens, and paper

Mis aspiraciones

Written Activity

TASK Students write a letter about their experiences as an immigrant in a Latin American country.

PURPOSE to use **Vocabulario** expressions, to use grammatical reflexives, to use the preterite and imperfect, and to use the indicative with habitual past actions

ACTIVITY Have students choose a city or town in a Latin American country and do research online to learn about the average teenager. They should find out about home and school life, preferred activities, language, music, and any other relevant information. Students should print out pictures of the city or town, the country, teenagers' activities, statistics or weather reports to use in a visual presentation about life in their Latin American country. Then, students imagine that they moved there one year ago. Have them write a letter to the class, explaining their experiences as a newly arrived immigrant, comparing and contrasting life in the United States to that in their new country, any obstacles they have had to face, and how they have overcome them. Students will present their project to the class.

MATERIALS access to online sources, scissors, glue, paper, and posterboard

Oral Activity

TASK Students will write and perform a short play about achievement or failure.

PURPOSE to use **Vocabulario** and **Gramática** expressions, to use grammatical reflexives, to use the preterite and imperfect, to use the subjunctive with future actions, and to use the indicative forms of verbs with habitual past actions

ACTIVITY Divide the class into four groups. Each group must write and perform a short play about success or failure, using the **Vocabulario** and **Gramática** expressions. The play can be about achieving a goal, succeeding in a career, overcoming obstacles, or failing at a task. Each member of the group must write and perform their lines. Students should be given time to write and rehearse. On the day of the play, the students can bring in props or simple costumes to aid with their performance.

MATERIALS paper, props, costumes

¿A qué te dedicas?

Written Activity

TASK Students write a formal letter of interest in response to a want ad.

PURPOSE to use expressions from **Vocabulario,** the conditional tense of verbs, the subjunctive with hypothetical statements, and indirect object pronouns

ACTIVITY Have students look through the classifieds section of various newspapers, or research online want ads. Students should choose a job or career that interests them, research the requirements for their chosen profession, and cut out or print out a want ad that will be added to a visual aid for their presentation. The visual aid should contain information on job requirements, benefits and prerequisites, and a copy of the want ad. Students will write a formal letter of interest in response to the want ad, explaining the position they are interested in, their educational and field experience, and what they would be able to contribute to the company.

MATERIALS access to online want ads, newspapers, posters, glue, scissors, and paper

Oral Activity

TASK Students will take part in a job interview.

PURPOSE to use expressions from **Vocabulario,** the conditional tense of verbs, the subjunctive with hypothetical statements, and indirect object pronouns

ACTIVITY Choose a position and company for which students will be interviewing. (Example: editor for the international magazine, *Hispanos de Hoy*) Briefly explain what the job entails and any educational or practical requirements for the position. Divide the class into two teams. One team will play the role of the interviewers and the other team will play the role of the candidates. Each interviewer will write at least two questions that they will ask candidates during the interview. The interviewers will write a job description, a list of educational and practical requirements, and a list of work benefits for their company. The team of candidates will prepare by writing down possible interview questions and rehearsing their answers with teammates. In addition, candidates will prepare a one-page resume that details their education, work experience, and skills. Each candidate's resume should be different. On the day of the interview, students should be dressed for an interview and have typed copies of all their material.

MATERIALS paper

Huellas del pasado

Written Activity

TASK Students create a story about something that happened a long time ago.

PURPOSE to use chapter vocabulary, to use functional expressions to set the scene of a story, to use the preterite and imperfect in storytelling

ACTIVITY Students imagine that they have just returned from a trip. They should write a letter describing in detail what happened. They should also compare the myths and traditions of the country that they visited with their own. Finally, students should make a recommendation to a friend about a trip that they should take, showing them pictures from a magazine.

MATERIALS pencils, markers, scissors, magazines

Oral Activity

TASK Students imagine that they are going to see a play about a myth. They have different ideas about what the play will be like.

PURPOSE to use the imperfect and preterite tenses for storytelling, to use functional expressions for setting the scene and continuing and ending a story, to use the subjunctive mood

ACTIVITY Students should take turns describing what they think will happen in the play.

MATERIALS pencil, paper

El mundo en que vivimos

Written Activity

TASK Students create a slide show that describes a natural disaster.

PURPOSE to use chapter vocabulary, to use **haber** and progressive tenses to describe scenes, to use the present perfect, to use the subjunctive and indicative with doubt, denial, and feelings

ACTIVITY Have students create "slides" from index cards and either sketch the "pictures" in their slide show or cut out pictures from a magazine. They should describe the scenes and tell where they were. They should also compare several disasters and talk about the ones they consider to cause the most destruction.

MATERIALS index cards, pencils, markers, scissors, glue, magazines

Oral Activity

TASK Students imagine that they are the mayor of a large city and need to create programs to fight the problems of pollution, unemployment, and crime.

PURPOSE to use expressions for predictions and warnings, the future tense, and the subjunctive with recommendations

ACTIVITY Students should take turns proposing measures or laws using the proper verbs. Other students should say which one they prefer and why, or make a recommendation to the first student. Students should continue until they have decided on six laws (three per student). At least one pair of laws should be rejected completely by each student.

MATERIALS city maps, pencil, paper

Performance Assessment

¡Adiós al verano!

Vocabulario 1/Gramática 1

ORAL ASSESSMENT Have students work in pairs to talk about what they did last summer. They should take turns asking each other questions and responding. Then have them tell about what they used to like to do during the summer when they were young. Tell them to comment on what they were like then and what they are like now. Do they still enjoy the same activities?

WRITTEN ASSESSMENT Have students imagine they are a tour guide for a group of Spanish exchange students visiting their community or another city for summer vacation. They should write a brochure describing the area and the activities in which students could participate. Have them suggest activities for specific interests. Tell them to be sure to include a section at the end of the brochure telling who they are, where they are located, and what they look like, so students can find them.

Vocabulario 2/Gramática 2

ORAL ASSESSMENT Have students work in groups of two. Each student will invent a problem, and they will take turns describing the problem to their partner and asking for advice. The partner will respond by giving advice and recommending activities in which the student has never participated.

WRITTEN ASSESSMENT Have students imagine they are interviewing a famous high school athlete. They should ask the athlete for advice about how to do well in sports. Also have them write questions about the athlete's plans for the future and be sure to include the athlete's responses.

Repaso

ORAL ASSESSMENT Have groups of students imagine they are on vacation in Spain. Group 1 has just arrived in Spain and Group 2 has been there for a week. Group 2 tells about what they did during the past week and Group 1 asks questions about how they liked each activity and asks for advice about what to do while they are there. Group 2 gives them advice by comparing some of the activities they did last week and then they tell Group 1 what they plan to do during the following week.

¡A pasarlo bien!

Vocabulario 1/Gramática 1

ORAL ASSESSMENT Have students work in pairs to discuss the activities they enjoy. They should take turns inviting each other to do various activities this weekend until they come up with a plan. They should each turn down at least two activities before they agree on something.

WRITTEN ASSESSMENT Have students write a paragraph about what they used to do during their summer vacations. Once they have given some background, they should write a story about one particular summer. The story can be real or made up. Have them talk about three activities they were going to do over the summer and why they were not able to do them.

Vocabulario 2/Gramática 2

ORAL ASSESSMENT Have students imagine they are a famous actor. They have had an argument with a boyfriend or girlfriend and are being interviewed about it. Students should take turns playing the part of interviewer and actor. The interviewer will ask the actor what happened and will then ask the actor to comment on what he or she looks for in a boyfriend (girlfriend).

WRITTEN ASSESSMENT Have students imagine they are studying abroad in Spain. It has taken them a while to make new friends, but now they have made a new friend with whom they have a lot in common. They should write a letter to a friend or family member telling him or her about the new friend and describing the characteristics that make the person such a good friend.

Repaso

ORAL ASSESSMENT Have groups of students act out the following situation. A couple is trying to make plans for the weekend. The girl invites the boy to do several activities and he turns them all down because he is not interested and is very stubborn. She becomes angry and leaves. She then sees some of her friends, who ask her what is wrong. She explains that she is upset with her boyfriend for being so rude. They suggest that she look for a boyfriend who respects her feelings.

Todo tiene solución

PERFORMANCE ASSESSMENT

Vocabulario 1/Gramática 1

ORAL ASSESSMENT Have students work in pairs to talk about stereotypes in their school. They should discuss students' attitudes and opinions about different groups and talk about why certain groups have a good or bad image. Have them tell whether they agree or disagree with the image of each group. Ask them to discuss the reasons for mistaken impressions.

WRITTEN ASSESSMENT Have students write a letter to a younger friend to tell him or her about their school courses this year. They should tell the friend about the courses they like and complain about the courses they do not like. Have students tell what their parents, friends, and teachers want them to do this year, and what they prefer to do.

Vocabulario 2/Gramática 2

ORAL ASSESSMENT Have students work in pairs. They should imagine that one student has had an argument with a friend. The other student will listen to what happened and then make suggestions about what he or she should do to resolve the problem.

WRITTEN ASSESSMENT Have students imagine they have done something to upset a boyfriend or girlfriend. Tell them to write a letter to apologize. They should also explain what they will do differently in the future to avoid arguments or misunderstandings.

Repaso

ORAL ASSESSMENT Pass out situations to students. Situations might include: you failed your last math test, your boyfriend or girlfriend is not speaking to you, your teacher is giving you more homework than you can handle, you found a hundred dollars on the sidewalk, your classmates have a mistaken impression of you, a local company discriminates against women, a friend bases his or her opinions on stereotypes. Have students work in pairs and take turns describing their situation. The partner must react by agreeing, disagreeing, making suggestions, or apologizing, depending on the context.

Entre familia

Vocabulario 1/Gramática 1

ORAL ASSESSMENT Have students work in pairs. Ask them to imagine they have not seen each other in years. They should take turns asking about the latest news on family members and responding.

WRITTEN ASSESSMENT Have students imagine they are reporters and have just attended a Hollywood party. They found out all the gossip about the celebrities (who is engaged, who is divorced, who had a baby) and have to write an article telling the latest news and expressing their reactions to the news.

Vocabulario 2/Gramática 2

ORAL ASSESSMENT Have students work in small groups. Ask them to imagine they are at a dinner party. The host serves the food, describing each dish. The guests should take turns commenting on the food. If they make a negative comment about the food, the host should explain and give excuses.

WRITTEN ASSESSMENT Have students imagine they are writing an interview with a famous chef. Have them write the questions they would ask the chef. They should include questions about his most famous dishes and how he prepares them, as well as his biggest disasters in the kitchen. Students should also write the chef's response to each question.

Repaso

ORAL ASSESSMENT Have groups of students imagine they are at a family reunion. Assign roles such as grandparents, parents, children, cousins, couples. You may wish to provide nametags identifying each family member. Students should talk to various family members, ask each other about the latest news, and react to news. They should also comment on the food being served, while those who prepared the food explain and give excuses.

El arte y la música

Vocabulario 1/Gramática 1

ORAL ASSESSMENT Have students act out a situation in which a group of friends is talking about famous buildings and their architecture. They use the passive voice to say who designed the buildings. Other friends in the conversation ask for and give opinions about the architecture.

WRITTEN ASSESSMENT Have students imagine they are interviewing a famous artist. Students should write the interview questions first and then write the artist's responses. The interview should ask the artist about several issues, and use expressions to change the topic of conversation.

Vocabulario 2/Gramática 2

ORAL ASSESSMENT Have students work in groups of two. One student will use gestures and body language to communicate actions or feelings, and the other student will narrate the action. For example, **Student A** mimes a violin player, then mimes someone covering his or her ears because the music is shrill. **Student B** will say that **Student A** went to a concert, but did not like the music.

WRITTEN ASSESSMENT Have students write a review of a school play or a band performance. Have students describe the music, the instruments, and how the music sounded to them. They could also make a recommendation for someone to go and see the next play or band performance.

Repaso

ORAL ASSESSMENT Students act out a conversation in which a group of friends is looking for something they can do together. The problem is that someone in the group is busy, has other plans, or does not care for the event the other friends suggest. Several suggestions are made, and invitations are turned down. Finally the group agrees to attend a rock concert that is coming to the area soon.

¡Ponte al día!

Vocabulario 1/Gramática 1

ORAL ASSESSMENT Have students work in pairs. Ask them to imagine that they watched the same documentary on television last night, but have very different points of view on the reporter and how the topic was covered. They should take turns giving their opinions and agreeing or disagreeing with their partner's point of view.

WRITTEN ASSESSMENT Have students write a short essay about how they stay informed. They should include the media sources they prefer, the quality of the news stories, which television programs they watch and why, which controversial topics they know a lot about, and which topics they know nothing about.

Vocabulario 2/Gramática 2

ORAL ASSESSMENT Have students work in small groups. Ask them to imagine that they are reading the Sunday paper with their family. Students should ask each other to pass a different section of the newspaper and explain why they prefer or need to read that section. As another student passes the requested item, he or she should give an opinion about that section of the newspaper.

WRITTEN ASSESSMENT Have students write an essay agreeing or disagreeing with one of the headlines below, and explaining why they agree or disagree.

"La crisis ambiental es una realidad, pero tiene solución"
"Las artes no son importantes para la educación de los niños"
"Hay mucha violencia en la televisión"
"Todos los programas de televisión son informativos"
"Hoy en día, los estudiantes no aprenden nada en el colegio"
"La censura es buena para la prensa"
"Los políticos deben leer las noticias con enfoque mundial"

Repaso

ORAL ASSESSMENT Have students work in pairs. Ask them to imagine that they are both reading the newspaper and come across several shocking headlines and articles. Students will take turns relaying the information to their partner, telling them what they read and where they read it. The partner will react to the information expressing certainty or doubt about the writer, the headline, or the article.

Mis aspiraciones

Vocabulario 1/Gramática 1

ORAL ASSESSMENT Have students work in pairs. Students tell their partner about their cultural heritage. They should explain where their ancestors are from, when they came to this country, and any customs or traditions their families have maintained. Students will then explain their partner's cultural heritage to the class.

WRITTEN ASSESSMENT Have students write an essay about an obstacle they have overcome either in school, sports, or their personal life. They should explain the problem and how it was overcome, using **Vocabulario** and **Gramática** expressions.

Vocabulario 2/Gramática 2

ORAL ASSESSMENT Have students work in pairs. Students will take turns asking and answering questions about their plans for the coming school year. Students should explain what their goals are and how they plan to achieve them.

WRITTEN ASSESSMENT Have students write an essay on one of the following topics, using **Vocabulario** and **Gramática** expressions:

La educación bilingüe
Si tuviera un millón de dólares
El sueño de mi vida
Mi rutina diaria
La vida de un inmigrante
El verano pasado
En cuanto cumpla los dieciocho años
Estoy orgulloso(a) de mi herencia

Repaso

ORAL ASSESSMENT Divide the class into two groups. Have them debate the following topic: "La educación bilingüe no es necesaria para los estudiantes americanos." Have the groups take turns stating their point of view and using **Vocabulario** and **Gramática** expressions. Have a post-activity discussion on the subject. You can include information on current bilingual education legislation, population statistics, government and foreign relations, job opportunities, OPEC, NAFTA or the International Red Cross.

¿A qué te dedicas?

Vocabulario 1/Gramática 1

ORAL ASSESSMENT Have students work in pairs. Ask them to imagine that they could not use common technological devices like televisions, computers or cell phones for one day. They should explain in detail how their daily lives *would* or *would not* change.

WRITTEN ASSESSMENT Have the students write a short story about a day in the life of a teenager in the future. Students can write about a future in which humans are technologically advanced or have lost all technology due to a catastrophic event. Students can embellish technological devices from **Vocabulario** to write about technology in the future.

Vocabulario 2/Gramática 2

ORAL ASSESSMENT Have students work in pairs. Have them take turns asking each other about their parents' careers. Students should explain their parents' position in the company, their job requirements, any education or experience they have, and any benefits they receive.

WRITTEN ASSESSMENT Have students write an essay on one of the following topics:

Las ventajas o las desventajas de la tecnología
La tecnología y la medicina
Cómo mi vida cambiaría con un robot
El trabajo voluntario
El trabajo ideal
Tengo talento para...
Lo que me gustaría hacer este verano
Lo que me gustaría estudiar
Lo que siempre he querido hacer
Si fuera rico(a)...
Si tuviera tiempo...

Repaso

ORAL ASSESSMENT Have students work in pairs. Students should think of a technological device that has not been invented. They should explain to their partners what device they would invent and what would be some of the advantages to having that device.

Huellas del pasado

PERFORMANCE ASSESSMENT

Vocabulario 1/Gramática 1

ORAL ASSESSMENT Have students work in groups of two. Each student will create a myth and explain it to his/her partner.

WRITTEN ASSESSMENT Have students imagine they are interviewing an actor in a play about a fairy tale. They should ask the actor what he has learned from the play. Have students write their questions and the actor's answers.

Vocabulario 2/Gramática 2

ORAL ASSESSMENT Have students work in pairs to talk about war, and why they think it may be necessary or not. They should take turns asking each other questions and responding. Then have them talk about the consequences of war. Tell them to take turns giving their point of view on war.

WRITTEN ASSESSMENT Have students imagine they are reporters and soldiers. Have the reporters interview the soldiers that are fighting to protect their country.

Repaso

ORAL ASSESSMENT Have groups of students create a fairy tale. The first student begins the fairy tale with a sentence and starts the second one. The second student finishes the sentence and starts the next one. Have another student write the sentences in the fairy tale. Once all students in the group have contributed a sentence to the fairy tale, call on a volunteer to share the group's story with the class.

CAPÍTULO

El mundo en que vivimos

PERFORMANCE ASSESSMENT

Vocabulario 1/Gramática 1

ORAL ASSESSMENT Have students work in pairs to talk about natural disasters. They should take turns asking each other questions and responding. Then have them talk about the consequences and the reactions of people in a disaster situation.

WRITTEN ASSESSMENT Have students imagine that they are members of a rescue team working in the area of a natural disaster. They should write a report describing the area and the destruction caused by the event. Have them suggest ways they could lessen the hardships of the residents in the affected areas. Tell them to be sure to include a section at the end telling who they are, where they are located, and what they look like so the people in need can find them.

Vocabulario 2/Gramática 2

ORAL ASSESSMENT Have students work in groups of two. Each student will invent an environmental problem, and take turns describing the problem to their partner and asking for advice about possible solutions. The partner will respond by giving advice and possible solutions.

WRITTEN ASSESSMENT Have students imagine they are interviewing a famous environmental activist. They should ask the activist to give them recommendations about how to conserve the environment. Also, have them write questions about the group's plans for the future, and include the activist's responses.

Repaso

ORAL ASSESSMENT Have groups of students imagine that they live in a very polluted city. **Group 1** supports cars fueled with gasoline. **Group 2** is against gasoline, and supports public transportation and the use of electric cars. Have them discuss their points of view, presenting examples and facts to try and persuade the other group to change its stance.